Marriage in Medieval England

LAW, LITERATURE AND PRACTICE

Marriage in Medieval England

LAW, LITERATURE AND PRACTICE

Conor McCarthy

THE BOYDELL PRESS

First published 2004
The Boydell Press, Woodbridge

The Boydell Press is an imprint of Boydell & Brewer Ltd
PO Box 9, Woodbridge, Suffolk IP12 3DF, UK
and of Boydell & Brewer Inc.
PO Box 41026, Rochester, NY 14604–4126, USA
website: www.boydellandbrewer.com

ISBN 1 84383 102 3

A CIP catalogue record for this book is available
from the British Library

Library of Congress Cataloging-in-Publication Data

McCarthy, Conor. 10054809949
    Marriage in medieval England : law, literature, and practice / Conor McCarthy.
        p. cm.
Includes bibliographical references (p.) and index.
    ISBN 1–84383–102–3 (acid-free paper)
1. Marriage – England – History – To 1500. 2. Marriage law – England –
History – To 1500. 3. Marriage in literature. 4. Marriage customs and rites,
Medieval – England. 5. Great Britain – History – Medieval period, 1066–1485.   I. Title.
HQ615.M38 2005
306.81′09′02 – dc22   2004005028

This publication is printed on acid-free paper

Printed in Great Britain by
Antony Rowe Ltd., Chippenham, Wiltshire

Contents

Acknowledgements

It is a pleasure to thank once again some of the many people who offered support or advice on my work on medieval marriage. Most of all, I am indebted to Gerald Morgan, who supervised my postgraduate research on the subject at Trinity College, Dublin, and was a source of encouragement and advice both then and afterwards. Thanks also to the examiners of that postgraduate work, Alcuin Blamires and John Scattergood, who offered advice that has found its way into the argument here. I am also grateful to former colleagues at the National University of Ireland, Galway, and the University of Durham, particularly to Corinne Saunders for help towards this book. Much appreciated assistance with Latin texts by Kathleen Coleman and Robert Carver is acknowledged at the appropriate places in the footnotes. For the helpfulness of their staff, and use of their resources, I am indebted to the library of Trinity College, Dublin, and the Fisher Library, University of Sydney. At Boydell & Brewer, thanks in particular to Caroline Palmer for editorial suggestions that helped this book to take its current form.

Personal thanks are due to family and friends for support and encouragement: particularly my parents Michael and Nuala McCarthy, my brothers Michael and David McCarthy, Anne van den Dungen, Dario and Juliette Brollo, Darren and Emily Brollo, Niamh Walsh and Lisa Carey. Thanks for timely assistance with computers to Margot Durcan and Niamh Durcan. Most gratitude, in return for most help, goes to Deidre Brollo with love and thanks.

All errors of fact and judgment remain my own.

Some of the material below has previously appeared in print, as follows. Part of chapter two was published as 'Marriage and Mede in Passus 2 to 4 of *Piers Plowman,*' *Nottingham Medieval Studies* 44 (2000), 152–66. Parts of chapter four previously appeared in 'Love, Marriage, and Law: Three Canterbury Tales,' *English Studies* 83 (2002), 503–18. Parts of chapter seven have been previously published as 'The Position of Widows in the Later Fourteenth Century English Community and the *Wife of Bath's Prologue,*' in *Authority and Community in the Middle Ages,* ed. D. Mowbray, R. Purdie, I. P. Wei (Stroud: Sutton, 1999), pp. 101–15. Portions of the argument throughout have been reworked from my unpublished Ph.D. thesis, 'Representations of Marriage in Later Medieval England' (Trinity College, Dublin, 1997). I am grateful to Oxford University Press for permission to reprint copyright material from *Councils and Synods with Other Documents relating to the English Church, AD 1205–1313,* ed. F. M. Powicke and C. R. Cheney (London: Oxford University Press, 1964).

Conor McCarthy
Sydney
January 2004

Abbreviations

EETS	Early English Texts Society
HMSO	Her/His Majesty's Stationery Office
MED	*Middle English Dictionary*
OED	*Oxford English Dictionary*
o.s.	original series
e.s.	extra series
OE	Old English
MnE	Modern English

Introduction

Literature, law and marriage

This book is about marriage in medieval England, the ways in which marriage is represented in medieval English legal and literary texts, and the relationship of these representations to actual practice. Both legal and literary texts have a great deal to say on the subject of marriage, and therefore provide us with a rich source of evidence. Where English legal writings are concerned, texts from the seventh-century laws of Æthelbert onwards contain regulations concerning marriage, albeit cryptically expressed, and later Anglo-Saxon laws show the influence of developing ecclesiastical thinking on marriage. From the point where William the Conqueror divides the ecclesiastical and secular jurisdictions, we see two sets of law intervening in marriage: the ecclesiastical courts take control of marriage in all of its spiritual aspects, leaving the secular jurisdiction to judge only those aspects of marriage relating to property and the inheritance of landed property. As for literature, it is true that literary writing on marriage from the early medieval period is thin. As Christine Fell observes, 'neither sex nor marriage is central to Old English literature, and romance plays a very small part.'[1] Nonetheless, evidence offered in passing by Old English poems such as *Beowulf* and *The Wanderer* can be illuminating on topics that are not their central concern. In the later Middle Ages, topics such as sex, marriage, and romance *are* a central concern: as David Lampe comments, 'Old English (or, if you prefer, Anglo-Saxon) seems to show very little interest in sex and Middle English has almost too much.'[2] The difficulty here is not how to make inferences from scant evidence, but how to make use of a very large body of writing about marriage, some of it very sophisticated.

The definition of 'legal' and 'literary' texts adopted here is broader than would apply to modern equivalents. Medieval law has a very broad scope. As Richard

---

[1]   Christine Fell, *Women in Anglo-Saxon England* (London: British Museum, 1984), p. 66.
[2]   David Lampe, 'Sex Roles and the Role of Sex in Medieval English Literature,' in *Handbook of Medieval Sexuality*, ed. Vern L. Bullough and James A. Brundage (London: Garland, 1996), pp. 401–22.

Firth Green argues, citing John Alford, 'people in the Middle Ages regarded divine, natural and human law as merely different aspects of a single ordering principle,' in contrast to the usual contemporary secular position which sees law as occupying a different sphere from morality or theology.[3] It is not possible to draw hard and fast distinctions between theological and legal traditions in Christian thinking about marriage. Canon law texts draw on a variety of materials in their thinking about marriage, and in particular they draw upon theological sources. The canonist Gratian, for example, draws heavily upon the writings of the theologian St Augustine. Gratian's thinking on marriage is challenged in turn by the theologian Peter Lombard, whose work influences the legal decisions of Pope Alexander III. Consequently, Augustine and Peter Lombard are discussed below for their influence on ecclesiastical marriage law.[4]

Where secular law is concerned, there is significant difficulty in relating legal texts to actual practice, to law as people might have experienced it. This is not simply the result of resistance to legal intervention, though that no doubt existed for secular and ecclesiastical law alike. Rather, it relates to problems of evidence. For early medieval England, there is the problem of relating the available written evidence to legal practice, in the light of Patrick Wormald's recent assertion that 'early medieval England was not a *pays du droit écrit*.'[5] For later medieval England, the various forms of evidence available to us (statute law, the evidence of legal manuals, local customs with the status of law) do not add up to form a coherent whole: the parts often contradict one another. To quote S. F. C. Milsom, 'in the fourteenth century there was no law of England, no body of rules complete in itself with known limits and visible defects; or if there was it was not the property of the common law courts or any others.'[6] Consequently, we need to speak of secular laws rather than secular law.

If medieval and modern notions of law do not quite match, a similar proposition may be posed concerning literature. As J. A. Burrow observes, literature is 'an honorific term with strong evaluative implications,' reserved nowadays for the most part to three forms of writing: prose fiction, poetry, and drama.[7] But as Burrow goes on to point out, much of what we consider to constitute the canon of

---

[3]   Richard Firth Green, 'Medieval Literature and Law,' in *The Cambridge History of Medieval English Literature*, ed. David Wallace (Cambridge: Cambridge University Press, 1999), pp. 407–31 (pp. 410–11).

[4]   I am well aware that none of the writers just cited are English, but the Church's law of marriage was (more or less) uniform and universal throughout western Christendom, and consequently requires discussion in a broader context. In the discussion below, however, I have focused where possible on local English ecclesiastical legislation.

[5]   Patrick Wormald, *The Making of English Law: King Alfred to the Twelfth Century. Volume I: Legislation and its Limits* (Oxford: Blackwell, 1999), p. 483.

[6]   S. F. C. Milsom, *Historical Foundations of the Common Law*, 2nd ed. (London: Butterworths, 1981), p. 83.

[7]   J. A. Burrow, *Medieval Writers and Their Work: Middle English Literature and its Background, 1100–1500* (Oxford: Oxford University Press, 1982), p. 12.

'medieval English literature' does not fit these categories. The discussion below does of course discuss texts which would meet a contemporary categorization of literature, poetry for the most part. But it also appropriates as literature other sorts of text which would not be categorized within literature's narrow margins if they were written today, such as hagiographical narratives and letter collections.

Having allowed that the boundaries of the legal and literary in the discussion here differ from contemporary usage, it remains necessary to justify reading what are usually assumed to be two very different categories of text in tandem. In fact, there is the justification of precedent, for medieval law and literature are often read against one another. But such readings usually leave the boundaries between the legal and the literary intact. As Emily Steiner and Candace Barrington comment: 'law and literature are assumed to be separate disciplines, a post-Romantic assumption that programatically distributes law and literature into oppositional categories, such as the scientific and the expressive or the instrumental and the aesthetic, prior to formulating an analogy between the two.'[8] Recent work on law and literature has taken a very different approach. Patrick Wormald and Robin Chapman Stacey have each argued recently for reading legal texts *as* literature: in Stacey's words, adopting 'approaches that resist [. . .] the traditional tendency of legal historians and literary specialists alike to regard the lawbooks as more or less dispassionate descriptions of social institutions and customary practice.'[9] Richard Firth Green has advocated 'regarding the law and literature as parallel forms of discourse.'[10] Noël James Menuge, in her study of legal and literary materials relating to wardship, argues that we should 'break down the distinct generic barriers which force us to view romance as literature and legal cases and treatises as legal history, and instead view each as related fictions with consciously constructed narratives and ideological agendas which serve specific purposes.'[11] Recent interdisciplinary studies of legal and literary texts, then, have emphasised similarities between the methods and objectives of legal and literary texts. Obviously, differences between the workings of legal and literary texts remain. But this recent shift in opinion on the relationship between the legal and the literary allows us to ask new questions of what legal and literary texts are doing when they address the same issues.

Ideology and overdetermination

In the discussion below, I intend to discuss both sorts of text as embodying and representing ideologies that attempt to determine the actual practice of marriage

[8] *The Letter of the Law: Legal Practice and Literary Production in Medieval England*, ed. Emily Steiner and Candace Barrington (Ithaca and London: Cornell University Press, 2002), p. 2.
[9] Robin Chapman Stacey, 'Divorce, Medieval Welsh Style,' *Speculum* 77 (2002), 1107–27 (p. 1107); Wormald, pp. 416–76.
[10] Green, 'Medieval Literature and Law,' p. 407.
[11] Noël James Menuge, *Medieval English Wardship in Romance and Law* (Cambridge: Brewer, 2001), p. 21.

in medieval England. In using the word 'ideology,' I am thinking of the definition formulated by the Marxist philosopher Louis Althusser, who defines ideology as 'the imaginary relationship of individuals to their real conditions of existence.'[12] In other words, ideologies are the ideas through which people live out the actions of their lives. Althusser makes it clear that ideologies are ideas which are expressed through actual material practices, and that there is no human activity which does not require an intellectual construction to enable it to take place.[13]

To put it very simply, in the case of marriage: a couple getting married in the twenty-first century may do so in a ceremony of consent not dissimilar to that of a fourteenth-century couple. They express consent to marriage to one another, in front of witnesses, perhaps in a religious context. They may exchange very similar words of consent to marriage. They may even be married in exactly the same building. It is more than likely that each of the two couples will cohabit, have sexual intercourse, share property, perhaps raise children. But it is ideology which defines the cultural meaning carried by these various actions. How the two couples conceive of marriage as a social institution is likely to differ enormously. The actions performed are superficially similar, but their cultural context, and hence their meaning (both to the individuals concerned and their broader society), are very different.

Ideology determines practice – it exercises an influence upon it.[14] Both legal and literary texts, in discussing marriage, are offering ideological suggestions as to what marriage is, and how people ought to act in relation to it. They address similar problems, from different perspectives. Certainly, the way in which each attempts to impose its ideology differs: legal texts often operate through the raw exercise of power, sanctioning penalties that may be exacted against their opponents. Literary texts cannot do this: they must persuade more gently, and depend upon subjective acceptance of their position. But both types of text, in discussing marriage, try to define it and its boundaries, and to shape the behaviour of the married. They are ideological texts attempting to determine practice. An important point in Althusser's theory of ideology is that several ideologies can be brought to bear on any one practice, each determining that practice in some way. This, Althusser argues, leads to overdetermination, a contradiction arising from 'the accumulation of effective determinations.'[15] The thesis that I wish to present in this book is that marriage in medieval England is overdetermined – essentially overregulated and overgoverned – and that this overdetermination of marriage leads to contradiction, and hence perhaps to unexpected consequences.

---

[12] Louis Althusser, *Essays on Ideology* (London: Verso, 1984), p. 37; for other definitions of ideology, see Raymond Williams, *Keywords: A Vocabulary of Culture and Society* (Glasgow: Fontana, 1976), pp. 126–30. Williams makes it clear that the term ideology need not necessarily carry the pejorative sense of 'false consciousness,' and in using Althusser's definition I am not referring to this sense of ideology as illusion.

[13] Althusser, *Essays*, pp. 35, 40, 44.

[14] For definitions of 'determine' see Williams, *Keywords*, pp. 87–91.

[15] Louis Althusser, *For Marx*, trans. Ben Brewster (Harmondsworth: Penguin, 1969), pp. 112–13.

In arguing for contradiction and overdetermination in the regulation of marriage in medieval England, the argument here might seem close to that of Georges Duby, who famously argued in his analysis of marriage in twelfth-century France that:

> The codes by which marriage is governed [. . .] belong to two differ-
> ent orders: the profane, and what we may call the religious. Normally
> the two systems adapt to, and reinforce one another. But there are
> times when they are in conflict, and such temporary discord causes
> marriage practices to change and evolve towards a new equilibrium.[16]

If we were to look at twelfth-century England, we may agree that there are two systems of law in operation, ecclesiastical and secular, which have jurisdiction over, respectively, the bond of marriage and property transfers relating to that bond. However, each of these embody fragmented attitudes towards marriage and encompass a multiplicity of ideologies, making it impossible to reduce the influences upon medieval marriage practices to a binary. It is possible to trace not only contradictions *between* the ecclesiastical and secular attitudes to marriage, but also contradictions *within* them.

Duby's argument for the existence of two competing 'models' of marriage in twelfth-century France was questioned by David Herlihy, who found the suggestion problematic. Herlihy asked whether the efforts of powerful laymen to bend the Church's rules might really be considered an alternative model of marriage, comparable to that of the Church, or whether it might simply be regarded as misbehaviour? Did evidence of resistance to the Church's theory of marriage necessarily imply a rival model?[17] Looking at medieval England, we may agree with Duby that there is a coherent lay aristocratic agenda, essentially based upon the idea that marriage is important for the transfer of property within and between families, and that this agenda lies, explicitly or latently, behind much secular law in medieval England. In contrast to this, the ecclesiastical view of marriage in the central and later Middle Ages is not based on family or property interests, but upon the freely given consent of individuals to be married. But Herlihy is correct in suggesting that these were not two coherent, opposed, alternative medieval models of marriage. Rather, the two coexisted by dividing the jurisdiction of marriage between them. The Church, by and large, did not interfere in secular matters relating to marriage, and the secular jurisdiction left spiritual matters to the ecclesiastical courts.[18] Sometimes the dividing line became unclear, and the jurisdictions clashed (disputes on questions of legitimacy and on the testamentary rights of married women, for example, are discussed in chapter two). More fundamentally, the two jurisdictions had very different notions

---

[16] Georges Duby, *The Knight, the Lady, and the Priest: The Making of Modern Marriage in Medieval France*, trans. Barbara Bray (New York: Pantheon, 1983), p. 19.

[17] David Herlihy, *Medieval Households* (Cambridge, MA, and London: Harvard University Press, 1985), p. 86.

[18] R. H. Helmholz, *Marriage Litigation in Medieval England* (London: Cambridge University Press, 1974), p. 3.

of the purpose of marriage – contradictory notions, even – but these contradictory notions coexisted. The argument of this book seeks to demonstrate this coexistence of contradictory notions, and examine its consequences.

This book

Much has already been written about marriage in medieval England, and particularly about marriage in the central and later Middle Ages, far too much to summarize here. James A. Brundage has surveyed the canon law of Christendom as it related to all forms of sexual behaviour.[19] Michael M. Sheehan has written several articles on the legislation of the English Church in the later Middle Ages, and the effects of that legislation on marriage and family.[20] Richard H. Helmholz has surveyed the marriage litigation which took place in the Church courts of later medieval England.[21] The canon law of marriage as it relates to medieval literature, and in particular to the work of Chaucer, has been discussed by Henry Ansgar Kelly.[22] Marriage has long been recognized as an important topic in Chaucer's work, and classic articles include G. L. Kittredge's 'Chaucer's Discussion of Marriage,' now almost a century old, and D. S. Brewer's 'Love and Marriage in Chaucer's Poetry.'[23] Since Kelly's book, there have been two other book-length studies of marriage as represented in Middle English literature – M. Teresa Tavormina's book on marriage in Langland, and Neil Cartlidge's on the literature of the twelfth and thirteenth centuries.[24] And although sex, marriage, and family are not central concerns in Old English writing, Christine Fell devotes two chapters to these subjects in her book on Anglo-Saxon women, and Carole Hough in a series of articles has been re-evaluating the gender politics of Old English legal texts.[25] As well as all of this writing on marriage and its representation in legal and

---

[19] James A. Brundage, *Law, Sex and Christian Society in Medieval Europe* (Chicago and London: University of Chicago Press, 1987).

[20] Collected in Michael M. Sheehan, *Marriage, Family and Law in Medieval Europe: Collected Studies*, ed. James K. Farge (Toronto: University of Toronto Press, 1996).

[21] Helmholz, *Marriage Litigation*.

[22] Henry Ansgar Kelly, *Love and Marriage in the Age of Chaucer* (Ithaca and London: Cornell University Press, 1975).

[23] G. L. Kittredge, 'Chaucer's Discussion of Marriage,' in *Chaucer Criticism*, ed. R. J. Schoeck and Jerome Taylor, 2 vols (Indiana: University of Notre Dame Press, 1960), I, 130–58 (first published in *Modern Philology* 9 (1911–12), 435–67); D. S. Brewer, 'Love and Marriage in Chaucer's Poetry,' *The Modern Language Review* 49 (1954), 461–64.

[24] M. Teresa Tavormina, *Kindly Similitude: Marriage and Family in Piers Plowman* (Cambridge: Brewer, 1995); Neil Cartlidge, *Medieval Marriage: Literary Approaches, 1100–1300* (Cambridge: Brewer, 1997).

[25] Fell, chapters 3, 4; Carole Hough, 'Alfred's *Domboc* and the Language of Rape: A Reconsideration of Alfred ch. 11,' *Medium Aevum* 66 (1997), 1–27, 'A New Reading of Alfred, ch. 26,' *Nottingham Medieval Studies* 41 (1997), 1–12, 'The Widow's *Mund* in Æthelbert 75 and 76,' *Journal of English and Germanic Philology* 98 (1999), 1–16, 'Two Kentish Laws Concerning Women: A New Reading of Æthelbert 73 and 74,' *Anglia* 119 (2001), 554–78.

literary texts, there is also an enormous literature on related topics. Particularly prominent are books on medieval women and their representation, books on love in the Middle Ages, and books offering feminist readings of medieval texts.[26] But there are also books on households and family structure, many on sex (including same-sex sex), books on medieval childhood, on prostitution, on mothering, on widowhood, and so on.[27] All of this is to say nothing of studies of other medieval European cultures.

Despite this vast output of writings on medieval marriage, however, the subject does not yet seem exhausted, and indeed this book makes no claim to be the last word on any of the topics that it touches on. What it will attempt to do is to offer something of an overview of legal and literary writing relating to medieval England.[28] In covering a broad topic over a very long period in a short book, it attempts to draw

[26] On medieval women, among others, see Angela M. Lucas, *Women in the Middle Ages: Religion, Marriage and Letters* (Brighton: Harvester, 1983), *Women's Lives in Medieval Europe: A Sourcebook*, ed. Emilie Amt (London: Routledge, 1993), *Woman Defamed and Woman Defended: An Anthology of Medieval Texts*, ed. Alcuin Blamires (Oxford: Oxford University Press, 1992), *Women and Writing in Medieval Europe: A Sourcebook*, ed. Carolyne Larrington (London: Routledge, 1995). On love, see C. S. Lewis, *The Allegory of Love: A Study in Mediaeval Tradition* (Oxford: Oxford University Press, 1936), Roger Boase, *The Origin and Meaning of Courtly Love: A Critical Study of European Scholarship* (Manchester: Manchester University Press, 1977), Peter L. Allen, *The Art of Love: Amatory Fiction from Ovid to the Romance of the Rose* (Philadelphia: University of Pennsylvania Press, 1992). On feminist readings of Old English literature, see Jane Chance, *Woman as Hero in Old English Literature* (Syracuse, NY: Syracuse University Press, 1986), of Middle English literature, *Feminist Readings in Middle English Literature: The Wife of Bath and All her Sect*, ed. Ruth Evans and Lesley Johnson (London: Routledge, 1994), of Chaucer, Carolyn Dinshaw, *Chaucer's Sexual Poetics* (London: University of Wisconsin Press, 1989), Jill Mann, *Geoffrey Chaucer* (London: Harvester, 1991), Elaine Tuttle Hansen, *Chaucer and the Fictions of Gender* (Oxford: University of California Press, 1992).

[27] On medieval families, see Herlihy, *Medieval Households*, Jack Goody, *The Development of Marriage and the Family in Europe* (Cambridge: Cambridge University Press, 1983). On sexuality, research up to 1990 is discussed in Joyce E. Salisbury, *Medieval Sexuality: A Research Guide* (New York: Garland, 1990); see also the bibliographies in *Handbook of Medieval Sexuality*, ed. Vern L. Bullough and James A. Brundage (London: Garland, 1996). On same-sex sex, see Allen J. Frantzen, *Before the Closet: Same Sex Love from Beowulf to Angels in America* (Chicago and London: University of Chicago Press, 1998), Carolyn Dinshaw, *Getting Medieval: Sexual Communities Pre- and Post-Modern* (Durham, NC: Duke University Press, 1999). On medieval childhood, see Shulamith Shahar, *Childhood in the Middle Ages*, trans. Chaya Galai (London: Routledge, 1990); there is a survey of research in Barbara A. Hanawalt, 'Medievalists and the Study of Childhood,' *Speculum* 77 (2002), 440–60. On prostitution, see Ruth Mazo Karras, *Common Women: Prostitution and Sexuality in Medieval England* (Oxford: Oxford University Press, 1996). On mothering, see *Medieval Mothering*, ed. John Carmi Parsons and Bonnie Wheeler (London: Garland, 1996). On widowhood, see *Upon my Husband's Death: Widows in the Literature and Histories of Medieval Europe*, ed. Louise Mirrer (Ann Arbor: University of Michigan Press, 1992), *Wife and Widow in Medieval England*, ed. Sue Sheridan Walker (Ann Arbor: University of Michigan Press, 1993).

[28] A broader overview of medieval European ideas of marriage already exists in C. N. L. Brooke's *The Medieval Idea of Marriage* (Oxford: Oxford University Press, 1989).

attention to broad thematic continuities and significant contradictions, focus attention on local English legislation (such as local ecclesiastical statutes and customary law, for example), and offer some detailed readings of literary texts. It is formatted not in chronological order, but thematically, treating subjects that might be thought to be important across the medieval period to differing degrees: consent to marriage, the property implications of marital union, the role of marriage in forging alliances, the relationship of love and marriage, the place of sex within marriage, models of family and family roles, and, finally, the ending of marriage through divorce or bereavement. This thematic structure should allow the reader to follow threads of continuity across the span of the period. In part, a structure based on continuities may prove useful because the actual argument of this book will spend a great deal of time emphasizing differences and contradictions.

Multiple inheritances

Before moving on to the subject proper, some background discussion may be useful. Medieval England inherited traditions relating to marriage from three major sources: from Roman law, from the Judaeo-Christian tradition, and from Germanic society. The three traditions are not entirely separate and distinct. Christian and Roman tradition necessarily influence one another after Christianity becomes the official religion of Rome and its empire. The marriage practices of the Germanic peoples who occupied the western empire between the late fourth and early sixth centuries differ from those of the Romans, but our only written evidence concerning Germanic laws comes from texts influenced by Latin culture.[29] Germanic marriage practices are also influenced by Christianity after conversion to the new faith.

Rome

Roman society, its marriage practice, and its broader sexual ethic, differs significantly from that of the Christian Middle Ages. Although Roman marriage was monogamous, and Roman law punished extramarital sex which fell into the categories of *stuprum*, 'fornication,' and *adulterium*, 'adultery,' only certain sorts of extramarital sex were condemned. Fornication between men and unmarried free women was punished, as was adultery between married women and anyone other than their husbands. But intercourse between upper-class men and lower-class women, concubines, and prostitutes was ignored.[30] The medieval Church, in contrast, attempted to prohibit all extramarital intercourse

---

[29] Amt, p. 38.

[30] Brundage, *Law, Sex and Christian Society*, pp. 28–32; on the meaning of the terms *stuprum* and *adulterium* (approximating to 'fornication' and 'adultery') see Susan Treggiari, *Roman Marriage: Iusti Coniuges from the Time of Cicero to the Time of Ulpian* (Oxford: Oxford University Press, 1991), pp. 262–64; on the sexual 'double standard,' see Treggiari, pp. 299–311.

as sinful. Roman law also permitted the existence of concubinage as an alternative to marriage,[31] while the medieval Church attempted to combat concubinage by appropriating it to marriage proper.[32] Roman law permitted divorce on a number of grounds, including adultery, the capture or enslavement of a spouse, sexual impotence, and insanity.[33] The medieval Church, in contrast, sought to prohibit divorce, although all of these reasons for divorce in Roman law constituted grounds for separation and remarriage at some point during the Middle Ages.[34] The understanding of marriage promoted by the Church in the Middle Ages, then, was much more restrictive than Roman law concerning extramarital sexual behaviour, divorce, and remarriage. In other areas the Church extends liberties, giving freedom to marry to people unable to do so in Roman society, such as slaves.[35]

Despite substantial differences in outlook, however, the medieval canon law of marriage was indebted to Roman law for two fundamental notions. The medieval canon law's insistence that it is consent that creates marriage is a legacy of Roman law. Whose consent, that of the individuals to be married or that of their families, may vary somewhat, but Susan Treggiari argues that 'in classical law the woman's consent, both to engagement and to marriage, is essential.' She suggests that the prospective spouses have at the very least a veto concerning their marriages, and at times may have much more than that.[36] The second notion of importance that the canon law inherits from Roman law is that of *maritalis affectio*. Marital affection was related to consent in that it was the will to be, and to remain, married – perhaps with an emotional tinge.[37] Both consent and marital affection are important in the medieval canon law of marriage as it was developed by Gratian and subsequent writers of the later Middle Ages.

---

[31] Brundage, *Law, Sex and Christian Society*, pp. 40–44.

[32] James A. Brundage, 'Concubinage and Marriage in Medieval Canon Law,' in *Sexual Practices and the Medieval Church*, ed. Vern L. Bullough and James A. Brundage (Buffalo, NY: Prometheus, 1982), pp. 118–28.

[33] Brundage, *Law, Sex and Christian Society*, p. 39.

[34] Fornication by a wife is grounds for a man to obtain a divorce in the Anglo-Saxon *Penitential of Theodore* 2.12.5. The text is a penitential guide associated with Theodore of Tarsus, archbishop of Canterbury (668–90). The subsequent clause makes it clear that the same liberty is not extended to wives whose husbands are fornicators, and the next clause again suggests that a legal marriage may not be broken except by the consent of both parties. The *Penitential of Theodore* 2.12.21–25 provides for remarriage if a spouse is taken into captivity, and discusses the problems that may arise from the subsequent return of the captured spouse: *Medieval Handbooks of Penance*, ed. and trans. J. T. McNeill and H. M. Gamer (New York: Columbia University Press, 1938; repr. New York: Octagon, 1965), pp. 208–10. Impotence and insanity remain impediments to marriage into the later medieval period, and marriages contracted by the impotent and insane might be legitimately dissolved: see chapter seven.

[35] Brundage, *Law, Sex and Christian Society*, p. 36.

[36] Treggiari, pp. 147, 170–80.

[37] John T. Noonan, Jr., 'Marital Affection in the Canonists,' *Studia Gratiana* 12 (1969), 479–509 (pp. 486–89).

The Judaeo-Christian tradition

Marriage and reproduction were compulsory for adult Jewish men in Biblical times.[38] Divorce was permitted, sometimes on very lax grounds, and fornication tolerated.[39] Adultery, however, was severely punished, at least in the case of women, who could expect to be stoned to death along with their partners in adultery.[40] Adulterous men got off much more lightly:[41] here, as in ancient Rome and Anglo-Saxon England, a sexual double standard seems to apply where adultery is concerned. Concubinage existed in Biblical-era Judaism, but disappeared from Jewish law during the Middle Ages.[42] Its earlier existence was nonetheless problematic for medieval Christian commentators: that Old Testament example posed a difficulty for the rather different Christian model of monogamous marriage is clear from a number of medieval texts. Augustine is forced to defend the Church fathers against the charge of unchastity in *De bono coniugali*.[43] In the twelfth century, Giraldus Cambrensis notes that the Irish justify their marriage practices according to the apparent (but not the true) example of the Old Testament.[44] In the fourteenth, Chaucer's Wife of Bath justifies her multiple marriages through pointing to the example of Abraham.[45]

Jesus did not have a great deal to say about marriage, except to prohibit divorce on grounds other than adultery.[46] In the absence of much direct commentary by Jesus on the subject of marriage and the family, medieval commentators discussed Gospel episodes and teaching such as his presence at the marriage of Cana, and the parable of Luke 14:20 – the wedding feast where the guests do not attend. There are also a number of statements in the Gospels which seem to suggest that Christianity and the family are incompatible, for example Matt. 19:29:

> 19:29. Et omnis qui reliquit domum vel fratres aut sorores aut patrem aut matrem aut uxorem aut filios aut agros propter nomen meum centuplum accipiet et vitam aeternam possidebit.

---

[38] Brundage, *Law, Sex, and Christian Society*, p. 52.

[39] Brundage, *Law, Sex, and Christian Society*, pp. 53–54.

[40] Brundage, *Law, Sex, and Christian Society*, p. 55.

[41] Brundage, *Law, Sex, and Christian Society*, p. 55.

[42] Brundage, *Law, Sex, and Christian Society*, p. 54.

[43] E.g. Augustine, *De bono coniugali, de sancta virginitate*, ed. and trans. P. G. Walsh (Oxford: Clarendon, 2001), p. 31.

[44] Giraldus Cambrensis, *The History and Topography of Ireland*, trans. John J. O'Meara (Harmondsworth: Penguin, 1982), p. 98.

[45] Reference to the works of Chaucer is to *The Riverside Chaucer*, ed. Larry D. Benson and others (Boston: Houghton Mifflin, 1987).

[46] Brundage, *Law, Sex, and Christian Society*, pp. 57–58, 74; John Boswell, *Christianity, Social Tolerance, and Homosexuality: Gay People in Western Europe from the Beginning of the Christian Era to the Fourteenth Century* (London: University of Chicago Press, 1980), pp. 114–15.

19:29. And every one that hath left house or brethren or sisters or father or mother or wife or children or lands, for my name's sake, shall receive an hundredfold and shall possess life everlasting.[47]

Jack Goody comments that 'the Gospels thus provide the scriptural basis for a rejection of family ties in favour of membership of the sectarian community,' and links this to the need to convert people from their previous beliefs.[48] David Herlihy argues that such apparently antifamilial comments in the Gospels were later reinterpreted to fit in with the idea of an *ordo caritatis*, which suggested that different degrees of love were appropriate for different persons and things. Love of family was not condemned, but should be superseded by love of God.[49]

It is not in the teachings of Jesus that we find the formulation of an early Christian position on marriage, however. That is to be found in the writings of St Paul. In 1 Corinthians 7, Paul formulated the basic Christian position on the relationship between the three grades of chastity, stating that while marriage was inferior to widowhood and to virginity, it was not condemned outright:

> 7:7. Volo autem omnes homines esse sicut me ipsum sed unusquisque proprium habet donum ex Deo alius quidem sic alius vero sic.
> 7:8. Dico autem non nuptis et viduis bonum est illis si sic maneant sicut et ego.
> 7:9. Quod si non se continent nubant melius est enim nubere quam uri.
> 7:7. For I would that all men were even as myself. But every one hath his proper gift from God; one after this manner, and another after that.
> 7:8. But I say to the unmarried and to the widows; it is good for them if they so continue, even as I.
> 7:9. But if they do not contain themselves, let them marry. For it is better to marry than to be burnt.

1 Corinthians 7 likewise outlines the basic position on marital sex, prescribing that each spouse owed a bodily debt to the other which they were obliged to pay:

> 7:3 Uxori vir debitum reddat similiter autem et uxor viro.
> 7:4 Mulier sui corporis potestatem non habet sed vir similiter autem et vir sui corporis potestatem non habet sed mulier.
> 7:3. Let the husband render the debt to his wife; and the wife also in like manner to the husband.

---

[47] All Biblical references are to the Douai-Rheims translation of the Vulgate.

[48] Goody, p. 90; David Herlihy, 'The Family and Religious Ideologies in Medieval Europe,' in David Herlihy, *Women, Family and Society in Medieval Europe: Historical Essays 1978–1991*, ed. A. Molho (Oxford: Berghahn, 1995), pp. 154–73 (p. 158) (first published in *Journal of Family History* 12 (1987), 3–17).

[49] David Herlihy, 'Family,' in David Herlihy, *Women, Family and Society in Medieval Europe: Historical Essays 1978–1991*, ed. A. Molho (Oxford: Berghahn, 1995), pp. 113–34 (pp. 123–24) (first published in *The American Historical Review* 96 (1991), 1–15).

> 7:4. The wife hath not power of her own body; but the husband. And in like manner, the husband also hath not power of his own body; but the wife.

It also formulates the basic position concerning the prohibition of divorce:

> 7:10. His autem qui matrimonio iuncti sunt praecipio non ego sed Dominus uxorem a viro non discedere.
> 7:11. Quod si discesserit manere innuptam aut viro suo reconciliari et vir uxorem ne dimittat.
> 7:10. But to them that are married, not I, but the Lord, commandeth that the wife depart not from her husband.
> 7:11. And if she depart, that she remain unmarried or be reconciled to her husband. And let not the husband put away his wife.

Elsewhere, Paul formulates the basis for a Christian tradition of love between married partners, in Ephesians 5:

> 5:28. Ita et viri debent diligere uxores suas ut corpora sua qui suam uxorem diligit se ipsum diligit.
> 5:29. Nemo enim umquam carnem suam odio habuit sed nutrit et fovet eam sicut et Christus ecclesiam.
> 5:30. Quia membra sumus corporis eius de carne eius et de ossibus eius.
> 5:31. Propter hoc relinquet homo patrem et matrem suam et adherebit uxori suae et erunt duo in carne una.
> 5:32. Sacramentum hoc magnum est ego autem dico in Christo et in ecclesia.
> 5:28. So also ought men to love their wives as their own bodies. He that loveth his wife loveth himself.
> 5:29. For no man ever hated his own flesh, but nourisheth and cherisheth it, as also Christ doth the Church.
> 5:30. Because we are members of his body, of his flesh and of his bones.
> 5:31. For this cause shall a man leave his father and mother; and shall cleave to his wife; and they shall be two in one flesh.
> 5:32. This is a great sacrament; but I speak in Christ and in the Church.

Paul's writings exercise an influence on all subsequent Christian thinking about marriage.

The early Church was deeply influenced by ascetic attitudes, which led to a suspicion of sexual intercourse even within a marital context.[50] It was the problem of the relationship of marriage to virginity that led to some of the decisive formulations of Christian marriage doctrine. Towards the end of the fourth century, a monk named Jovinian wrote a work, now lost, which suggested that

---

[50] Vern L. Bullough, 'Introduction: The Christian Inheritance,' in *Sexual Practices and the Medieval Church*, ed. Vern L. Bullough and James A. Brundage (Buffalo, NY: Prometheus, 1982), pp. 1–12.

marriage was equal in merit to virginity. Jovinian's work drew a response from St Jerome, whose defence of the superior status of virginity appeared in his *Adversus Jovinianum*, 'Against Jovinian' in 393. The problem with Jerome's work was that in condemning Jovinian's position, he seemed also to condemn marriage. He defends himself from this charge in letters to his friend Pammachius, but Pammachius and his other friends in Rome had (unsuccessfully) tried to suppress the publication of 'Against Jovinian' in Rome because of the views it contained.[51] Jerome's work is important in itself, but has added importance in that it provokes St Augustine to write a defence of marriage: *De bono coniugali*, 'On the Good of Marriage' (c. 401). Augustine's early writings on marriage are also an attempt to refute Jovinian, but, wary of Jerome's example, Augustine also takes care to praise marriage as good. Augustine praises marriage as a relative rather than an absolute good, and formulates three goods that marriage contains (fidelity, offspring, and the sacrament).[52] These goods mean that Christian marriage is indissoluble, monogamous, and directed towards procreation, and this formulation of Augustine's becomes an authoritative one. Augustine's ambiguity about marital intercourse, however, means that marital sex remains a problem for later Christian writers. The early Christian tradition, then, defends marriage as good, but in the context of an ascetic school of thought which is suspicious of sexual intercourse. Marriage therefore occupies the lowest position among the three grades of chastity, but is still relatively good in comparison with unchastity.

'Germanic' tradition

While it is easy to posit the existence of pre-Christian Anglo-Saxon customs and beliefs relating to marriage, their recovery is problematic. The earliest source for the marriage customs of a Germanic society is the *Germania* of Tacitus, from the end of the first century. Tacitus portrays a society which is largely monogamous, with only the uppermost reaches of society excepted, where adultery is rare and severely punished, and where virginity is preserved until marriage.[53] But these comments may not be so much an accurate portrait of what Tacitus found among the Germans as a portrait of what he found to condemn in his contemporary Roman audience.[54] Early legal texts from Germanic societies also tend to be influenced by Roman example.[55]

---

[51] The letters to Pammachius are in St Jerome, *The Principal Works of St Jerome*, trans. W. H. Fremantle (Oxford: James Parker, 1893), pp. 66–80.

[52] Sacramentality, in the sense in which Augustine uses it, refers to indissolubility: Dyan Elliott, *Spiritual Marriage: Sexual Abstinence in Medieval Wedlock* (Princeton: Princeton University Press, 1993), p. 47.

[53] Amt, pp. 36–38.

[54] Roberta Frank, 'Marriage in Twelfth- and Thirteenth-Century Iceland,' *Viator* 4 (1973), 473–84, in commenting on a society that converted very late to Christianity, observes wryly of Tacitus's comment on monogamy that 'Tacitus was not known in medieval Iceland' (p. 479).

[55] Amt, p. 38.

But there are presumably early practices that we can see enduring after conversion. Margaret Clunies Ross portrays Anglo-Saxon concubinage in a way that does not contradict Tacitus: it is a sort of polygyny available within a society which is broadly monogamous. She argues that in the early Anglo-Saxon period at least, there is evidence that the concubine was a member of a man's household, and able to inherit. The Church attempted to impose monogamy by trying to make it impossible for illegitimate children to inherit: this is the implication of a legatine commission of 786 which urges that children of recognized but not fully legal unions should be declared illegitimate and prevented from inheriting the kingship.[56] As we shall see later, however, the Church had difficulty in stamping out concubinage among the clergy, never mind the laity. This example suggests that pre-conversion Anglo-Saxon society may well have left an enduring heritage of marital customs somewhat at odds with a Christian emphasis on monogamy and indissolubility.

European contexts

Having established some background, it may also be helpful to glance quickly at some contexts. Although the Church attempts to impose a more or less uniform ethic of marriage across western Christendom, contrasts do exist between countries, and marriage and its circumstances in medieval England are not necessarily identical with practice in other medieval European countries. Both Ireland and Iceland, for example, have marriage regimes at odds with the Christian model of the monogamous, exogamous, indissoluble marriage well into the later Middle Ages.[57] Italy's marriage regime does conform with canon law, but economic and social circumstances may mean that marriage in later medieval Italy looks rather different from marriage in later medieval England.

Ireland
Reform-minded clerics of the eleventh and twelfth centuries were outraged by the marital arrangements of the Irish, and frequently expressed their outrage in writing. In 1074, Lanfranc, archbishop of Canterbury, wrote to king Toirdelbach ua Briain to complain about divorce and incest among the Irish. A similar letter was sent by his successor, Anselm, to Muirchertach, Toirdelbach's son.[58] The failure of the Irish to conform to the reform Church's ideas on marriage and sexual behaviour plays a part in the papal sanction of Henry II's

---

[56] Margaret Clunies Ross, 'Concubinage in Anglo-Saxon England,' *Past and Present* 108 (1985), 3–34 (pp. 6, 27–28); cf. Goody, p. 76.

[57] 'Exogamy' is marriage outside the kin group.

[58] Cited in Bart Jaski, 'Marriage Laws in Ireland and on the Continent in the Early Middle Ages,' in '*The Fragility of Her Sex*'? *Medieval Irishwomen in their European Context*, ed. Christine Meek and Katharine Simms (Dublin: Four Courts, 1996), pp. 16–42 (p. 16).

intervention in Ireland in 1171. Pope Alexander III writes to Henry (probably in 1172) applauding his actions, in part because he may reform a country where men allegedly mate with their stepmothers, with their sisters-in-law, and with the daughters of mothers they have deserted.[59] It is a few years later that Giraldus Cambrensis (Gerald de Barry), whose relatives were involved in that Anglo-Norman intervention of the late 1160s and early 1170s, makes his observation that the Irish do not contract marriages, or avoid incest, and that the men debauch the wives of their dead brothers, following the apparent (but not the true) doctrine of the Old Testament.[60] Anglo-Norman intervention did not bring reform to all of the Irish church, however, and in the later Middle Ages, two marriage regimes existed among the two 'nations' of medieval Ireland, the Irish and the English.[61]

But this great difference between Irish behaviour concerning marriage and sexual practices and the laws of marriage evident on the European continent and in England did not exist a few centuries earlier. There were differences between the marriage regime of early Ireland and that of the rest of the early medieval Church, but, as Donnchadh Ó Corráin writes, 'the similarities are, in practice, much more significant than the differences, and if Ireland was remarkable it was in the persistence of early medieval patterns of marital behaviour into the later Middle Ages and beyond.'[62]

What is striking about the early Irish laws (c. eighth century) are the number of different sorts of union they allow for. Marriages can be contracted in a variety of ways, and can be contracted on the basis of property contribution from either or both of the parties. Non-dowry marriage could be used to acquire secondary wives, wives of low status, and concubines. Various non-marital sexual relationships also received some sort of classification in the legal texts.[63] Part of the issue here may be inheritance strategies. Ó Corráin argues that occasional endogamous tendencies in early medieval Ireland may have been related to inheritance. A *banchomarba*, an heiress, could only hold a life interest in her inheritance, and in order to pass on an interest to her children might be best off to marry one of the ultimate heirs, necessarily a relative, a first or perhaps a second cousin. The result is parallel cousin marriage as found in the Old Testament.[64] David Herlihy notes the existence of 'resource polygyny' in early medieval Ireland, where the rich and powerful men in society tended to accumulate women. Herlihy argues that this accumulation of women

---

[59] *English Historical Documents, Volume 2: 1042–1189*, ed. David C. Douglas and George W. Greenaway (London: Eyre & Spottiswoode, 1953), p. 779.

[60] Giraldus Cambrensis, p. 98.

[61] Art Cosgrove, 'Marriage in Medieval Ireland,' in *Marriage in Ireland*, ed. Art Cosgrove (Dublin: College Press, 1985), pp. 35–50 (p. 35).

[62] Donnchadh Ó Corráin, 'Marriage in Early Ireland,' in *Marriage in Ireland*, ed. Art Cosgrove (Dublin: College Press, 1985), pp. 5–24 (p. 5); cf. Jaski, p. 41.

[63] Ó Corráin, pp. 6–7, 17–18.

[64] Ó Corráin, p. 11.

around men in the upper strata of society leads to a shortage elsewhere, that this results in sexual promiscuity and the consequent blurring of lines of descent through males, and the consequent importance of lines of descent through women.[65] But polygyny might also be considered to originate in an aristocratic strategy of heirship, for all recognized sons have the same rights of inheritance as the sons of the chief wife.[66] In accumulating women, propertied men increase their chances of generating heirs. Such strategies of heirship were incompatible with the Church's model of monogamous, exogamous marriage, and in the central Middle Ages we see the emergence in most of Europe of an alternative heirship strategy among the European aristocracy – the patrilineage.[67] In failing to adapt to developments in the rest of Europe, Ireland came to seem immoral to contemporaries in England and elsewhere.[68]

Iceland

Iceland, like Gaelic Ireland, operated a marriage regime largely outside the control of the Church. The canon law of marriage did exercise a very small degree of influence on thirteenth-century Iceland: Roberta Frank notes that an Icelandic episcopal statute of 1269 finally states the principle that the consent of both parties was necessary to create a valid marriage. The first evidence of the principle being enforced, however, appears in 1429.[69] Medieval Iceland seems to have ignored the Christian insistence on the indissolubility of marriage, allowing for divorce on a number of grounds: a slap, a family feud, incompatibility, nonconsummation, a compromising wound, a fatal illness, cross-dressing, and a mocking verse are all shown to be reasons for divorce in Icelandic sagas.[70] Concubinage survived into the thirteenth century, as did the sexual double standard which treated adultery as a predominantly female crime.[71] Iceland is of interest for the study of medieval European marriage because perhaps, as Roberta Frank argues, 'the situation in Iceland may be taken as representative of what happened in other rural districts of medieval Europe where both the Church and the world of classical letters were remote.'[72] Lay behaviour in Gaelic Ireland and in Iceland, at the fringes of Europe, may hint at concealed lay ideologies elsewhere in Europe wherever the Church's authority failed to reach.

---

65 Herlihy, *Medieval Households*, pp. 38–43.
66 Fergus Kelly, *A Guide to Early Irish Law* (Dublin: Dublin Institute for Advanced Studies, 1988), p. 102.
67 Herlihy, *Medieval Households*, pp. 83–88 argues that the triumph of monogamy was a precondition for patrilineage, but not its principal cause, which he suggests was economic.
68 Jaski, p. 42.
69 Frank, p. 474.
70 Frank, p. 478.
71 Frank, p. 479.
72 Frank, p. 473.

Italy

Ireland and Iceland are of interest because their marriage regimes display possibly archaic features due to relative independence from ecclesiastical control, and they suggest possibilities for alternatives to the Church's model of marriage at the relatively neglected margins of western Christendom. Later medieval Italy is of interest as a contrast to England because while it too has the same consensual model of marriage, and consequently experiences some similar difficulties with problems such as clandestine marriage,[73] different social and economic circumstances exercise an influence upon its marriage regime. In a classic article on marriage patterns, J. Hajnal argued that 'European' marriage patterns involved late marriage for women with a relatively small gap in age between men and women on first marriage.[74] Hajnal argued on the basis of studies of the 1377 poll tax that the English population was non-European, or a mixture of European and non-European with a wider variation of age at first marriage than is found later.[75] Other studies, however, have suggested the existence of Hajnal's European marriage pattern in later medieval England. Richard M. Smith points out that, in Hajnal's European system of marriage, both sexes marry late, establish an independent household, and before marriage often circulate between households as servants. In the alternative, joint-household system, men and women both marry earlier, there is likely to be a significant age gap between them, and the couple live with the husband's family. Smith notes that the circulation of young people as servants before marriage in England is compatible with Hajnal's 'European' pattern, and he contrasts the situation in Italy, where 60% of servants were married or widowed, and brides in their late teens married husbands a decade older.[76] Service in England preceded later marriage, service in Italy followed early marriage and perhaps early widowhood: work patterns give us an insight into patterns of marriage, and maybe a glimpse at the nature of those marriages, for the English pattern suggests companionate marriage, with a small gap in age between spouses, whereas the Italian suggests the opposite. P. J. P. Goldberg's analysis of service patterns based on witness depositions in marital disputes at York leads him to suggest a picture not dissimilar to Smith's, with a usual urban age of marriage

---

[73] On which see Gene Brucker, *Giovanni and Lusanna: Love and Marriage in Renaissance Florence* (Berkeley: University of California Press, 1986).

[74] J. Hajnal, 'European Marriage Patterns in Perspective,' in *Population in History: Essays in Historical Demography*, ed. D. V. Glass and D. E. C. Eversley (London: Edward Arnold, 1975), pp. 101–53 (pp. 118–20).

[75] For criticism of the studies of the 1377 poll tax that Hajnal relied upon, see Barbara A. Hanawalt, *The Ties that Bound: Peasant Families in Medieval England* (Oxford: Oxford University Press, 1986), pp. 95–96; for criticism of tax evidence as a source, cf. Brooke, p. 14.

[76] Richard M. Smith, 'Geographical Diversity in the Resort to Marriage in Late Medieval Europe: Work, Reputation and Unmarried Females in the Household Formation Systems of Northern and Southern Europe,' in *Woman is a Worthy Wight: Women in English Society, c. 1200–1500*, ed. P. J. P. Goldberg (Stroud: Sutton, 1992), pp. 19–59 (pp. 26–27, 30, 39).

in the mid twenties, slightly earlier for rural deponents, with a small difference in age between spouses at first marriage.[77]

Barbara A. Hanawalt, however, argues that economic and social conditions in England might have caused patterns of servitude and agricultural help to change substantially in the later Middle Ages. Where a labour surplus might have driven young people into service prior to marriage in the early fourteenth century, Hanawalt suggests, the post-plague economic environment might have made service a less appealling option, and we can see pressure on pay and conditions for servants and labourers. In the late sixteenth and early seventeenth centuries, however, labour supply once again outstripped demand, and service and the postponement of marriage again became an attractive option for young people.[78] If Hanawalt's analysis is correct, this suggested contrast between England and Italy might not be an absolute one, but variable depending on economic circumstances.

In both theory and practice, then, medieval English marriage displays debts to multiple inheritances in Roman, Judaeo-Christian, and Germanic ideologies of marriage. It exists in a broader European context where multiple ideologies of marriage lead to a wide variety of practice. The rest of this book will seek to demonstrate that variety in marital ideology and practice is also something that is to be found in medieval England.

---

[77] P. J. P. Goldberg, 'Marriage, Migration and Servanthood: The York Cause Paper Evidence,' in *Woman is a Worthy Wight: Women in English Society, c. 1200–1500*, ed. P. J. P. Goldberg (Stroud: Sutton, 1992), pp. 1–18.

[78] Hanawalt, *The Ties that Bound*, pp. 165–66.

1

The Principle of Consent

The Early Middle Ages

When the Church canonists of the central Middle Ages considered the question of what created a marriage between two people, the conclusion that they came to was that it was the consent of the persons to be married which created the marital bond. It was not necessary for a public ceremony to be held, or for their families to consent, although these things were seen as desirable, and were recommended by the Church. Nor were people considered to be married simply because of long cohabitation, or the birth of children. Rather, the bond of marriage was created through each person speaking words of consent in the present tense–'I N. accept you as mine.'[1]

The notion of consent as an important factor in the making of marriages was not a new one when the medieval Church formulated its consensual model of marriage: indeed the emphasis on consent in the canonists' formulation may owe something to the Roman emphasis on consent as a fundamental aspect of the marriage bond.[2] We can also see evidence of the importance of consent (albeit as one of a number

---

[1] This formula, 'Ego N. accipio te in meum,' is from the English statute 1 Salisbury 84, printed in *Councils and Synods with Other Documents relating to the English Church, AD 1205–1313,* ed. F. M. Powicke and C. R. Cheney (London: Oxford University Press, 1964), I, 87–88. It is also found in the *Corpus Iuris Canonici*: Friedberg, II, 672. But Jean Dauviller, *Le Mariage dans le Droit Classique de L'Église depuis le Decrét de Gratien (1140) jusqu'a la mort de Clément V (1314)* (Paris: Sirey, 1933), p. 31, argues that this formula (which contains no specific reference to marriage) is not offered as an example of the words to be spoken by those contracting, but rather as an example of present consent that could not be confused with future consent. Helmholz, *Marriage Litigation,* pp. 45–46 finds that all clandestine contracts required a specific reference to marriage in order to be accepted by an English ecclesiastical court.

[2] Percy Ellwood Corbett, *The Roman Law of Marriage* (London: Oxford University Press, 1930), p. 91; Brundage, *Law, Sex and Christian Society,* pp. 34–37; Michael M. Sheehan, 'Choice of Marriage Partner in the Middle Ages: Development and Mode of Application of a Theory of Marriage,' in Michael M. Sheehan, *Marriage, Family, and Law in Medieval Europe: Collected Studies,* ed. James K. Farge (Toronto: University of Toronto Press), pp. 87–117 (p. 92) (first published in *Studies in Medieval and Renaissance History* 1: 1–33).

of factors) in the making of marriages in Anglo-Saxon England. The text *Be wifmannes beweddunge,* 'Concerning the Betrothal of a Woman' (c. 975–1030), a pre-scriptive text describing how marriage agreements are to proceed, begins by stating that if a man wishes to betroth a maiden or a widow, the proposal must please her *and* her kinsmen.[3] Similarly, 2 Cnut 74 (c. 1020–23) states that no woman should be forced to marry a man that she dislikes or be given in marriage for money.[4]

And in an Old English marriage agreement from Kent (c. 1016–20) we are told:

> Her swutelaþ on þysan gewrite þa foreward þe Godwine worhte wið Byrhtric þa he his dohter awogode, þæt is ærest þæt he gæf hire anes pundes gewihta goldes wið þonne þe heo his spæce underfenge, 7 he geuþe hire þæs landes æt Stræte mid eallan þon þe þærto herð, 7 on Burwaramersce oðer healf hund æcera, 7 þærto þrittig oxna, 7 twentig cuna, 7 tyn hors . 7 tyn ðeowmen.

> Here in this document is made known the agreement which Godwine made with Brihtria when he wooed her daughter; first, namely, that he gave her a pound's weight of gold in return for her acceptance of his suit, and he granted her the land at Street with everything that belongs to it, and 150 acres at Burmarsh and in addition 30 oxen, and 20 cows, and 10 horses and 10 slaves.[5]

The reference to 'her acceptance of his suit' is to the recipient of the money and property, i.e. to Brihtria's daughter. Christine Fell comments that it is clear that 'we are dealing with acceptance of the suit by the woman herself, not by her kins-men on her behalf.'[6]

The fact that these are late Anglo-Saxon texts might lead us to speculate that these texts are not a reliable guide to earlier marriage practices in Anglo-Saxon soci-eties. But there is evidence for earlier ecclesiastical opinion, at least, in the *Penitential of Theodore* (a seventh-century text, with later additions). One canon, providing for cold feet on the part of either party to a betrothal, states that if the woman refuses to live with the man to whom she is betrothed, the money which he gave should be paid back to him with an extra third. If it is he who refuses, however, he loses the

---

[3]   *English Historical Documents, 500–1042*, ed. Dorothy Whitelock, 2nd ed. (London: Eyre Methuen, 1974), p. 431.

[4]   Whitelock, p. 429; Clunies Ross, p. 8, suggests that this refers to an ideal situation which is unlikely to have represented the true state of affairs, especially for young women at first mar-riage; Lorraine Lancaster, 'Kinship in Anglo-Saxon Society,' *British Journal of Sociology* 9 (1958), 230–50, 359–77 (p. 241 and n. 42) offers the same view; Michael M. Sheehan, 'Marriage and Family in English Conciliar and Synodal Legislation,' in Sheehan, *Marriage, Family, and Law*, pp. 77–86 (p. 84) (first published in *Essays in Honour of Anton Charles Pegis*, ed. J. Reginald O'Donnell (Toronto: Pontifical Institute of Mediaeval Studies, 1974), pp. 205–14) argues for ecclesiastical influence here.

[5]   *Anglo-Saxon Charters*, ed. and trans. A. J. Robertson (Cambridge: Cambridge University Press, 1956), p. 150; the English translation here is from Whitelock, p. 548.

[6]   Fell, p. 58.

money. In another canon, different manuscripts offer differing statements regarding the age at which a girl (rather than her parents) has power over her own body – thirteen, fourteen, sixteen, and seventeen years. The subsequent canon states that a boy is in the power of his father until he is fifteen, and after that he can make himself a monk. Similarly, a girl is in the power of her parents until the age of sixteen or seventeen, and after that she can become a nun, and her father cannot give her in marriage against her will.[7]

It is obvious that the consent of the persons to be married is not the only factor to be considered in the making of marriages in early eleventh-century England. And statements like that of Cnut prohibiting practices such as forcing women to marry or giving them for money suggests perhaps that such things did take place, although not that they were the norm.[8] But it is also clear from these texts that the consent of the persons to be married was a factor recognized by the law and by actual agreements representing contemporary practice. Anglo-Saxon England could be a harsh place, however, and at the opposite end of the spectrum from the discussions of marital consent just cited we find suggestions of the grim realities of rape and abduction in texts from across the period.[9] The *Penitential of Theodore* discusses the possibility of remarriage where a spouse has been taken into captivity.[10] Wulfstan's (admittedly polemical) *Sermo Lupi ad Anglos*, from the eleventh century, describes how ten or twelve Vikings might rape a thegn's wife, daughter, or kinswoman, while he looks on, disgraced.[11] In a context of warfare and unrest, in the medieval era as in our own, all social norms and ideals are cast aside.

Consent and canon law

The consensual model of marriage was one that was arrived at slowly, but its starting point may be seen in the canon law text assembled around the year 1140 by

---

[7] The *Penitential of Theodore* 2.12. 35–37, in McNeill and Gamer, p. 211.

[8] Discussion of the existence of 'marriage by purchase' in Anglo-Saxon England often focuses on a much earlier law, Æthelbert 77, 'Gif mon mægþ gebigeþ, ceapi geceapod sy, gif hit unfacne is', 'If a man buys a maiden, the bargain shall stand, if there is no dishonesty': *The Laws of the Earliest English Kings*, ed. and trans. by F. L. Attenborough (Cambridge: Cambridge University Press, 1922), pp. 14–15. Carole Hough, 'The Widow's *Mund*' (p. 13 and n. 37) argues that Old English *gebigan* is not identical to Modern English 'to buy', and that this (common) interpretation may be inappropriate. See the discussion at the beginning of chapter 2, below.

[9] Corinne Saunders, *Rape and Ravishment in the Literature of Medieval England* (Cambridge: Brewer, 2001), pp. 47–48, argues that the distinction between rape and abduction in Anglo-Saxon law was eroded by a broader ecclesiastical emphasis on fornication in general, and by a revival of interest in Roman law.

[10] The *Penitential of Theodore* 2.12.21–25 in McNeill and Gamer, pp. 208–10.

[11] *Anglo-Saxon Prose*, ed. and trans. Michael Swanton (London: Dent, 1975), p. 120; Saunders, p. 45, comments that in Wulfstan's text, 'the woman is objectified and her rape is an offence against the man, a means of causing him shame and loss. Rape is constructed entirely in terms of the public, patriarchal politics of warfare, as an action of enemy against enemy.'

the canonist Gratian: the *Decretum*, or *Concordance of Discordant Canons*, which contained an extensive discussion of marriage. For Gratian, the creation of the marital bond took place in two stages. The first stage is consent, the second, consummation. In this passage from causa 27 of the *Decretum*, Gratian is discussing the difference between *sponsalia* (engagement) and marriage:

> Apparet ergo, hanc non fuisse coniugem, cui vivente sponso alteri nubendi licentia non negatur. Quomodo ergo secundum Ambrosium at reliquos Patres sponsae coniuges appellantur, et his omnibus argumentis coniuges non esse probantur? Sed sciendum est, quod conigium desponsatione initiatur, commixtione perficitur. Unde inter sponsum et sponsam coniugium est, sed initiatum; inter copulatos est coniugium ratum.[12]

> It is apparent, therefore, that she was not a wife, since she is not denied permission to marry someone else by the mere fact of her betrothed being alive. How therefore are engaged people referred to as spouses by Ambrose and the other Fathers, and from all of these arguments they are not to be regarded as spouses? Because it must be understood that betrothal begins a marriage, sexual union completes it. Therefore between a betrothed man and a betrothed woman there is marriage, but begun; between those who have had intercourse, marriage is established.

For Gratian, then, the formation of the bond of marriage has two parts: the exchange of verbal consent between the persons to be married initiates marital union, and sexual intercourse between them completes it. Gratian also asserts that it is the consent of the persons to be married that is important, not the consent of their families (although it seems that he might have anticipated a context where both individuals and families should be involved in the giving of consent).[13] In response to the question of whether or not a daughter could be given in marriage against her will, he responds, *Hiis auctoritatibus evidenter ostenditur, quod nisi libera voluntate nulla est copulanda alicui*, 'By these authorities it is evident that no woman should be married to anyone except by her free will.'[14] In this, he goes further perhaps than the authorities that he cites in support.[15]

Later twelfth-century writers produced a different model of the creation of the marital bond. The most important of these was the theologian Peter Lombard (c. 1095–1160), later bishop of Paris, who rejected Gratian's inclusion

---

[12] Gratian, *Decretum* c. 27 q. 2 c. 3, printed in Friedberg, I, 1073; I am grateful to Dr R. H. F. Carver for his revision of the translation here.

[13] Sheehan, 'Choice of Marriage Partner,' pp. 96–97.

[14] Gratian, *Decretum*, c. 31 q. 2 c. 4, printed in Friedberg, I, 1114; English translation here from Sheehan, 'Choice of Marriage Partner,' p. 96.

[15] On the use that Gratian makes of his evidence on this question, see John T. Noonan, 'Power to Choose,' *Viator* 4 (1973) 419–34; Sheehan, 'Choice of Marriage Partner,' pp. 92–97.

of a sexual requirement, and championed a purely consensual definition. He writes in the *Sentences*:

> Efficiens autem causa matrimonii est consensus, non quilibet, sed per verba expressus; nec de futuro, sed de praesenti. – Si enim consentiunt in futurum, dicentes: Accipiam te in virum, et ego te in uxorem, non est iste consensus efficax matrimonii. Item, si consentiant mente, et non exprimant verbis vel aliis certis signis, nec talis consensus efficit matrimonium. Si autem verbis explicatur, quod tamen corde non volunt, si non sit coactio ibi vel dolus, obligatio illa verborum quibus consentiunt, dicentes: Accipio te in virum et ego te in uxorem, matrimonium facit.[16]

> But the efficient cause of marriage is consent, not any consent, but expressed in words; not concerning the future, but in the present tense. – For if by consent in the future tense, saying: I will accept you as my husband, and I you as my wife, this consent does not effect marriage. Likewise, if they consent mentally, and they do not express consent through words or other clear signs, neither does such consent effect marriage. But if it is expressed in words, which nonetheless are not heartfelt, provided there is no duress or deceit present, that pledge of words through which they consent, saying: 'I accept you as my husband, and I you as my wife,' makes marriage.

It was this consensual definition, in modified form, which became the basis of the marriage doctrine of Pope Alexander III (c. 1105–81). Alexander's mature marriage theory allowed for two modes of contracting: either the exchange of words of consent in the present tense (present consent), without any consummation being necessary to complete the contract of marriage, or alternatively the exchange of words of consent in the future tense (future consent), which would constitute a marriage if followed by sexual intercourse. According to James Brundage, Alexander expressed his mature marriage theory most clearly in the decretal *Veniens ad nos*, addressed to Bishop John of Norwich. The case is undated, but probably from the 1170s.[17] *Veniens ad nos* presents a complicated case in which a man has agreed to marry two women. The first woman was someone with whom he had previously had children: she came to his house, and he agreed to take her as his wife in the presence of witnesses. But he then spent the night at his neighbour's house, and when the neighbour happened to come across him in bed with his daughter, he forced him to agree to marry *her*, and the words spoken on this occasion were in the present tense. The pope has been asked to decide which of these women he should be husband to.

---

[16] Peter Lombard, *Sententiae in IV Libris Distinctae*, ed. Pontificale Collegium S. Bonaventurae Ad Claras Aquas (Rome: Grottaferrata 1971–81), II, 422–23; I am grateful to Dr R. H. F. Carver for his revision of the translation here.

[17] Brundage, *Law, Sex, and Christian Society*, p. 333.

Alexander's decision instructs the bishop to obtain two pieces of information, and to act accordingly. If the man has had sexual intercourse with the first woman after agreeing that he would marry her at some future date, then he was to remain with her, for future consent followed by intercourse made marriage. If that was the case, then his pledge to the second woman was invalid, for if he was already married to the first woman, he could not legally marry the second. So the question of intercourse is a crucial one in this case. But if he had not had intercourse with the first woman after his promise, then he was merely betrothed or engaged, rather than married, at the time of giving his consent to the second woman, and in that case, because his pledge to *her* was made in the present tense, this second pledge then made a marriage. Or, at least, he was married to her if he had not been forced into the union, for force and fear invalidate consent and so constitute an impediment to the creation of the marriage bond. And so the second thing that the bishop needs to decide upon is the extent to which the neighbour really did force the man in this case to marry his daughter.[18]

Alexander's formulation of what constitutes a marriage clearly owes a debt to Peter Lombard in its first definition: that the giving of consent in the present tense creates a marriage without anything further being required.[19] But it may also owe something to Gratian in its second formulation: that future consent to marriage is ratified by subsequent intercourse.[20] Alexander's judgments on the formation of the bond became the basis of subsequent law, and his marriage decretals were incorporated in the *Decretals of Gregory IX* or *Liber Extra* (which formed the second part of the *Corpus Iuris Canonici*, alongside the *Decretum*) when it was compiled in 1234.

There are convenient theological reasons why an emphasis on consent as the fundamental requirement for creating a marriage might be preferred to an emphasis on coition. Elizabeth A. Clark, writing on the marriage theory of St Augustine, notes his conclusion that Mary and Joseph were husband and wife, despite their failure to have intercourse, in contrast to St Jerome's assertion that Joseph was Mary's guardian rather than her husband.[21] Gratian also notes that

---

[18]   *Veniens ad nos* is in the *Decretals of Gregory IX*, lib. 4, tit. 1, c.15, printed in Friedberg, II, 666–67.

[19]   Intercourse does retain a role, though, in that impotence was seen as an impediment to matrimony, and it was possible to secure a divorce *a vinculo* (from the marital bond) because of it: Friedberg, II, 705; Helmholz, *Marriage Litigation*, pp. 87–90.

[20]   Dauviller, pp. 56–57 argues that Alexander III follows Gratian in the formulation of this second means of contracting marriage, but notes that the canonist Huguccio, rejecting such a model, argued that intercourse between people who had exchanged future consent itself constituted present consent. In practice, both models meant that future consent followed by intercourse was marriage.

[21]   Elizabeth A. Clark, ' "Adam's Only Companion": Augustine and the Early Christian Debate on Marriage,' in *The Olde Daunce: Love, Friendship, Sex and Marriage in the Medieval World*, ed. Robert R. Edwards and Stephen Spector (Albany: SUNY Press, 1991), pp. 15–31 (pp. 22–23).

if sexual intercourse made marriage, then no marriage existed between Mary and Joseph.[22] He solved the dilemma that this posed for his model of marriage by stating:

> Beata Mariae proposuit se conservaturam votum virginitatis in corde, sed ipsum votum virginitatis non expressit ore. Subiecit se diuinae dispositioni, dum proposuit se perseueraturam virginem, nisi Deus ei aliter reualeret. Conmittens ergo virginitatem suam diuinae dispositioni consensit in carnalem copulam, non illam appetendo, sed diuinae inspirationi in utroque obediendo. Postea vero filium genuit quod corde conceperat simul cum uiro labiis expressit, et uterque in virginitate permansit.

> The Blessed Mary proposed that she would preserve a vow of virginity in her heart, but she did not express that vow of virginity with her mouth. She subjected herself to divine disposition when she proposed that she would preserve virginity, unless God revealed to her otherwise. Therefore, committing her virginity to divine disposition, she consented to carnal union, not by seeking it, but by obeying divine inspiration in both the one case and the other. But it was after she bore a son that she expressed with her lips what she had conceived with her heart, together with her husband, and each remained in virginity.[23]

Peter Lombard adopts this passage from Gratian, but argues that, when Mary and Joseph married, she consented to conjugal society, but not to intercourse, unless it was pleasing to God.[24]

St Thomas Aquinas also asks if a 'true marriage' existed between Mary and Joseph.[25] He states that a marriage is true when complete, and distinguishes between two types of completion: the first being the form which gives something specific character (here the union of souls), the second through the operation by which the thing achieves its purpose (here the birth and training of children). He concludes that their consent to the marital bond (but not to sexual union unless it was pleasing to God) fulfilled the first requirement, and that although their marriage was not consummated, it fulfilled the second form of completion regarding the bringing up of children. He then quotes Augustine as saying that all the goods of marriage were found in the marriage of Christ's parents.[26] A consensual theory of marriage, then, allows Aquinas, following Augustine and contemporary legal theory, to argue for the completion of the marriage of Mary and Joseph.

---

[22] Friedberg, I, 1063.

[23] Friedberg, I, 1063; English translation from Elliott, p. 178.

[24] Peter Lombard, II, 439–40.

[25] St Thomas Aquinas, *Summa Theologiae*, ed. T. Gilby and others, 61 vols (London: Blackfriars, 1964–81), LI, 63.

[26] Aquinas, LI, 65–67.

English ecclesiastical legislation

A large body of evidence concerning the English Church's intervention in marriage practices in the later Middle Ages exists in the conciliar and synodal legislation produced in England between 1215 and the end of the fourteenth century.[27]
As Michael M. Sheehan writes in his survey of the conciliar legislation and diocesan statutes of later medieval England:

> [. . .] Synodal regulations and other collections published directly by
> the bishops were to provide one of the major means by which import-
> ant developments in the understanding and practice of marriage were
> implemented during the thirteenth century.[28]

The statutes achieved wide circulation: in the thirteenth century and afterwards,
each diocesan had to have a copy of legatine and provincial canons, and regular
prelates and lower clergy were obliged to possess some sections of the law.[29] The
function of the statutes was, to some extent, to repeat and amplify law already current in the great legal texts of the western Church, the *Corpus Iuris Canonici* and
its commentaries.[30] But, as R. H. Helmholz comments:

> Much of the scope of the jurisdiction exercised by the English Church
> was based immediately upon local custom and synodal legislation. In
> fact, this appears to have been true in many parts of Western Europe.
> The ecclesiastical courts did not always enforce all of the law found in
> the *Corpus Iuris Canonici*.[31]

On the question of the formation of the marital bond, it is the two methods of
contracting developed by Alexander III that we encounter in the local legislation
of thirteenth- and fourteenth-century England. 1 Salisbury 84 (1217 × 1219)
reads:

> De (recta) forma contrahenda.
> Item, precipimus quod sacerdotes doceant personas contrahentes

---

[27] On the terms 'council' and 'synod', C. R. Cheney, 'Legislation of the Medieval English
Church,' *English Historical Review* 50 (1935), 193–224, 385–417 (p. 196) writes: 'Although by
a convenient custom modern writers usually apply "synod" to diocesan meetings, reserving
"council" for assemblies of wider scope, no formal distinction was made in the middle ages.'

[28] Michael M. Sheehan, 'Marriage Theory and Practice in the Conciliar Legislation and
Diocesan Statutes of Medieval England,' in Sheehan, *Marriage, Family, and Law*, pp. 118–76
(p. 123) (first published in *Mediaeval Studies* 40 (1978) 408–60).

[29] Cheney, 'Legislation,' p. 213; but cf. William Langland's satirical comment on a slothful
parish priest's ignorance of the canon law in *Piers Plowman* B. 5. 416, 422.

[30] Cheney, 'Legislation,' p. 202.

[31] R. H. Helmholz, *Canon Law and the Law of England* (London: Hambledon, 1987),
Introduction, p. ix.

hanc formam verborum in Gallico vel Anglico: Ego N. accipio te in meam. Similiter et mulier dicat: Ego N. accipio te in meum. In hiis enim verbis consistit vis magna et matrimonium contrahitur. Nec sine trina denuntiatione in ecclesia facta publice et sollempniter presumat sacerdos aliquas personas coniungere matrimonialiter; pro quibus denunitaitionibus faciendis nichil omnino exigatur. Et si utraque persona coniungenda fuerit omnino incongnita, nullo modo prestet sacerdos auctoritatem tali contractui, nisi prius ei legittime constiterit quod persone legittime fuerint ad contrahendum. Similiter si altera illarum fuerit incongnita, habeat literas testimoniales quod legittime possit contrahere et quod trina denuntiatio facta fuerit in parochia illius.[32]

Concerning the (correct) form of contracting a marriage. Similarly we command that priests should teach the persons contracting a marriage this form of words in French or English: I N. accept you as mine. And similarly the woman must say: I N. accept you as mine. For in these words great force exists, and marriage is brought about. A priest should not presume to join any persons matrimonially without making an announcement three times, publicly and solemnly in the church; for making these announcements, no fee should be demanded. And if either of the persons to be married is entirely unknown, in no way ought the priest to be responsible for the authorization of such a marriage unless it was legally proved beforehand that they were legitimate persons for the purpose of being married. Similarly, if one of them was unknown, he must have a letter of testimony that he can legally get married, and that a threefold announcement has been made in his parish.

Although there are a number of conditions attached to this 'correct' form of contracting a marriage, the formula 'for in these words great force exists, and marriage is brought about,' makes it clear that it is the giving of consent, expressed in the present tense, that creates the marriage. 2 Salisbury 23 has a similar formula:

Precipimus etiam quod adveniente die nuptiarum in facie ecclesie sacerdos palam interroget contrahentes si sibi invicem consentiant et si ad consensum extorquendum vis vel metus sit illatus; et tunc cessante quolibet impedimento instruant eos in wlgari quod se invicem accipiant hoc modo: Accipio vel recipio in meam, et: Ego te in meum, per que vel per similia verba coniugalis contractus forma designatur.[33]

Also we command that when the day of marriage arrives, in front of the church the priest should publicly interrogate the persons contracting if they mutually consent to each other and whether force or fear

---

[32] Powicke and Cheney, I, 87–88; I am grateful to Professor Kathleen M. Coleman for her revision of the translations from the English statutes offered here.
[33] Powicke and Cheney, I, 376.

was applied to extract their consent; then, there being no impediment, they should tell each other in the vernacular that they mutually accept each other in this way: I accept, or I receive you as mine, and: I you as mine, by these or by similar words the contract of marriage is to be signified.

Regarding future consent, 1 Canterbury 55 (1213 × 1214), the Constitutions of a Certain Bishop 60 (1225 × 1230?) and 1 Chichester 28 (1245 × 1252) all state that oaths of betrothal followed by intercourse would be regarded as marriage by the Church.[34]

Clandestine marriage

The problem with the consensual theory of marriage, requiring as it did only an exchange of consent between parties for a marriage to be valid, is that it has been seen as conferring legitimacy upon privately contracted unions that ignore the ecclesiastical regulations with regard to contracting in front of the church, in the presence of a priest, subsequent to the threefold announcement of the banns,[35] etc. If 1 Salisbury 84 prescribes the 'correct' way of contracting a marriage, it is clear that its explicitly enshrining the creation of the marriage bond in the exchange of words of consent also creates a large number of 'incorrect', but nonetheless canonically valid, ways of contracting a marriage, and the problem of clandestine marriage, condemned by Gratian and subsequently by 4 Lateran 51 in 1215, is (along with clerical concubinage) the single largest concern of English ecclesiastical marriage legislation in the thirteenth and fourteenth centuries.

This interpretation, which sees the consensual theory as a loophole by which clandestine marriages are validated is, however, disputed by Jack Goody, who sees the acceptance of clandestine marriage by the Church as being a reflection of its difficulties in imposing its own model of contracting.[36] Certainly clandestine marriage was an enormous problem: of 122 cases surveyed by Sheehan in the diocese of Ely between March 1374 and March 1382, 89 were clandestine marriages; R. H. Helmholz's survey of Canterbury cases between 1411 and 1420 likewise turns up 38 clandestine marriages out of 41 contracted by words of present consent.[37]

---

[34] Powicke and Cheney, I, 34–45, 190–91, 457; Sheehan, 'Marriage Theory,' p. 431 argues that this method of contracting did not appear in a greater number of statutes because 'the main purpose of the statutes was not to teach that such a union established a valid marriage but to forbid it.'

[35] The banns are a threefold public announcement of the impending marriage which allow the public to raise any potential objections before the wedding takes place.

[36] Goody, p. 148.

[37] Michael M. Sheehan, 'The Formation and Stability of Marriage in Fourteenth Century England: Evidence of an Ely Register,' in Sheehan, *Marriage, Family, and Law*, pp. 38–76 (p. 61) (first published in *Mediaeval Studies* 33 (1971) 228–63); Helmholz, *Marriage Litigation*, p. 28.

2 Salisbury 23 (1238 x 1244) could be interpreted either as showing how the consensual theory leads to acceptance of clandestine marriage, or how acceptance of clandestine marriage leads to the expansion of the Church's control over marriage. It opens by admitting that consent alone can create a marriage, but stresses the priority of the Church's authority over marriage. Hence clandestine marriages are not valid unless they are 'tolerated with permission':

> Licet verum matrimonium per legitimum viri et mulieris consensum contrahatur, necessaria tamen sunt quantum ad ecclesiam verba vel signa consensum exprimentia de presenti, ex quo manifestissime apparet quod sine auctoritate ecclesie, cuius iudicio approbandus est contractus vel reprobandus, non sunt matrimonia contrahenda, licet alias quandoque contracta ex permissione tollerentur.[38]

> But although marriage can be contracted by the lawful agreement of a man and a woman, nevertheless with respect to the Church there are essential words or signs expressing present consent, from which it appears most clearly that without the authority of the Church, by whose judgment the contract is to be approved or rejected, marriages are not to be contracted, although unions which are otherwise contracted are sometimes to be tolerated with permission.

Hence, presumably, Helmholz's assertion that by far the most common matrimonial case in medieval Church courts was the suit brought to enforce a marriage contract, where one person wished to prove the existence of their marriage to another.[39] This assertion is supported by Charles Donahue's analysis of cases in the court of York, which finds that 78% of the 88 fourteenth-century cases and 85% of the 125 fifteenth-century marriage cases surviving from this court were suits to enforce a contract.[40]

All of the statutes seem to accept the validity of clandestine marriage, excepting those which simply mention in passing that it is prohibited (e.g. Lincoln 42 (1239?), Norwich 39 (1240 × 1243), and 2 Winchester 57 (1247?)),[41] although they are careful to follow 4 Lateran 51 in condemning the practice, insisting that Church approval is necessary, and prescribing penance. 1 Salisbury 85 reads:

> De clandestinis matrimoniis.
> Prohibemus similiter clandestina matrimonia, precipientes quod publice fiant in facie ecclesie, presente sacerdote ad hoc vocato. Si vero secus actum fuerit non approbetur, nisi de nostra specialia auctoritate.

---

[38] Powicke and Cheney, I, 375.

[39] Helmholz, *Marriage Litigation*, p. 25.

[40] Charles Donahue, Jr., 'Female Plaintiffs in Marriage Cases in the Court of York in the Later Middle Ages: What Can We Learn from the Numbers?,' in *Wife and Widow in Medieval England*, ed. Sue Sheridan Walker (Ann Arbor: University of Michigan Press, 1993), pp. 183–213 (pp. 185, 186, 198).

[41] Powicke and Cheney, I, 274, 351, 412.

> Sacerdos qui tales coniunctiones prohibere contempserit vel talibus interesse presumpserit, vel quilibet alius regularis, secundum statuta concilii ab officio per triennium suspendatur, gravius puniendus si culpe quantitas postulaverit. Set et qui taliter copulari presumpserint, etiam in gradu concesso, hiis condigna penitentia iniungatur.[42]

> Concerning clandestine marriages.
> We similarly prohibit clandestine marriages, ordering that they shall be made in public in front of the church, in the presence of a priest who has been called for this purpose. If it has actually been done otherwise, it is not to be approved, except by our special authority. A priest who has refused to prevent unions of such a kind or who has presumed to be present at such, or any other person subject to a rule, according to the statutes of the council is suspended from office for three years, and must be more harshly punished if the size of the fault demands it. But a suitable penance must be demanded of those who have presumed to couple in this manner, even in the permitted grades.

There is, however, a further interpretative problem in that the term 'clandestine marriage' can cover a variety of circumstances. James Brundage cites the canonist Hostiensis as distinguishing between six different types, but such a division does not seem to neatly correspond with the usages found in the English statutes.[43]

Rather, the English councils and synods seem to deal mainly with four potential types of clandestine contract:

1. The exchange of present consent by two parties outside of any ceremonial setting, possibly with few or no witnesses.

2. The contracting of marriages without the threefold announcement of the banns having preceded them.

3. The celebrating of marriage ceremonies in secret circumstances or locations.

4. The celebrating of marriage ceremonies where the persons to be married are unknown.

For example, in 1 Salisbury 85, quoted above, the first sentence orders that marriages should not take place unless in public, in front of the church, in the presence of a priest. This seems to be an injunction against clandestine marriage of our first sort, clandestinity in what Sheehan calls 'the older and narrower sense.' But it also goes on to prescribe penance for priests who participate in or fail to prohibit clandestine marriages, and clearly a different sense of clandestinity applies here.[44] Possibly what is meant is marriage without the announcement of

---

[42] Powicke and Cheney, I, 88.
[43] Brundage, *Law, Sex, and Christian Society,* pp. 440–41.
[44] Sheehan, 'Marriage Theory,' p. 155.

the banns, our second type, or our third, marriage in secret ceremonies or locations. But 1 Salisbury 85 certainly includes more than one meaning for the term
'clandestine marriage'.

Inadvertent marriage

Because a clandestine marriage involving the exchange of consent between two
parties outside of any ceremonial setting could be valid (our first category of clandestine marriage), the Church was particularly concerned that such marriages
should not occur accidentally. And so legislation requires that priests should be
present whenever a promise was made concerning marriage, including betrothals
as well as marriages. There seems to be concern that in intending to become
betrothed, which should occur through making a promise to marry in the future
tense, the parties might instead speak in the present tense, and find themselves not
engaged, as they had intended, but securely married instead. 1 Salisbury 83 is the
first English statute which requires a priest to be present at betrothals:[45]

> De reverentia matrimonii.
> Propter hoc precipimus quod matrimonia cum honore celebrentur et
> reverentia, non cum risu et ioco, non in tabernis, potationibus publi-
> cis seu commenssationibus. Nec quisquam annulum de iunco vel alia
> vili materia vel pretiosa iocando manibus innectat muliercularum, ut
> liberius cum eis fornicetur, ne dum iocari se putat, honeribus matri-
> monialibus se astringat. Nec de cetero alicui fides detur de matrimo-
> nio contrahendo, nisi coram sacerdote et tribus aut quatuor personis
> fidedingnis, propter hoc convocatis (Quod si secus actum fuerit, et
> fides pro nulla habeatur et carnalis copula etiam si sit subsecuta).
> Nichilominus, quoniam non mediocriter turbant ecclesiam dei et
> pericula animabus ingerunt taliter contrahentes, statuimus ut tales ad
> nos transmittantur, et nos illos ad apostolicam sedem transmittemus,
> tanquam perturbatores ecclesiastice pacis et contemptores ecclesiasti-
> corum mandatorum. Et hoc statutum precipimus omni die dominico
> populo denuntiari.[46]

> Concerning the reverence of marriage.
> On account of this we command that marriages are to be celebrated
> with honour and reverence, not with laughter and ribaldry, not in tav-
> erns, with public drinking and eating together. Nor should anyone
> bind women's hands with a noose made of reed or any other material,
> be it cheap or expensive, so as to fornicate with them more freely, for
> fear that while he considers himself to be joking, he binds himself

---

[45] Sheehan, 'Marriage Theory,' p. 138; Dauviller, p. 133, notes that legislation against clandestine betrothals was usually local.

[46] Powicke and Cheney, I, 87. For the influence of this statute, see Sheehan, 'Marriage Theory,'
pp. 138, 141–42. The sentence in parentheses appears as a cancelled sentence in one ms.

with the rites of marriage. Nor should a promise be given to anyone from now on if not in the presence of a priest and three or four persons of good faith who have been called together for this purpose (But if it has happened differently, a promise is not deemed to have been made to any woman, even if copulation has occurred). Nevertheless, since people entering into unions in this way trouble the church of God not a little and inflict dangers on souls, we have decided that such people should be handed over to us, and we will hand them on to the Holy See, as disturbers of the ecclesiastical peace and despisers of ecclesiastical orders. And we order this statute to be read out to the people every Sunday.

The second sentence here seems to be a warning against the inadvertent exchange of present consent. The binding of someone's hands is presumably a symbol of marriage.[47] The statute then attacks clandestine betrothals, and a cancelled sentence declares these promises not to hold. The prohibition on marriages being celebrated in taverns is partly about the dignity of the institution,[48] but perhaps also an expression of concern regarding the giving of consent to marriage while drunk: 3 Worcester 23 (1240) states that pledges of betrothal should be made with a dry mouth.[49] The suggestion that men should not make gestures of marriage towards women 'so as to fornicate with them more freely' probably describes a fairly common practice, and perhaps finds an echo in a much later case, from fifteenth-century Yorkshire. John Walkar allegedly made a contract with Alice Walkar, saying to her that he would take no other for wife than her, by his faith. This pledge was followed by intercourse. Such a form of words might only constitute betrothal, but, as we have seen, betrothal followed by intercourse was regarded as marriage, and, as we shall see shortly, the declaration that clandestine betrothals were to be disregarded did not outlast the thirteenth century. Alice was nonetheless prosecuted for fornication, possibly because John denied the contract, but although the case ends without recording the judgment, the editor offers evidence from other cases that suggests they might have married after all, although John's habits seem not to have changed: a John Walkar was prosecuted for adultery in 1462.[50]

---

[47] Helmholz, *Marriage Litigation*, pp. 45–46 cites a case where a man and a woman are said to have 'clasped hands in the manner of contracting a marriage, but no words were spoken.' The court held against the contracting of a marriage, but it is clear that an exchange of consent could involve signs as well as words. Sheehan, 'Formation and Stability,' pp. 56, 58–59, cites other cases of clandestine marriage including gestures as well as words.

[48] Helmholz, *Marriage Litigation*, p. 29, records marriages taking place under an ash tree, in a bed, in a garden, in a small storehouse, in a field, in a blacksmith's shop, near a hedge, in a kitchen, by an oak tree, at a tavern, and on the King's Highway.

[49] Powicke and Cheney, I, 302.

[50] *Before the Bawdy Court: Selections from Church Court and Other Records relating to the Correction of Moral Offences in England, Scotland, and New England*, ed. Paul Hair (London: Elek, 1972), p. 226.

The Constitutions of a Certain Bishop 59 echoes the cancelled sentence of 1 Salisbury 83 and declares clandestine marriages (in our first sense) to hold, but denies the validity of clandestine betrothals:

> Nec clamdestina contrahantur matrimonia, set pupplice et in facie ecclesie, presente sacerdote. Si vero secus actum fuerit, factum non admittatur in ecclesia, nisi de speciali auctoritate nostra. Sacerdos autem qui contra huius statuti nostri formam aliquos matrimonio copulaverit ab omni officio suspendatur, nec relaxetur nisi de speciali mandato nostro. Nec fides de aliqua desponsanda detur nisi presente sacerdote. Quod si aliter factum fuerit, decernimus contractum non tenere et persone legittime punientur.[51]

> Marriages should not be contracted clandestinely, but publicly and in front of the church, in the presence of a priest. But if it happens otherwise, what has been done is not admitted in the church, except by our special authority. But a priest who has joined people in matrimony in defiance of the contents of this statute of ours is to be suspended from all his duties, and is not to be pardoned except by our special mandate. Nor should pledges from anyone to be betrothed be given, except in the presence of a priest. If this has been done otherwise, we declare the contract not to hold, and the persons are to be punished legally.

The following canon, no. 60, declares betrothal following intercourse to be marriage,[52] perhaps implying that clandestine betrothal followed by intercourse is not, echoing 1 Salisbury 83. The declaration in these statutes that clandestine betrothals will not be recognized does not endure: 3 Worcester 23 (1240) orders priests to prevent clandestine betrothals, but does not declare them invalid.[53] 2 Salisbury 25 (1238 × 44) and the Provincial Constitutions of Walter Raynold, archbishop of Canterbury (1322), both prescribe excommunication for those who engage in clandestine betrothals, but neither deny the validity of the practice.[54]

The Church's nervousness about people unwittingly exchanging present consent, and thus becoming married when they might intend merely to become engaged, is perhaps based on a lack of popular awareness of the importance of the distinction in the eyes of the Church courts. R. H. Helmholz argues for a difference between formal law and popular attitude regarding the consensual model of marriage, and he argues that many lay people continued to regard a contract of marriage through words of present consent merely to constitute betrothal.[55] In one

---

[51] Powicke and Cheney, I, 190.
[52] Powicke and Cheney, I, 190–91.
[53] Powicke and Cheney, I, 302.
[54] Powicke and Cheney, I, 376; *Concilia Magnae Brittaniae et Hiberniae*, ed. David Wilkins (London, 1737), II, 58.
[55] Helmholz, *Marriage Litigation*, p. 31.

case from about 1200, an account of the testimony of Robert Parage, the brother of one of the litigants, reveals that he did not know the form of words to be used in the contracting of a marriage, even though he had himself been married earlier in the year.[56] So the attack on clandestine betrothal in the statutes may be an attempt to prevent the unwitting exchange of present consent, and hence clandestine marriage of our first sort.

In part, the problem is that, in practice, the consensual model, which we might imagine to be concerned primarily with the intentions of the persons to be married, is reduced to a formula of words spoken by one person to another. It is words, not intentions, that the Church courts will take into account in deciding whether or not a bond of marriage existed between two persons. In an early discussion of what constitutes a marriage, St Augustine asks if a man and a woman cohabit and have sex with one another, simply because they cannot control their lust, can this be called a marriage? He decides that if they are faithful to one another, and do not use contraception, and agree to live together until the death of one of them, then this can be called a marriage. Then he asks what the case is if the intention of one of the parties is different from that of the other (in a passage which seems to recall some of his own biography as described in the *Confessions*).[57] Augustine's discussion of what makes a marriage here is all about intentions: what the parties to the union see themselves as doing, what their respective views of the relationship and its purpose are. But the ecclesiastical legislation of the central and later Middle Ages is concerned only with actions. In Peter Lombard's words, already quoted above, giving consent mentally but not expressing it in words does not create a marriage. But if the words of consent are spoken, even if the person speaking does not mean what they say, and speaks them insincerely, they still have the effect of creating a marriage.[58] Likewise, according to 1 Salisbury 83, no one should jokingly offer to marry someone in order to have sex with them, for the words will bind irrespective of the intention.[59] For the most part, then, 'consent' in the consensual model of marriage is not about intentions but about a verbal formula.

Impediments to consent

There were certain conditions, however, which could prevent that verbal formula from holding. The Church recognized a number of impediments to marital consent. Incest, in the sense of consanguinity (relationship of blood) and affinity

---

[56] *Select Cases from the Ecclesiastical Courts of the Province of Canterbury, c. 1200–1301*, ed. Norma Adams and Charles Donahue, Jr. (London: Selden Society, 1981), p. 23.

[57] St Augustine, ed. and trans. Walsh, pp. 11–13; cf. St Augustine, *Confessions*, trans. R. S. Pine-Coffin (Harmondsworth: Penguin, 1961), p. 131.

[58] Peter Lombard, II, 422–23.

[59] Powicke and Cheney, I, 87.

(relationship through marriage or sexual intercourse), created an impediment to marriage, the latter being an innovation of the Church, along with the spiritual relationships which impeded marriage. Jack Goody demonstrates clearly the alteration in English kin terms to include affinal relationships (hence father-in-law, sister-in-law, etc.) and spiritual relationships (godmother, godfather) in the eleventh century due to the introduction of the Church regulations.[60] The rules of consanguinity as modified in 4 Lateran 50 (1215) meant that any persons with an ancestor in common in the previous four generations were forbidden to marry.[61] Likewise the rules of affinity meant that anyone whose ancestors had married or had intercourse in the previous four generations could not marry.[62] Several other impediments are discussed in 1 Salisbury 86 – vows, holy orders, and disparity of cult (meaning that Christians cannot marry non-Christians):

> (Ne sortilegia vel maleficia fiant in nuptiis)
> In nuptiis semper prohibeatur sub pena excommunicationis sortilegia fieri et maleficia, et sub tali pena teneantur omnes qui celant impedimenta matrimonii: votum, ordinem, consanguinitatem, affinitatem, disparem cultum, compaternitatem. Et hec tantum iiii[or] personas excludit a matrimonio: compatrem, commatrem, filiolum, fratrem vel sororem spiritualem, scilicet, filium vel filiam patrini. Et ista comminatio in singulis parochiis frequentur recitetur.[63]

> That sorcery or wickedness are not made in relation to marriage. In relation to marriage is always to be forbidden the practice of sorcery and witchcraft, under threat of excommunication, and under such a penalty are to be included all those who conceal impediments to matrimony: vows, orders, consanguinity, affinity, disparity of cult, sponsorship. And this excludes only four sorts of people from marriage: godfathers, godmothers, godchildren, and spiritual brothers and sisters, that is to say, the sons and daughters of godparents. And that prohibition should be read aloud frequently in each parish.

Clandestine marriages of the second sort discussed above, marriages without the threefold announcement of the intention to get married, seem to have taken place

---

[60] Goody, pp. 269–70.

[61] On calculations of relationships of consanguinity and affinity, see Goody, pp. 136–37.

[62] On the modification of the rules of affinity in 4 Lateran 50, see Frederick Pollock and Frederic William Maitland, *The History of English Law Before the Time of Edward I*, 2nd ed., 2 vols, (Cambridge: Cambridge University Press, 1898), II, 405.

[63] Powicke and Cheney, I, 88. A final impediment in addition to these, the 'impediment of crime', appears in 1 Salisbury 79: It states that adulterers may not marry if they have agreed to marry during the lifetime of a spouse or if they plotted the death of a spouse: Powicke and Cheney, I, 85–86. This is not an influential canon (Sheehan, 'Marriage Theory,' pp. 131–32), but it does derive from authoritative sources (cf. Peter Lombard, II, 472; Friedberg, II, 687–88; discussion in Dauviller, pp. 158–59). I argue for its relevance to Chaucer's *Wife of Bath's Prologue* in chapter 7, below.

in order to avoid the problems posed by impediments. This is implicit in the declaration of the Provincial Council at Canterbury (1328):

> De matrimonio non solemnizando absque bannorum editione. Item, quia ex contractibus matrimonialibus absque bannorum editione praehabita initis, nonnulla pericula proveniunt, et manifestum est indies provenire; omnibus et singulis suffrageneis nostros praecipimus statuendo, quod decretalem: 'Cum inhibitio Extr. de clandestin. de sponsal.' qua prohibetur, ne qui matrimonium contrahant, bannis non praemissis, in singulis ecclesiis parochialibus suae diocesis pluribus diebus sollenibus, cum major populi affuerit multitudo, exponi faciant in vulgari, ipsamque faciant firmiter observari, quibusvis sacerdotibus etiam parochialibus vel non parochialibus, qui contractibus matrimonialibus ante sollenem editionem bannorum initis, praesumpserint interesse, poenam suspensionis ab officio per triennium infligendo; et huiusmodi contrahentes etiam, si nullum subsit impedimentum, poena debit percellendo.[64]

Concerning marriage that is not to be solemnized without the banns having been published.

Likewise, because dangers arise as a result of contracts of marriage that are entered into without the banns having been published in advance and it is clear that these arise on a daily basis; we order to be declared by each and every suffragan of ours, this decree: 'Since the external constraints on clandestine betrothals', whereby it is forbidden that anyone should contract a marriage, without publishing the banns beforehand, and in each parish church of their diocese on several Sundays, with most of the people present, they are to cause it to be proclaimed in the vernacular, and that they are to cause it to be strictly observed by any parish priests or priests without parishes who dare to be present at marriage contracts initiated before proper publication of the banns, the penalty of suspension from office for three years is to be inflicted; and there is a penalty of flogging for persons contracting like this, even if no impediment is at hand.

The implication here is that there usually was an impediment, as there was for example in the case of William de Hypsconys and Matilda Swyninton. A papal letter of 1390 to the bishop of Lichfield directs him to absolve this couple from the excommunication they incurred by marrying in a private chapel, without banns.[65] They were related in the third and fourth degrees of consanguinity, which would impede them from marrying. This reveals the purpose of the banns, which were intended to determine whether or not an impediment to the marriage existed. Of course, impediments to the marriage which had not been revealed by the

---

[64] Wilkins, II, 554.
[65] *Calendar of Entries in the Papal Registers Relating to Great Britain and Ireland. Papal Letters. Vol. IV. AD 1362–1404*, ed. W. H. Bliss and J. A. Twemlow (London: HMSO, 1902), p. 372.

announcement of the banns might still come to light after the wedding, as is shown in the case of William de Tenderyng and Catherine Mylde. A papal letter of 1397 to the bishop of Norwich describes how William, a knight, and Catherine, a noblewoman, had married in the prescribed manner, after the threefold announcement of the banns. The declaration of the banns, however, failed to unearth the fact that the two were related in the third and fourth degree of kindred. Having married in ignorance of this fact, its subsequent discovery led them to apply for permission to remain in the marriage: the pope granted this and declared their offspring legitimate.[66]

2 Salisbury 25 also suggests that people contract clandestinely in order to avoid impediments:

> Canones Lateranensis concilii exequentes clamdestina coniugia penitus inhibemus, prolem ex huiusmodi coniunctione in gradu prohibito etiam ignoranter susceptam prorsus illegitimam nuntiantes. Quod etiam de illis sentimus quorum parentes impedimentum scientes legitimum, preter interdictum de facto in facie ecclesie contraxerunt.[67]

> Following the canons of the Lateran Council we forbid clandestine marriage, asserting that offspring from such a union in the forbidden degree, even when conceived in ignorance, are still illegitimate. We also feel this concerning children whose parents, knowing a lawful impediment, effectively contracted in front of the church, despite the ban.

In practice, some people seem to have contracted, and then arrived at the Church courts with the forbidden marriage as a *fait accompli*, which the courts would then be reluctant to dissolve. An example of this deliberate contracting despite knowledge of an impediment is found in the papal letter of 1391 to the bishop of Lichfield dispensing John de Dalton, a knight, and Isabella Rogeri, a widow, to remain in the marriage that they had contracted (despite an impediment in the fourth degree of consanguinity) in the hope of more easily receiving a licence from Rome to remain in a marriage than to contract one.[68]

Sheehan's survey of the consistory court records in Ely from 1374 to 1382 has twelve cases dealing with objections to marriage following the reading of the banns out of 122 matrimonial cases. Five opposed an impediment of affinity, one of consanguinity.[69] Helmholz suggests that there are few cases of divorce on these grounds because people did not generally marry outside the prohibited degrees, and he suggests that evidence showing that large numbers of people married outside their own parishes confirms this.[70] But his argument that there were a large

---

[66] Bliss and Twemlow, p. 72.
[67] Powicke and Cheney, I, 376.
[68] Bliss and Twemlow, pp. 412–13.
[69] Sheehan, 'Formation and Stability,' pp. 46–47.
[70] Helmholz, *Marriage Litigation*, pp. 79–80.

number of cases where persons attempted to engage in 'self-divorce' and remarry, almost always with some canonical reason for repudiating the first marriage,[71] might suggest an alternative view of the evidence: that there are a low number of divorces on these grounds not because people obeyed the rules, but because they attempted to resolve the situation without recourse to the Church courts. Hence 1 Winchester 59 (1224):

> Districte prohibemus ne in controversia que inter virum et mulierum orta fuerit super contractum matrimonii vel sponsalium aliqua compositio fiat nisi talis quod vir mulierem habeat in uxorem dum modo constet quod sint legitime persone ad contrahendum; quoniam si separatio talis contractus fieri debet, oportet quod fiat per sententiam et non per compositionem. Preterea cum de inpedimento matrimonii orta fuerit questio, nulla penitus admittatur compositio sed per sententiam dirimatur.[72]

> We strictly forbid that there should be any settlement in a dispute which has arisen between a man and a woman about a contract of matrimony or betrothal, unless it takes the form of the man having the woman as his wife as long as it is agreed that they are persons legally allowed to marry; seeing that if separation of such contracts has to happen, it is proper that it should be made through judgment and not through settlement. Moreover, when a question has arisen about impediments to marriage, no settlement is to be fully implemented but it must be superseded by judgment.

The existence of legislation prohibiting people from making their own settlements in such cases suggests the existence of the practice it seeks to prohibit, although to what extent it is difficult to judge.

To briefly discuss our two remaining categories of clandestine marriage: type three refers to secret ceremonies or locations. The First Statutes of Fulk Basset for the diocese of London (1245 × 1259) condemns such marriages, interestingly referring to the possibility of lay persons usurping the priestly role in performing such marriages.[73] The Constitutions of John Thoresby, archbishop of York (1367) also condemns those who 'flee the public view, embracing the night' for the contracting of clandestine marriages.[74] The Provincial Council at Canterbury under Simon Mepham (1328) forbids the celebration of marriages in unauthorized locations, as does the Council of London (1342), echoing it.[75] The most notable example of an attack on persons marrying where they were unknown, our fourth category of clandestine marriage, comes in the Council of London's frequently

---

[71] Helmholz, *Marriage Litigation*, p. 58.
[72] Powicke and Cheney, I, 135.
[73] Powicke and Cheney, I, 135.
[74] Wilkins, III, 71.
[75] Wilkins, II, 554, 704.

cited canon, *Humana Concupiscentia*. Ten of Sheehan's 122 cases deal with violations of *Humana Concupiscentia*, with one case, that of John Anegold and Joan Andrew, corresponding exactly to the circumstances described.[76] The motivation here is, again, the avoiding of impediments:

> De celebrantibus matrimonia clandestina in ecclesiis, oratoriis, vel capeliis.
> Humana concupiscentia, semper ad malum procliva, quod est prohibitum, frequenter ardentius appetit, quam quod licet: unde personae variae, quae propter consanguinitatem, vel affinitatem, seu alia impedimenta legitima matrimonialiter adinvicem de jure nequeant copulari, multoties desiderant id de facto, ut sub matrimonii contecti velamine possint carnis operam perniciosam et illicitam liberius adimplere; qui sua scientes impedimenta nota fore in parochiis, in quibus degent, quia parochiales presbyteros propter huiusmodi impedimenta notoria, seu famam impedimenti vehementem, ad sollenizandum matrimonium inter tales paratos non inveniunt, ad loca remota, et praecipue ad civitates, et municipia populosa, in quibus praemissorum non habetur notitia, transferunt se ad tempus; et illuc quandoque, bannis publice non editis, nec horis nec temporibus opportunis, aliquoties in ecclesiis, aliquando in capeliis, seu oratoriis matrimonia inter ipsos de facto sollenizari procurant, et ibidem morantes, vel ad partes proprias postea redeuntes, et adinvicem cohabitantes ut coniuges, quia locorum ordinarii et populares alii, prae timore vexationum et sumptuum, ipsos super illicita copula nolunt, aut non audeant impetere, seu eorum denunciando crimina propolare, illicite remanent adinvicem copulati, in suarum interitum animarum.[77]

> Concerning those who celebrate clandestine marriages in churches, oratories, or chapels.
> Human desire, always inclined towards evil, frequently desires more ardently what is forbidden than what is allowed: whence different people, who on account of consanguinity, or affinity, or another impediment are unable to contract mutually by law a legal marriage, oftentimes desire it *de facto*, that under the veil of a concealed marriage they are able more freely to perform the destructive and illicit work of the flesh; such people, knowing that their impediments will be known in the parishes in which they live, because on account of such notorious impediments or a strong rumour of an impediment they cannot find parish priests ready to solemnize marriage between such persons, such people move temporarily to a remote place, and especially to cities and well populated towns in which they do not have an advance reputation; and to that place at some time, without

---

[76] Sheehan, 'Formation and Stability,' p. 51.
[77] Wilkins, II, 707.

banns having been given publicly, at inappropriate times and on inappropriate dates, several times in churches, sometimes in chapels or oratories, they manage *de facto* to solemnize marriage between them; and lingering in the same place, or afterwards returning to their own place, and cohabiting like married persons because the ordinaries of those places and the rest of the population, on account of fear of ill treatment and expense, do not desire or would not dare to challenge them concerning their illicit connection, or, by denouncing them, publicize their crimes – they remain mutually joined illicitly, to the ruin of their souls.

But by far the largest obstacle that the acceptance of clandestine marriage posed was the ability of persons to contract more than one marriage. A previous contract rendered a subsequent one void, and Helmholz notes from his survey of cases that the allegation of a pre-existing clandestine marriage was the most frequent way in which existing marriages were dissolved in the medieval courts.[78] Allegations that defendants were bigamists, or about to become bigamists in the case of an objection subsequent to the banns, make up 49 of Sheehan's 122 cases. Sheehan notes that in some cases a second, third, or sometimes even more clandestine marriages were alleged and often proved.[79] The Church courts were vulnerable to manipulation in such cases: a papal letter to the bishop of Lincoln in November 1367 mentions a case where false and corrupt witnesses and forged documents were presented where precontract was alleged. A letter of June 1368 to the archbishop of Canterbury refers to the same case. The person alleging precontract is said to have demanded a hundred pounds and an annual pension of five pounds from the couple he was taking action against.[80] Sheehan presents another case where William Chilterne colludes with Joan Squire in order to have his marriage to Amicia Nene annulled: William and Joan declare to the court that they were previously married and that they had children together. The ecclesiastical court corruptly annuls the marriage, but the case is reopened and the judgment reversed when Joan subsequently marries someone else.[81] Little wonder that the statute 3 Worcester 22 states that errors in contracting marriages lead to 'execrable lawsuits.'[82]

Exceptions to the consent model

There were very visible exceptions to the Church's consensual model of marriage in actual medieval practice. This is unsurprising: although the Church had gained

[78] Helmholz, *Marriage Litigation*, pp. 57, 64.
[79] Sheehan, 'Formation and Stability,' pp. 62, 63.
[80] Bliss and Twemlow, pp. 70–71.
[81] Sheehan, 'Formation and Stability,' pp. 63–64.
[82] Powicke and Cheney, I, 301.

control of decision making on the formation of the marital bond, its ideology of consensual marriage had to compete with other important factors involved in the making of marriage. Although marriage was a means of uniting individuals, it was also important to families, both in the transmission of property within families and in the making of alliances between them. As John T. Noonan comments concerning marital consent:

> The standard set scarcely maximised free choice. It did nothing to liberate a son or daughter from psychological or social pressure. It did not disturb the prevailing pattern of parentally arranged marriages. [. . .] Nonetheless, in recognizing an area of freedom where parents should not trespass, the canons acknowledged rights of the individual not dependent on family.[83]

But not only is the consensual model under pressure from other vested interests in marriage, the Church itself sometimes ignores it in the interests of social regulation. Recidivist fornicators were forced into marriage by the Church, a practice known as abjuration *sub pena nubendi*. In 1 Winchester 54[84] the pledge that fornicators were forced to make is one of betrothal, as it is in 1 Winchester 58:

> Si aliquis ad aliquem mulierem consuetudinem habeat et hoc fit publicum, sacerdos suus eum conpellat per excommunicationem ad alterum istorum: scilicet ut in presentia quatuor aut quinque testium eadem muliere presente fidem det quod eam pro uxore semper *habeat* si eam decetero carnaliter cognoverit, et mulier hoc idem ex parte sua promittat fide media; quod si ad hoc induci non possunt per fidem et fideiussores promittant penam pecuniaram pro facultatibus suis si decetero conveniant in eadem domo. Et si inventi fuerint in una domo vel facti evidentia vel per legittimos testes probari possint, pena statim exigatur. Occulti autem fornicatiores occulta correctione castigentur. Cum vero fornicatio fuerit manifestata per prolem vel alio modo et non fuerit consuetudinaria, ad predicta non compellantur fornicatores sed solummodo moneantur, et aliis modis saluti eorum consulatur sicut visum fuerit expedire.[85]

> If anyone habitually has intimacy with a woman and this should become public, his priest should compel him under threat of excommunication to one of the following courses of action: namely that in the presence of four or five witnesses, the same woman being present, he should give his pledge that he will always *have* her as his wife if he should henceforth know her carnally, and the woman should likewise on her part truly promise this in public; but if it is not possible to induce them to this, through a pledge and persons giving security

---

[83] Noonan, 'Power to Choose,' p. 433.
[84] Powicke and Cheney, I, 134.
[85] Powicke and Cheney, I, 135.

they should promise a financial penalty according to their means if henceforth they should meet in the same house. And if they are found in one house, and this can be proved by evidence of the deed or through legitimate witnesses, the penalty is to be immediately demanded. But secret fornicators are to be punished with secret correction. When, in truth, fornication has become clear through offspring or other means, and was not habitual, with respect to the aforementioned the fornicators should not be compelled but only warned, and their safety is to be ensured in other ways as has seemed appropriate.

This is the form of contract found in the case of Richard de Bosco and Johanna de Clapton from 1269–71.[86] Later cases also exist: Robert Poppe and Isabella Copyn were contracted in court after their conviction for fornication at Kirby-le-Soken in Essex in 1458.[87] By the time of Wells 13 (1258?) the contract has become a conditional one contracted through words of present consent:

> Rubrica. De forma abiurandi.
> Abiurationes autem fornicariarum sub pena peccuniaria fieri prohibemus omnino; set delinquentes iuramento prestito se astringant quod si se in iudicio confiteri contigerit vel convinci passos fuisse postea recidivum, pene corporali pro personarum suarum conditione et qualitate delicti ibidem statim presidentis arbitrio exponende, sine contradictione aliqua subiacebunt. Si vero penam illam incurrerint et tertio super recidivo huiusmodi convicti fuerint vel confessi, tunc vir et mulier absque iuramento contrahant sub hac forma: Ego accipio te ex nunc in meam, si decetero te cognoscam carnaliter, et: Ego te in meum, si a te decetero fuero cognita carnaliter. Et ut certius procedatur in huiusmodi negotiis, que acta fuerint precipimus fideliter redigi in scripturam; quam quidem formam contrahendi, sine conditione tamen, in veris contractibus precipimus observari.[88]

> Rubric. Concerning the form of oaths.
> But oaths that are made for fornication we forbid altogether under financial penalties; but transgressors, having made an oath, bind themselves, but if they happen to admit in court or are convicted of having a relapse afterwards, they must be exposed to corporal punishment in accordance with the condition of their persons and the type of crime they have committed, without contradiction in any way they will undergo it. But if they have incurred that penalty and have been convicted of a third lapse of this type or they have acknowledged their guilt, then the man and the woman by taking an oath contract a marriage under this formula: I accept you as mine from now, if I

---

[86] Adams and Donahue, p. 97.
[87] Hair, p. 167.
[88] Powicke and Cheney, I, 598.

know you carnally from now on, and: I accept you as mine, if from now on I have carnal knowledge of you. And so that there can be a more definite procedure in cases of this kind, we order what has been done to be recorded faithfully in writing; we order that this formula of marriage, without having any conditions attached, be observed in actual contracts.

The opening sentence here seems to echo 1 Salisbury 83's opposition to the swearing of oaths of marriage for ease of fornication, and insists that fornicators undergo corporal punishment. That forcing fornicators to marry seems to run against the idea that marriage should be contracted by the free exchange of consent was not lost on contemporaries. A similar formula in the statute 2 Exeter 7 is glossed in one manuscript as follows:

> Nota quod hec constitutio est contra iura et naturalem equitatem, quia de iure libera debent esse matrimonia et sponsalia [. . .].[89]

> Note that this regulation is against the law and the just claim of nature, because by law marriage and betrothal should be free [. . .].

Charles Donahue, in his survey of fourteenth-century cases at the court of York, comments, 'it is hard to escape the sense that the institution of abjuration *sub pena nubendi* was not favored by the York court, particularly at the end of the fourteenth century.'[90] Nine of the fourteenth-century cases examined by Donahue, or 10% of the total, involved abjuration *sub pena nubendi*, in contrast with two, or 2%, of the fifteenth-century cases.[91] Helmholz suggests that the practice had disappeared by the end of the fifteenth century.[92] The consensual model, then, important as it is, is subject to modification by the Church's need to exert social control.[93]

Furthermore, although the Church had declared the use of 'force and fear' to extract consent to invalidate any consent given, there is evidence that such things did of course happen in practice, and, as in the case of *Veniens ad nos* discussed at

---

[89] Powicke and Cheney, II, 999 n. 4.
[90] Donahue, p. 194.
[91] Donahue, p. 187.
[92] R. H. Helmholz, 'Abjuration *Sub Pena Nubendi* in the Church Courts of Medieval England,' in R. H. Helmholz, *Canon Law and the Law of England* (London: Hambledon, 1987), pp. 145–55 (p. 154) (originally published in *The Jurist* (1972): 80–90).
[93] There is a Middle English poem from ms. Harley 2253, edited in *Alliterative Poetry of the Later Middle Ages*, ed. Thorlac Turville-Petre (London: Routledge, 1989), in which the narrator describes being brought to the ecclesiastical court and forced to contract in this way. The poem is discussed in Thorlac Turville-Petre, 'English Quaint and Strange in "Ne mai no lewed lued"', in *Individuality and Achievement in Middle English Poetry*, ed. O. S. Pickering (Cambridge: Brewer, 1997), pp. 73–83, and in John Scattergood, 'The "Lewed" and the "Lerede": A Reading of *Satire on the Consistory Courts*,' in John Scattergood, *The Lost Tradition: Essays on Middle English Alliterative Poetry* (Dublin: Four Courts, 2000).

the outset of this chapter, part of what comes into question in such cases is how much force can be judged to be necessary to force consent? An example of the extremes to which people went to in practice may be seen in a papal letter of June 1364 to the bishop of Lichfield, instructing him to make a decision in the case of Isabella de Scaresbrok, who was betrothed at the age of ten to Henry Molineux, but carried off by John de Yorke and terrified by him into a clandestine marriage for John's financial gain. She was subsequently freed by her relations, and was married to Henry when she reached an appropriate age, but John, alleging pre-contract, took legal action. John is subsequently alleged to have so treated the advocates and proctors that no one dared defend Isabella, and she feared to appear in person before the archbishop because of the danger posed by John.[94]

As with the prohibition on forced marriage, the Church's ban on underage marriages (the issue being the ability to consent, the age set usually being puberty)[95] is repeated in the synodal legislation, for example, 2 Salisbury 23.[96] But a sizeable number of underage marriages do appear in papal letters and petitions to the pope from Britain. Some appear because they are repudiated by the parties on reaching the age of consent. An example is the papal letter of 1354 to the bishop of London allowing Roger Germeyn and Cicely le Haute to stay in the marriage they contracted aged ten or eleven, Cicely having been contracted to a boy at the same age who failed to consummate the marriage, and from whom she was canonically separated on reaching the age of discretion (Roger was unaware of this union).[97] This case also gives evidence of the sort of dealing on the marriage market that obviously under-lies cases of this sort. A particularly obvious case of parental manipulation is that described in a papal letter of 1354 to the bishop of Moray. Cristin Macrath com-pelled Marjory, then of marriageable age, to marry his seven-year-old son. Cristin himself subsequently knew her carnally, and, on his son's death, married her. The papal letter declares that the contract of marriage between Cristin's son and Marjory is not an impediment to her marriage to Cristin.[98] These cases are hardly typical. Papal documents and Church court records are far more likely to reveal evidence of aberrations than norms, but it is clear nonetheless that the doctrine of consent was not as absolute in practice as it might appear from reading the canon law texts.

Internal dissent: Clerical concubinage

The notion of legally valid clandestine marriage also created difficulties regarding the institution of concubinage – nonmarital unions in which couples cohabited and

---

[94] Bliss and Twemlow, p. 44.
[95] Minors could contract betrothals, but not marriage: Friedberg, II, 675–76.
[96] Powicke and Cheney, I, 376.
[97] *Calendar of Entries in the Papal Registers Relating to Great Britain and Ireland. Papal Letters. Vol. III. AD 1342–1362*, ed. W. H. Bliss and C. Johnson (London: HMSO, 1897), p. 537.
[98] Bliss and Johnson, p. 524.

had sexual relations. Such unions existed alongside marriage throughout the Middle Ages. Although the Church attempted to prohibit all nonmarital sex as sinful, its attempts to do so were complicated by the legal view of consent, for later medieval canon law took open cohabitation to represent marital consent, and therefore regarded concubinage as presumptive marriage.[99] Concubinage was therefore appropriated as marriage where possible, and, as we have just seen, the Church was prepared to force fornicators into public marriage. But concubinage could pose a problem where the parties concerned were not free to marry, and in particular it posed a problem where one of the parties in the relationship was a cleric.

Holy orders were an impediment to marital consent. But while the Church had attempted to outlaw clerical marriage since the fourth-century canons of Elvira, it had enjoyed little enough success in the early medieval period.[100] One of the aims of the Church reform movement of the central Middle Ages was to impose clerical celibacy, but we still find clerical concubinage a significant problem in later medieval England. It seems reasonable to assume that clerical resistance to the sexual ethics that the Church sought to impose would have undermined its attempts to impose its will upon the laity. The canons of the Legatine Council of London (1237) show concern for the public face of the Church, stating:

> Licet ad profugandum a laribus ecclesie putridum illud turpitudinis libidinose contagium quo decor ecclesie graviter maculatur studuerunt semper ecclesiastici correctores, ipsum tamen tante improbitatis existit ut semper se ingerat impudenter.[101]

> Even though the correctors of the Church always give attention to banishing from the bosom of the Church that putrid contamination of disgrace through lechery by which the beauty of the Church is seriously stained, nevertheless it consists of such evil that it always increases shamelessly.

But while the Church condemns clerical fornication, it does not seem to punish it harshly.[102] 1 Salisbury 81, attacking reports of fornication in prebendal churches, allows correction in the first instance by the chapter, and does not prescribe specific penalties:

> De fornicatione et adulteriis.
> Ad hec quoniam de fornicationibus, adulteriis, et incestuosis commixtionibus et aliis flagitiis in prebendis et ecclesiis prebendalibus frequenter commissis clamor ad aures nostras ascendit et ad aures domini sabaoth timemus ascendisse, que ad commonotionem et iussionem episcopi, secundum statuta concilii, infra terminum competentem per

---

[99] Brundage, 'Concubinage and Marriage,' p. 126.
[100] Brundage, *Law, Sex and Christian Society*, pp. 69–70, 150–51.
[101] Powicke and Cheney, I, 252–53.
[102] Brundage, *Law, Sex and Christian Society*, pp. 315–18.

capitulum corrigi debent, ne de manibus nostris sanguis animarum requiratur districte auctoritate concilii precipimus quod (infra festum sancti Iohannis) ea que correctione indigent per capitulum corrigantur; alioquin, deum habentes pre oculis (ex tunc) prout animarum cura requirit, pro officii nostri debito quod nostrum erit faciemus.[103]

Concerning fornication and adultery.

Furthermore, seeing that an outcry concerning fornication, adultery, incestuous intercourse and other crimes frequently committed in prebends and prebendal churches has come to our ears and we are afraid it has also come to the ears of the Lord God, sins which according to the strictures and command of the bishop, following the statutes of the council, ought to be corrected within the term deemed suitable by the chapter, so that the blood of souls is not sought at our hands, we command with rigour with the authorization of the council (before the feast of St John) that those sins which have need of correction shall be corrected by the chapter; in any case, having God before our eyes (from then) as the cure of souls requires, we shall act in accordance with the responsibility of the office which will be ours.

1 Canterbury 6 (1213 × 1214) prescribes specific and far from lenient penance only for priests who have intercourse with women whose confessions they hear: the penalty is fifteen years of penance followed by seclusion in a monastery. The statute notes that if a priest sins he causes his flock to sin, but the implication is that the penance is imposed for the transgression against the sacrament of penance, rather than the fornication – a parallel is drawn with sin committed against the sacrament of baptism.[104]

But if English statute legislation does not seem to deal very harshly with clerical fornication, beyond simple condemnation, this changes when the statutes turn to deal with clerical concubinage. Penalties are prescribed not just against priests who keep concubines, but also against the concubines themselves. 1 Salisbury 9 suggests that they should contract or enter a cloister, or, since they have sinned publicly, perform public penance. But if they cannot be persuaded to do any of these things, they should be excommunicated, and ultimately handed over to the secular jurisdiction for punishment.[105] The Constitutions of a Certain Bishop 35 also attacks concubines directly:

> Moneantur concubine eorum ut recedant ab ipsis; que nisi commonite recedant ab eisdem, post trinam ammonitionem, quoniam infamant ecclesiam, ab ecclesia expellantur et excommunicentur; nec ad ecclesiastica sacramenta admittantur set ab actibus legittimis repellantur ut infames.[106]

---

[103] Powicke and Cheney, I, 86.
[104] Powicke and Cheney, I, 26.
[105] Powicke and Cheney, I, 62–63.
[106] Powicke and Cheney, I, 187.

Their concubines should be warned to depart from them; if, having been reminded, they do not depart from the same, after three warnings, seeing that they bring the Church into ill repute, they are to be expelled and excommunicated from the Church; nor are they to be admitted to the sacraments of the Church, but kept away by legal action like people who are disgraced.

1 Exeter 5 (1225 × 1237) continues the attack on concubines, but also attacks clerics directly, and offers a reason for the specific focus on clerical concubinage, rather than fornication generally: the potential alienation of church property.[107] 3 Winchester 44 suggests a similar motivation for moves against clerical concubinage:

> Et ut huiusmodi vitium plenius detestemur, quantumcumque liberas esse velimus ultimas decedentium voluntates, testamenta clericorum omnium quo ad ea que focariis suis relicta fuerint vel legata carere decernimus robore firmitatis. Legata vero huiusmodi, si qua fuerint, per officiales nostros in usus pauperum volumus erogari.[108]

> And so that we may censure vice of this sort more fully, however much we desire the final will of the dying to be free, we decree that the wills of all clerics whereby their possessions were left to their concubines or willed to them lack the strength of validity. Truly such legacies, if there were such, we desire to be taken from them by our officials and used for the poor.

Since orders were an impediment to marriage, then, clerical concubinage seems to have provided a sort of *de facto* marriage arrangement for clergy. English statutes are concerned about this primarily for two reasons: the damage to the reputation of the Church (and, presumably, the consequent implications for governing the sexual behaviour of the laity), and the possibility of alienation of Church property. That it was a sizeable problem may be deduced from the substantial amount of local ecclesiastical legislation directed against it. On the broader issue of clerical sexual activity, we might note that of the forty cases of sexual offences mentioned in the record of the episcopal visitation of Canterbury from 1292 to 1294, twenty-one mention clergy.[109]

Clandestine marriage and Middle English literature

There have been a number of readings of Middle English poems which have suggested the presence of clandestine marriage. Perhaps the best known is Henry Ansgar Kelly's argument, in his book *Love and Marriage in the Age of Chaucer*, that

---

[107] Powicke and Cheney, I, 229–30.
[108] Powicke and Cheney, I, 710.
[109] Rothwell, pp. 705–20.

a clandestine marriage exists between the central characters of Chaucer's *Troilus and Criseyde*. Kelly argued that the exchange of pledges of *trouthe* between the two (at III. 1296–98 and 1512) and the exchange of rings makes them a married couple. His argument acknowledges that 'Chaucer took pains to avoid making their marital status explicit,' using ambiguities where his sources are clear-cut. Nonetheless, he argues, it does not take a great deal to contract a clandestine marriage, and 'Troilus and Criseyde could be married with no more than an "I take you as mine" or its spoken or unspoken equivalent.'[110]

The problem with Kelly's argument lies in the ambiguities which Chaucer seems to deliberately introduce, and with the specificity which English courts actually demanded in contracts of clandestine marriage. Kelly argues that the formula found in Alexander III and elsewhere, *Ego te accipio in meam*, is enough to create a marriage.[111] But others argue that this is simply an example of what present consent looks like (in contrast to future consent), and R. H. Helmholz's survey of matrimonial litigation finds that a specific reference to marriage was required to enforce a clandestine contract in an ecclesiastical court.[112] Kelly's argument rests partly upon intentions: for the most part, medieval ecclesiastical courts found intentions very difficult to measure, and so opted instead to rely upon measuring forms of words. Derek Brewer's review of Kelly's book refutes Kelly's argument through citing Helmholz's study (which, he acknowledges, appeared too late for Kelly to take account of). Brewer argues that 'the upshot is that had Troilus taken Criseyde to court, as so many men and women (though not of such high rank) in fourteenth-century England did to their all-too temporary partners in bed (and sometimes indeed at board) in order to enforce a marriage, he would have failed.'[113] The Chaucerian ambiguities traced by Kelly, then, obstruct his argument for the existence of a clandestine marriage because, in the marriage litigation of later medieval England, what the courts are looking for is a very specific verbal formula. But, as C. N. L. Brooke observes, Kelly has revealed an intriguing element in the poem – it may contain only echoes of married union, but the echoes are there.[114]

Kelly's argument for the presence of marriage pledges in another Chaucerian text, *The Legend of Good Women*, has found more favour.[115] Kelly demonstrates that many of the smooth-talking but footloose men in the poem offer their partners

---

110 Kelly, p. 230.

111 Kelly, pp. 99 and n. 48, 230.

112 Helmholz, *Marriage Litigation*, pp. 45–46; see also n. 1 above.

113 Derek Brewer, review of Kelly (1975), *Review of English Studies*, n. s. 28 (1977), 194–97 (p. 196); see also the discussion in Joseph Allen Hornsby, *Chaucer and the Law* (Norman, Oklahoma: Pilgrim, 1988), pp. 56–68.

114 Brooke, pp. 225–27.

115 Kelly, *Love and Marriage*, pp. 202–16; cf. Richard Firth Green, 'Chaucer's Victimized Women,' *Studies in the Age of Chaucer* 10 (1988), 3–21 (pp. 14–15 and nn. 41, 42), A. J. Minnis with V. J. Scattergood and J. J. Smith, *Oxford Guides to Chaucer: The Shorter Poems* (Oxford: Oxford University Press, 1995), pp. 417–21.

pledges of marriage, either through words of present or future consent. This passage is from *The Legend of Medea*:

> They been acorded ful bytwixe hem two
> That Jason shal hire wedde, as trewe knyght;
> And terme set to come sone at nyght
> Unto hire chambre and make there his oth
> Upon the goddes, that he for lef or loth
> Ne sholde nevere hire false, nyght ne day,
> To ben hire husbonde whil he lyve may,
> As she that from his deth hym saved here.
> And hereupon at nyght they mette in-feere,
> And doth his oth, and goth with hire to bedde;
>
> (*LGW*, 1635–44)

Despite its clandestine nature, the promise of marriage, that he 'shal hire wedde,' followed by intercourse means that they are married. Perhaps, as Kelly notes, the line 'As she that from his deth hym saved here' constitutes a condition, as it does in Gower's version of the tale, but the condition is fulfilled, and is in any case overridden by the subsequent intercourse.[116]

Dido and Eneas likewise seem to marry clandestinely:

> For there hath Eneas ykneled so,
> And told hire al his herte and al his wo,
> And swore so depe to hire to be trewe
> For wel or wo and chaunge hire for no newe;
> And as a fals lovere so wel can pleyne,
> That sely Dido rewede on his peyne,
> And tok hym for husbonde and becom his wyf
> For everemo, whil that hem laste lyf.   (*LGW*, 1232–39)

Later in the poem, Dido seems uncertain as to whether she is his wife (as she names herself at 1307) or whether he has simply sworn to take her as his wife (in line 1304). Perhaps it is a question of intentions – in the passage just quoted, Dido accepts *him* as her husband, but perhaps he offers *her* no guarantees beyond that of 'a fals lovere.' In any case, even a false lover's promise of marriage creates a binding union when followed by intercourse, and Dido is pregnant.

Perhaps Chaucer's portraits of these unfaithful men making pledges of marriage is a reference to contemporary practice, and the possibility of men entering into clandestine contracts with women in order to seduce and then abandon them. This is what the statute 1 Salisbury 83 seemed to be concerned about when it warned men that if they made promises to women in order 'to fornicate with them more freely' they might bind themselves in marriage. But some seem to have been serial offenders. Michael M. Sheehan finds cases where

---

[116] Kelly, *Love and Marriage*, pp. 205–6.

offenders were involved in two, three, or sometimes even more clandestine marriages.[117] And in *The Legend of Good Women*, Jason, having already married and deserted two women, 'wedded yit the thridde wif anon' (*LGW*, 1660). Clandestine marriage clearly offered opportunity, if not sanction, for serious licence on the part of the utterly unscrupulous.

The Church's proposition and enforcement of a consensual model of marriage, then, is fraught with problems. The consensual model legitimates clandestine marriage, a move which leads to differing views on how a marriage bond is formed and how legally enforced, and which leaves both potential spouses and the ecclesiastical courts open to deception and manipulation. 'Consent' becomes, in the courts, less a matter of inner intentions than a matter of verbal formulae, which may or may not reflect the inner feelings of the persons concerned. Furthermore, the Church often ignored its own insistence on free consent in the interests of maintaing social control: hence its forcing of recidivist fornicators into marriage through the practice of abjuration *sub pena nubendi*. The coexistence of such differing attitudes in the Church's attempts at intervention in marital practice means that that practice is overdetermined. Further to that, there is evidence that popular attitudes to marriage, in some respects at least, may have remained stubbornly different to the ecclesiastical model. Ecclesiastical insistence upon the freedom to consent, and the relationship of that insistence to actual practice, comes further into question in the face of the economic rights that lords claimed to have in the marriages of wards, tenants, and widows who were subject to them, which will be discussed in the next chapter.

---

[117] Sheehan, 'Formation and Stability,' pp. 250–51.

2

Marriage and Property

Although the Church in the later Middle Ages promoted marriage first and foremost as a consensual commitment between two individuals, marriage always had implications for the transfer of property between kin. Major redistribution of property within families tends to take place on two occasions – at the death or marriage of a family member. Along with inheritance strategies, marriages were the major means by which families sought to establish economic viability for the succeeding generation. Marriages, then, were occasions on which property transfers, both symbolic and real, took place within and between families.

What this meant in practice was that it was difficult to get married without access to sufficient property to establish an economically viable family unit. The question of who gives property to the married couple and their heirs, or how it is held by them, varied across medieval Europe: we find that brides bring dotal payments to their husbands in Roman society, followed by a reversal of direction in the late empire which persists throughout the earlier part of the Middle Ages, until there is once again a shift back to dowries given by the bride's family in the central and later Middle Ages.[1] But at all times and all social levels property is required in order to get married and establish some sort of household. George C. Homans argues on the basis of linguistic evidence that the landless were unable to marry. *Anilepiman* meant both 'single man' and 'landless man,' and *husbond* meant both 'husband' and, in northern and eastern England, the holder of a certain sort of (quite substantial) tenement.[2] At times, difficulties in obtaining access to land, whether because of population increase, changes in family strategies of property transfer, or other reasons, can result in later ages of marriage, or large numbers of persons who are unable to marry.

The Church's consensual model was at odds with this emphasis on the roles of property and the interests of the wider kin group in establishing marriages. It was also at odds with the notion that lords had an interest (sometimes merely

---

[1] Herlihy, *Medieval Households*, pp. 14–16, 98–103.
[2] George C. Homans, *English Villagers of the Thirteenth Century* (London: Norton, 1941, repr. 1973), pp. 136–37.

economic, sometimes more) in the marriages of their tenants, their wards, the widows who held property from them. But the consensual model did not replace these other interests. Rather, it coexisted with them.

Women as property: 'Bride purchase'

Perhaps the most obvious way in which marriage is thought to interrelate with property interests in the early medieval period is the notion, much disputed, that marriage may itself have been akin to a financial transaction in early Germanic societies. Discussion of the existence of 'bride purchase' in Anglo-Saxon England centres on the meaning of words sometimes interpreted to indicate purchase in texts such as this early seventh-century law, Æthelbert 77:

> Gif mon mægþ gebigeð, ceapi geceapod sy, gif hit unfacne is
>
> 'If a man buys a maiden, the bargain shall stand, if there is no dishonesty'[3]

This notion of 'marriage by purchase' in early medieval Germanic societies suggests a model of the family not dissimilar to that of ancient Rome, where two forms of marriage were recognized. In the first, older, form of marriage, called marriage *in manu*, the bride was transferred from the authority of her father to the authority of her husband. In the second, marriage *sine manu*, which became the norm after the second century A.D., the bride did not come under her husband's authority, but remained under the technical guardianship of her father, until she became entirely independent either through the father's death or the birth of three children.[4] In the older form, where the bride passed from the authority of her father to the authority of her husband, the transfer was effected in one of three ways. The first, socially restricted, involved the making of a sacrifice to Jupiter. The second, of most interest to us here, involved a token payment from the groom to the bride's father. The third simply involved cohabitation for a year or longer.[5] This second form of transfer from the authority of the father to the authority of the husband, a sort of imaginary sale, is what is sometimes called 'bride purchase.'[6] It implies a patriarchal society where women are given by fathers to husbands, with the payment of money marking the transfer of authority.

---

[3]   Attenborough, pp. 14–15.

[4]   Treggiari, p. 17, notes that the phrases 'marriage *cum manu*' and 'marriage *sine manu*,' although useful, are modern constructs. The Romans only speak of the wife coming into or being in *manus*.

[5]   This description of Roman marriage draws substantially on the discussion in Herlihy, *Medieval Households*, pp. 8–9; Herlihy draws a parallel between Roman and Germanic forms of marriage on p. 49.

[6]   That the *coemptio* is a kind of imaginary sale is attested by Gaius who describes it as *quondam imaginarium venditionem*: Treggiari, p. 25.

This idea that 'marriage by purchase' exists in early Germanic societies generally, and in early Anglo-Saxon England, leads to the argument that the position of
women within marriage improved later in the Anglo-Saxon period.[7]Anne L.
Klinck distinguishes between the compensation for rearing paid by a husband
to the family of his bride described in the late text *Be wifmannes beweddunge*
(c. 975–1030), a text with an implicit emphasis on the woman's consent, from the
'brideprice' of earlier texts such as Æthelbert 77.[8] But as David Herlihy argues with
reference to the purchase of the bride in ancient Rome:

> The act may once have constituted an authentic purchase of the bride,
> but most legal historians doubt that Roman marriages were ever truly
> sales (after all, the groom could not resell his wife, as he could any
> other purchased object). Rather the payment may once have repre-
> sented compensation to the father for his loss of authority over his
> daughter.[9]

In an Anglo-Saxon context, then, the 'buying' of a maiden in the seventh century,
and the paying of compensation for rearing to the bride's father in the tenth, may
not be very different after all.[10]

Others disagree on the translation of Old English *gebigan* in texts such as
Æthelbert 77, arguing that the word is not identical to Modern English 'to buy,'
and that this (common) interpretation may be inappropriate.[11] F. Mezger translates Æthelbert 77:

> If one makes a marriage agreement with regard to a virgin, be it
> agreed through exchange of the gift to the bride, if it (the transaction)
> is without fraud.[12]

In Mezger's translation, the notion of marriage by purchase no longer applies. The
same problems of translation apply to the possible references to marriage by purchase in the Old English *Maxims I* and *II*, where similar language is used.[13]

Other evidence from the laws of Æthelbert indicates that the position of
women in Anglo-Saxon society differs significantly from the suggested model

---

[7] Anne L. Klinck, 'Anglo-Saxon women and the Law,' *Journal of Medieval History* 8 (1982),
    107–21; Fell, p. 56 warns against reading the successive law-codes as embodying a natural,
    progressive development.

[8] Klinck, p. 113.

[9] Herlihy, *Medieval Households*, p. 8; Lancaster, p. 243, cites anthropological evidence against
    the interpretation of brideprice as purchase of the bride.

[10] Goody, p. 242, argues that this 'compensation for rearing' might in fact represent a payment
    to the bride via the father; Ó Corráin (p. 16) notes that in early medieval Ireland the payment
    made by the husband, the *coibche*, may have gone in part to the bride.

[11] Hough, 'The Widow's *Mund*,' p. 13 and n. 37.

[12] F. Mezger, 'Did the Institution of Marriage by Purchase Exist in Old Germanic Law?,'
    Speculum 18 (1943), 369–71 (p. 370).

[13] Cf. Klinck, p. 109.

where a woman exists under the authority of her husband. The following laws deal with the woman's right to leave the marriage, and the inheritance rules if the marriage is childless:

> 79. Gif mid bearnum bugan wille, healfne scæt age.
> 80. Gif ceorl agan wile, swa an bearn.
> 81. Gif hio bearn ne gebyreþ, fæderingmagas fioh agan ⁊ morgengyfe.

> 79. If she wishes to depart with her children, she shall have half the goods.
> 80. If the husband wishes to keep [the children], she shall have a share of the goods equal to a child's.
> 81. If she does not bear a child, [her] father's relatives shall have her goods, and the 'morning gift.'[14]

These laws suggest that the woman has the right to divorce her husband, and to claim some share of the couple's property.[15] Furthermore, they suggest that she remains a member of her father's kin, rather than passing entirely to her husband's. Christine Fell notes that Æthelbert 81 may be interpreted in two ways. If it refers to repudiation (which she thinks unlikely) it allows the woman to return to her kin with financial support. If it refers to a woman who dies childless, it means that if the marriage is childless, it is her father's kin who inherit her goods.[16] These laws would seem to contradict the notion of a purchased bride passing entirely under the authority of her husband. The evidence examined in the previous chapter from the *Penitential of Theodore* on the importance of the woman's consent also weighs against the notion of 'bride purchase,' literally interpreted. Furthermore, the husband's payment to the bride's father is not the only payment that he makes when he marries, for he also makes payments to the bride herself, both a dowry and the *morgengifu*, the 'morning gift,' paid after the consummation of the marriage. In addition, she might receive payments from her own family.[17] The wife's receipt of property in marriage seems to contradict the notion of the wife herself as a piece of property.

Despite all of these arguments against the idea of the sale of women in marriage, however, we do still find the idea of the woman as the husband's property appearing in later medieval literature. In the discussion of adultery in Chaucer's *Parson's Tale*, a wife's body is regarded as being the property of her husband:

> This synne is eek a thefte, for thefte generally is for to reve a wight his thyng agayns his wille. Certes, this is the fouleste thefte that may be, whan a womman steleth hir body from hir housbonde and yeveth it to hire holour to defoulen hire, and steleth hir soule fro Crist and yeveth it to the devel. (X. 877–78)

---

[14] Attenborough, pp. 14, 15.
[15] Fell, p. 57, notes that the woman's right to divorce is not repeated in later laws.
[16] Fell, pp. 74–75.
[17] Herlihy, *Medieval Households*, pp. 49–50.

When she commits adultery, she is a thief, because she has stolen her body from her husband, its rightful owner. A similar notion is visible in Gower's *Confessio Amantis*, which describes rape as 'Robberie,' and specifically the theft of another man's goods (V. 6118).[18]

Marriage and property: Dotal transfers

Dotal transfers (from the Latin *dos*) are transfers of property that took place at the contracting of the marriage. As David Herlihy observes, the direction of dotal gifts changes to and fro across the late classical and medieval period: it is the bride who brings property to the husband in Roman society, but the reverse in the late empire and early Middle Ages, and a return of dowries given by the bride's family in the central and later Middle Ages.[19] *Be wifmannes beweddunge* states that the husband to be must make a pledge for remuneration for rearing of the bride to the person to whom it is owed. Then he must announce what he grants the bride in return for her acceptance of his suit, and what he grants her if she should out-live him – her dower, in other words. The text then states what that grant of dower should be: it is appropriate that she should be entitled to half the goods. If they have a child together, she is entitled to all of them. These entitlements to dower are nullified if she marries again.[20] There are, then, two sorts of dotal gift here, both given by the husband.

In the central and later Middle Ages, also, two main varieties of dotal transfer occurred at marriage: the first being the transfer of property to the couple or to one member of the couple by third parties, and the second being the constitution of dower by the husband for his wife.[21] We shall deal firstly with dotal transfers of the first sort. *Bracton* defines the transfer of property called *maritagium* (a transfer of property from the wife's family to one or both of the couple) by dis-cussing the variety of ways in which land can be given because of marriage. The land can be given by the father or another close relative with the woman in mar-riage to the husband. Alternatively it can be given to both the husband and wife,

---

[18] Reference to the *Confessio Amantis* is to Gower, John, *The English Works of John Gower*, ed. G. C. Macaulay, EETS, e.s. 81, 82 (Oxford: Oxford University Press, 1900); discussion in Saunders, p. 118; Saunders, pp. 67–72, 75, demonstrates a growing concern with *raptus* as abduction with economic motives in later medieval England, in contexts where the economic objective is wardship or extortion, and argues for an ambiguity of definition which allows overlap between sexual and economic offences categorized as *raptus*.

[19] Herlihy, *Medieval Households*, pp. 14–16, 98–103.

[20] Whitelock, p. 431.

[21] The thirteenth-century legal treatise *Bracton* refers to both varieties of dotal transfers as *dos*, but I follow other commentators in referring only to the second type of transfer as 'dower.' Transfers of the first sort are not referred to as 'dower' or 'dowry' (the two English nouns derived from *dos*), but as *maritagium*, jointure, etc. depending on the way in which the grant was made.

and to their heirs, which *Bracton* says has the same effect. Again, it can be given to the woman alone, to facilitate her marriage. Finally, it can be given without any mention of marriage, a gift such as may be made to anyone. But if marriage is mentioned in giving the land, the property given is called a *maritagium*. *Bracton* states that such a gift may be made before marriage, at the marriage, or after it, and he distinguishes this gift from the constitution of dower made by the husband for his wife at the church door.[22] It is clear that according to the definition in *Bracton* that *maritagium* is always given by the wife's family, but that it may be given either to the husband alone and his heirs, to the wife alone and her heirs, or to both and their common heirs.[23] In any case, homage is not performed until the third heir enters into the inheritance.[24] Hence the *maritagium* may revert to the donor or to the donor's heirs if the heirs of the recipient fail. Milsom notes the popularity of restricting descent to limited heirs – to the heirs of the body in particular[25] – in contrast with the grant described in *Bracton* which is simply to 'their heirs'. Commenting on the hypothetical situation where the grant was to the woman being married and the heirs of her body, Milsom states that 'to take homage would create fee, so that when the woman's issue failed the land would not revert back to the central inheritance, but pass to heirs found among or through her brothers and the like.'[26] Implicit in the acceptance of homage after the entry of the third heir is the assumption that the line will now survive and that reversion to the central inheritance is unlikely.

Recipients of *maritagia* tried to get around the conditions attached to the grant which allowed it to revert to the giver. Edward I's statute 2 Westminster 1 (1285), the clause known as *De donis conditionalibus*, attempts to prevent recipients from alienating property granted with such conditions attached.[27] If the recipient sold the tenement, the potential gain that could be realized by the passing of the property to a third heir could be converted into an immediate gain: the proceeds of the sale of the property. The donor (or the donor's heir) would then be unable to recover the property even if issue did fail. Such an approach must have had obvious advantages for the recipients of such gifts before their alienation was outlawed by statute.

---

[22] *Bracton: On the Laws and Customs of England*, ed. G. E. Woodbine, trans. S. E. Thorne (Cambridge, MA: Harvard University Press, 1968–77), II, 77.

[23] *Bracton*, ed. Woodbine, trans. Thorne, II, 79.

[24] *Bracton*, ed. Woodbine, trans. Thorne, II, 77–79.

[25] Milsom, p. 173.

[26] Milsom, p. 171; Land held as a *feudum* or fee is held in tenure, and homage is a formal act of allegiance performed in this case by the recipient of the land to the person from whom the land is ultimately held, marking the irreversible transfer of tenure.

[27] *English Historical Documents, 1189–1327*, ed. Harry Rothwell (London: Eyre & Spottiswoode, 1975), pp. 228–29; the statute refers to 'frank-marriage,' which *OED* defines as 'a tenure in virtue of which a man and his wife hold lands granted to them by the father or other near relative of the wife, the estate being heritable to the fourth generation of heirs of their bodies, without any service other than fealty,' i.e. what *Bracton* calls *maritagium*.

K. B. McFarlane suggests, however, that *maritagium*, the land transfer from the wife's family to one or both of the couple, was dying out among the aristocracy by the end of the thirteenth century, to be replaced by the marriage portion, a money payment made directly from the bride's family to the groom's: a payment for the marriage rather than an endowment.[28] Land was then settled on the couple by means of the jointure, defined by McFarlane as 'land held in joint tenancy for their two lives by husband and wife and by the survivor alone after the death of one partner.'[29] Robert C. Palmer's study of evidence from the king's court from around the year 1300 also finds that land was often given by the husband's family to the bride or to the couple: he cites the late thirteenth-century case of Henry de Sindleston and his wife-to-be Sara. The friends of the latter agreed to the marriage only when Henry's father granted some land to the couple.[30]

Bracton places the *maritagium* in the context of other forms of dotal transfer, but all of these are made on the wife's behalf. These forms of transfer, and that known as *parapherna*[31] are distinguished from the second type of dotal transfer, which is the constitution of dower by a husband for his wife. Dower is the property of the husband that the wife will acquire if her husband predeceases her. She holds a life interest in the property, which *Britton* defines as being for the support of the wife and nurture of the children.[32] The amount of property is defined in *Magna Carta* (1217) as a third of all the land which her husband held in his lifetime, unless the endowment at the church door specified a smaller share.[33] W. S. Holdsworth suggests that it was not possible for a woman to accept less than her common law right of one third of her husband's land from early in the fourteenth century.[34] This limit of one third of the husband's property, referred to as reasonable or rightful dower, applied only to military fees, and was abolished from those in the fifteenth century.[35] Lower down the social scale, G. C. Homans finds that while the most frequent custom was for the widow to hold one third of her husband's tenement after his death, elsewhere the widow had the right to one half of the tenement or even the whole of it.[36] J. M. Bennett, in her study of pre-plague Brigstock, also finds that custom varied from village

---

[28] K. B. McFarlane, *The Nobility of Later Medieval England: The Ford Lectures for 1953 and Related Studies* (Oxford: Oxford University Press, 1973), pp. 64, 85.

[29] McFarlane, p. 65.

[30] Robert C. Palmer, 'Contexts of Marriage in Later Medieval England: Evidence from the King's Court circa 1300,' *Speculum* 59 (1984), 42–67 (p. 47).

[31] *Bracton*, ed. Woodbine, trans. Thorne, II, 266; *Fleta: Volume IV: Book V and Book VI*, ed. and trans. G. O. Sayles, Selden Society vol. 99 (London: Selden Society, 1984), p. 73, defines *parapherna* as 'what the wife has over and above her dower from whatever source, both before marriage and during marriage, whether made to the husband and wife together or to the wife alone.'

[32] *Britton*, ed. and trans. F. M. Nichols (London: Macmillan 1865), II, 236.

[33] Rothwell, p. 333.

[34] W. S. Holdsworth, *A History of English Law*, 3 vols (London: Methuen, 1909), III, 162.

[35] *Britton*, ed. Nichols, I, Introduction, p. xlii, II, 238.

[36] Homans, p. 18.

to village, and she too finds customs granting one third, one half, or all of the conjugal holding to the widow.[37] Roger, a priest testifying in the early thirteenth-century case of Alice and John the Blacksmith, describes John's endowment of Alice with half of all his goods, what he had and what he would get.[38] An example of a case where the widow receives all of the conjugal holding appears in a case cited in *Bracton*, where Isabella de Cursun receives the whole tenement of Thomas Fughelston in dower, according to Kentish custom.[39] What was achieved in the resort to jointure in military fees during the fourteenth century, as noted by McFarlane, was achieved through different means by other forms of tenure, including the tenures of many lower down the social scale, i.e. the securing of guaranteed tenure for the widow in landed property greater than the one third of the husband's property allowed by *rationabilis dos*, 'rightful' or 'reasonable dower', for military tenures.

The question of what property was to be taken into account for the granting of dower is somewhat ambiguous. *Bracton* and *Fleta* both hold that it is the land held by the husband on the day of the marriage, whereas *Magna Carta* (1217) states that it is the land held by him during his lifetime. F. M. Nichols considers *Britton* to be ambiguous on the subject, but argues that the right was held to have been granted by *Magna Carta*, and refers to a case from 1311 where the charter was cited in support of that right.[40] A gloss to a fourteenth-century manuscript of *Britton* asks whether or not a husband may refuse to endow his wife: the glossator concludes that he may not.[41] To endow a wife in chattels rather than land was pronounced legally impossible in the reign of Henry IV.[42]

Although clandestine marriages were recognized as valid by the Church (despite their condemnation), clandestine endowments were not recognized as valid by the secular courts, and the constitution of dower had to take place at the door of the church in order to be valid.[43] This is not a case of divergence between ecclesiastical and secular law, for the secular law was prepared to recognize clandestine marriages for the purpose of determining the legitimacy of heirs.[44] Rather, the secular law was choosing to apply a more stringent set of criteria for the awarding of dower to a widow than the awarding of an inheritance to an heir.

There were no exceptions to the requirement that the endowment take place at the church door. If the endowment was being made out of lands held by someone other than the husband, they were required to assent at the church door to the

---

[37] Judith M. Bennett, *Women in the Medieval English Countryside: Gender and Household in Brigstock before the Plague* (Oxford: Oxford University Press, 1987), p. 163.

[38] Adams and Donahue, p. 26.

[39] *Bracton*, ed. Woodbine, trans. Thorne, III, 382.

[40] *Britton*, ed. Nichols, II, 238, note 'c'; *Year Books: 5 Edward II*, Selden Society vol. 63 (London: Selden Society, 1944), p. 14.

[41] *Britton*, ed. Nichols, II, 236, note 'a.'

[42] Holdsworth, III, 158.

[43] *Bracton*, ed. Woodbine, trans. Thorne, II, 266.

[44] *Bracton*, ed. Woodbine, trans. Thorne, II, 266.

endowment.[45] Even if the endowment was made in writing at another location, it had to be repeated at the church door in order to be valid.[46] The condition applied even under an interdict.[47] The insistence upon the endowment taking place at this specific location was due to the presence of the words 'at the church door' in the writs used to bring dower cases to court.[48]

Bracton also states that the ecclesiastical ban on marriages between those related by consanguinity and affinity did not affect the constitution of dower.[49] This, again, is not an example of a difference between ecclesiastical and secular law, but rather an acknowledgement that the determination of the legitimacy of the marital bond does not belong to the secular jurisdiction (which will determine any action for dower) but the ecclesiastical. Hence the secular court would not concern itself with allegations of impediments to marriage, but only with the results of any judgments given by the ecclesiastical court in its determination of the validity of the marriage.

Women and property during marriage

Later medieval legal texts state that all authority over property was vested in the husband during marriage,[50] and he could alienate it freely. Under the common law, if a husband predeceased his wife, the wife could recover any of her landed property alienated by her husband without her consent after his death. If she did consent to the alienation of the property, that consent was only admissible in conveyances by fine in the king's court.[51] Conversely, the wife could not alienate property without the consent of her husband, since, as *Bracton* says, a wife may not dispute her husband's acts. A wife may not recall her husband's gift of property during his lifetime, but if she makes such a gift, the husband may revoke it at once.[52] *Britton* has a similar statement that married women cannot alien without their husbands, and that husbands may not make any gift from the inheritance of their wives that shall not be revocable by the wives if they survive their husbands.[53] Because married women could hold no property, they were unable to contract on their own behalf, although they could contract as agents of their husbands.[54]

---

[45] *Britton*, ed. Nichols, II, 244.

[46] *Britton*, ed. Nichols, II, 276.

[47] *Britton*, ed. Nichols, II, 268 and note 'm'.

[48] *Britton*, ed. Nichols, II, 265; *Novae Narrationes*, ed. E. Shanks and S. F. C. Milsom, Selden Society no. 80 (London: Quaritch, 1963), pp. 51, 224–26.

[49] *Bracton*, ed. Woodbine, trans. Thorne, II, 266.

[50] *Britton*, ed. Nichols, I, 227.

[51] *Bracton*, ed. Woodbine, trans. Thorne, IV, 30–31.

[52] *Bracton*, ed. Woodbine, trans. Thorne, II, 97.

[53] *Britton*, ed. Nichols, I, 223. Alienation of property was made considerably easier by the statute of 1290, *Quia emptores*: Rothwell, p. 466; Milsom, p. 115.

[54] Holdsworth, III, 411; Pollock and Maitland, II, 405.

Neither could wives take legal action without their husbands.[55] There was one limitation on the male partner's power: a husband could not sue on his own for land held in his wife's right.[56]

There is a passage in the early Middle English poem *The Owl and the Nightingale* which has previously been read as relating to clandestine marriage, but which has been reinterpreted recently as relating to female property rights within marriage. The passage concerns a young woman who has entered into a secret relationship, but who may bring it out into the open by accepting the bonds of the Church:

> Heo mai hire guld atwende
> A rihte weie þurþ chirche bende;
> An mai eft habbe to make
> Hire leofmon wiþute sake,
> An go to him bi daies lihte,
> Þat er stal to bi þeostre nihte.   (1427–32)[56a]

Janet Coleman has suggested that there is an argument here for the couple to contract in public what is very likely already a clandestine marriage. In offering this interpretation, Coleman reads *sake* in line 1430 to mean a cause for legal action or a dispute, which in the context of marriage would mean an impediment: 'She has given her consent, and there is no impediment. The Nightingale says she may go to her man, not in secrecy, but in daylight.'[57] But in an interesting recent reading, Bruce Holsinger has interpreted this passage very differently, and indeed as offering a subtle antimatrimonial argument. Holsinger's argument is based on a different reading of the word *sake*. He argues that *sake* has a legal meaning of the profits or fines from a piece of property – rights that a woman would lose in matrimony because of her husband's legal authority over her. To take a husband, then, means that a woman must go 'wiþute sake.'[58]

Statements concerning the legal disabilities of married women owe a great deal to antifeminist statements in the canonical collections of ecclesiastical law.[59] In insisting on the legal disability of wives, at least, the two jurisdictions were in agreement. But there are laws which modify the common law's insistence on the legal disability of wives. The common law is frequently altered by local custom with the status of law: customary law from Torksey (1345), Worcester (1467), Lincoln

---

[55] *Britton*, ed. Nichols, II, 339–40; *Bracton*, ed. Woodbine, trans. Thorne, III, 358–59; cf. Whittaker, p. 45.

[56] Pollock and Maitland, II, 408.

[56a] Reference is to *The Owl and the Nightingale: Text and Translation*, ed. and trans. Neil Cartlidge (Exeter: University of Exeter Press, 2001).

[57] Janet Coleman, '*The Owl and the Nightingale* and Papal Theories of Marriage,' *Journal of Ecclesiastical History* 38 (1987), 517–68 (pp. 538–39).

[58] Bruce Holsinger, 'The English Jurisdictions of *The Owl and the Nightingale*,' in *The Letter of the Law: Legal Practice and Literary Production in Medieval England*, ed. Emily Steiner and Candace Barrington (Ithaca and London: Cornell University Press, 2002), pp. 154–84 (pp. 162–63).

[59] See for example Gratian, *Decretum*, c. 33 q. 5; for the influence of this passage, see Elliott, pp. 155–56.

(1480–81), Hastings (1461–83) and Fordwich (fifteenth century) allow married women who are traders to sue and be sued without their husbands.[60] In some cases, however, the motivation in passing such laws is clearly to protect the husband's property. The Lincoln text reads:

> Femina cooperta potest implicari absque viro suo. And if ony woman that hase a husbonde use ony crafte within the cite werof hyr husbonde mellys not, sche schal be charged as a sole woman os touchyng suche thynges os longeth to hyr crafte. And yf a pleynt be takyn ageyn syche a woman, sche schall answer and plede as a sole woman, and make hyr law, and take other avauntege in courte by plee or otherwyse for hyr dyscharge. And if sche be condempnyd sche schall be commyt to preyson tyl sche be agrede with the pleyntyf. And noo godes nor catell that longeth to hyr husbonde schall be attached for hyr nor chargyd.[61]

Other customs, however, operated to the wife's advantage. Witnesses in an ecclesiastical court case of the thirteenth century testify to a local custom of community of goods between husband and wife, in contradiction of the common law's assertion that all power over property during the duration of the marriage was vested in the husband.[62]

T. F. T. Plucknett argues that local custom frequently accorded greater proprietary and legal rights to women than common law, an argument echoed by Mary Carruthers.[63] Some of the supporting examples offered by Carruthers as broadening the rights of women, however, do accord with rights available to women under the common law. In a 1327 case cited where the mayor and bailiffs of Oxford assert a wife's right 'to give and sell to whom she will' of her own property, it is clear that the wife in question is a widow, and that her right to dispose of her property exists under the common law also. Similarly the 1419 London custumal that prevents a husband from bequeathing a wife's property or property jointly held: the common law also prevents this. Carruthers's mention of the case of Margery Kempe, however, is certainly plausible: as she argues, 'John Kempe exacts a promise from his wife, Margery, to pay off all his debts before he will agree to a vow of connubial chastity; this incident strongly suggests that he had no right to use her property as he chose.'[64] Plucknett does point out the limitations on our

---

[60] Bateson, I, 227–28.

[61] Bateson, I, 227.

[62] Adams and Donahue, pp. 619, 621.

[63] Theodore F. T. Plucknett, *A Concise History of the Common Law* (London: Butterworths, 1956), p. 313; Mary Carruthers, 'The Wife of Bath and the Painting of Lions,' in *Feminist Readings in Middle English Literature: The Wife of Bath and All her Sect*, ed. Ruth Evans and Lesley Johnson (London: Routledge, 1994), pp. 22–53 (p. 25).

[64] Carruthers, p. 25 n. 11, cases cited from *Borough Customs*, ed. Mary Bateson, 2 vols (London: Quaritch, 1904–06), II, 102–8; the financial issues relating to Margery Kempe's marriage are discussed further in chapter 5, below.

knowledge of local customs, given that many custumals have not survived, and many more examples of customary law may never have been written down at all.[65] Not all customary law operated in women's favour, of course. The common law's protection of endowments made for wives is undermined by some custumals;[66] other custumals reassert the common law's prohibition of women making wills.[67]

Gifts between spouses were not legally valid under the common law.[68] *Bracton* justifies the ban on grounds of fear that the gifts should be motivated by the lust or excessive poverty of one of the parties.[69] *Britton* offers similar justifications.[70] The subsequent discussion in *Bracton* of the validity or otherwise of gifts made before marriage contains reference to the feelings that might motivate such gifts, frowning on gifts made because of love, *ob amorem*, as opposed to gifts made out of marital affection, presumably a substantially different attitude.[71]

Marriage and property: Inheritance

The vesting of all authority over property in the husband also prevented the wife from making a will. *Bracton* advocates the husband consenting to his wife's making a will, but states that if she is under her husband's authority, she will be unable to do so without his consent.[72] The Church, whose courts held testamentary jurisdiction in England, advocated freedom of consent for all. This may not have been for entirely selfless reasons: Michael M. Sheehan observes that the Church's testamentary jurisdiction stemmed from a theory of alms rather than a theory of family property.[73] Legislation enacted by English bishops prohibiting husbands from impeding their wives' testamentary capacity culminated in Archbishop John Stratford's Provincial Constitution of 1342, which drew a condemnation from parliament.[74] Sheehan does note a reasonable number of married women's wills

---

[65] Plucknett, p. 313.

[66] Bateson, II, 103–5.

[67] Bateson, II, 108–11; cf. the discussion of women's testamentary rights below.

[68] *Bracton*, ed. Woodbine, trans. Thorne, II, 97–99; *Britton*, ed. Nichols, I, 223, 227, 234.

[69] *Bracton*, ed. Woodbine, trans. Thorne, II, 97.

[70] *Britton*, ed. Nichols, I, 227.

[71] *Bracton*, ed. Woodbine, trans. Thorne, II, 98–99; for the distinction between *amor* and *maritalis affectio*, see chapter 4.

[72] *Bracton*, ed. Woodbine, trans. Thorne, II, 179; for the similar situation of Anglo-Saxon women regarding wills, see Klinck, p. 117.

[73] Michael M. Sheehan, 'The Influence of Canon Law on the Property Rights of Married Women in England,' *Mediaeval Studies* 25 (1963), 109–24 (p. 119) (reprinted in Michael M. Sheehan, *Marriage, Family and Law in Medieval Europe: Collected Studies*, ed. James K. Farge (Toronto: University of Toronto Press, 1996), pp. 16–37); cf. Goody, p. 155.

[74] Wilkins, II, 705–6; R. H. Helmholz, 'Married Women's Wills in Later Medieval England,' in *Wife and Widow in Medieval England*, ed. Sue Sheridan Walker (Ann Arbor: University of Michigan Press, 1993), pp. 165–82 (p. 166); Sheehan, 'Influence,' pp. 119–20.

in mid-fourteenth-century Rochester, but Helmholz suggests a decline in the following century.[75] Helmolz does offer a possible explanation for the decline, however, by suggesting that married women may have been holding their property in use (the ancestor of the modern trust) rather than in direct ownership.[76] This could potentially have bypassed both the husband's jurisdiction over the wife's property and her need to make a will.

Ironically, the husband's testamentary freedom grew larger in this same period. *Bracton* notes the regulation that a married man's will must leave one third of his chattels to his wife and one third to his children, leaving one third for him to dispose of as he wished.[77] These restrictions ceased to operate generally during the fourteenth century.[78] The husband's testamentary freedom expanded yet further with the rise of the use. The testator granted his lands, or a portion of them, to feoffees, to hold them to his use and to dispose of them as instructed in his last will.[79] This allowed him to sidestep the regulation of inheritance of land (through primogeniture, ultimogeniture, partibility, or whatever inheritance custom was attached to the form of tenure by which he held the land). The practice does not derive from any statute, and early enforcement seems to have been by means of the probate jurisdiction of the ecclesiastical courts.[80] McFarlane suggests that the aristocracy could have employed the use, as it did the entail, to keep property in the hands of male members of the family, bypassing potential female heirs. He cites in support the example of Thomas Beauchamp, earl of Warwick, whose eldest son died, leaving two daughters. Rather than have his granddaughters inherit, Beauchamp left all his property to his remaining sons by means of the use.[81] The use could also benefit women, however. It could be employed to bequeath land to wives other than that given in dower, bypassing all the restrictions discussed earlier on the transfer of landed property from husband to wife. An example is the will of Thomas Walwayn, made in 1415.[82] The use was also potentially the way around the wife's proprietary disability: by having lands held by others to her benefit, she could avoid her husband's jurisdiction over her property.[83]

If testamentary freedom was a source of contention between the ecclesiastical and secular jurisdictions, so was the issue of legitimacy. Bastardy was an issue

---

[75] Sheehan, 'Influence', p. 122; Helmholz, 'Married Women's Wills,' pp. 169–70.

[76] Helmholz, 'Married Women's Wills,' pp. 173–74.

[77] *Bracton*, ed. Woodbine, trans. Thorne, II, 180.

[78] Holdsworth, pp. 435–36, notes that the system endured in the province of York until 1692, in Wales until 1696, and in London until 1794.

[79] McFarlane, p. 69; Milsom, p. 200, notes that the noun 'use' has no connection with the modern verb 'to use', but is from Norman French *al oeps*, Latin *ad opus*, 'to his benefit'.

[80] McFarlane, p. 68; R. H. Helmholz, 'The Early Enforcement of Uses,' *Columbia Law Review* 79 (1979), 1503–13 (pp. 1504–7) (repr. in R. H. Helmholz, *Canon Law and the Law of England* (London: Hambledon, 1987), pp. 341–53).

[81] McFarlane, pp. 72–73.

[82] *The Fifty Earliest English Wills in the Court of Probate, London*, ed. F. J. Furnivall, EETS, o.s. no. 78 (London: Oxford University Press, 1964), pp. 24–26.

[83] Helmholz, 'Married Women's Wills,' p. 174; Pollock and Maitland, II, 433.

which belonged to the jurisdiction of the ecclesiastical courts, and hence was referred to the ecclesiastical jurisdiction by the secular when the issue was raised in the courts of the latter.[84] There was however, a difference between ecclesiastical and secular law on the subject of legitimacy. Whereas the Church recognized children born out of wedlock as legitimized by the subsequent marriage of the parents, the State did not, and would not regard such children as heirs capable of succeeding to the property of their parents.[85] Attempts to harmonize the two systems failed. The Statute of Merton (1236) shows the bishops refusing to answer enquiries from the secular courts as to whether litigants were born before or after marriage (as opposed to declaring whether or not they were legitimate) and the nobles refusing to alter the laws of England to accord with the laws of the Church.[86] Hence litigants in the secular court were required to allege bastardy specifically because of birth before marriage or otherwise.[87] If birth before marriage was alleged, the issue was determined in the secular court. If it was alleged that there was no marriage, it was sent to the ecclesiastical court.[88]

Another difficult issue relating to legitimacy is the question of the 'putative marriage,' where the ecclesiastical court decides that there is no marriage because of the existence of an impediment, but the parties (or one of the parties) contract in good faith, ignorant of the existence of the impediment. Canon law judged the children of such unions legitimate, as does *Bracton*, whose discussion is shown by Maitland to derive from canon law.[89] The offspring of clandestine unions contracted despite impediments, were, however, judged to be illegitimate.[90] Pollock and Maitland also demonstrate, that secular law ultimately diverges from canon law on this issue of the legitimacy of children from marriages which are dissolved by the ecclesiastical jurisdiction, and that in the reign of Edward III the legitimacy of children depended on their parents, while living, never having been divorced.[91]

In some cases, the law would not permit parents to acknowledge children born within wedlock as being legitimate and heirs to property. *Bracton* states such circumstances as including cases where husband and wife have not cohabited for a long time, cases where the husband is frigid or impotent, or if the husband was out of the realm or province for two years or more and returns to find a pregnant

[84] *Bracton*, ed. Woodbine, trans. Thorne, III, Introduction, p. xv.
[85] *Bracton*, ed. Woodbine, trans. Thorne, II, 186.
[86] *Bracton*, ed. Woodbine, trans. Thorne, III, Introduction, p. xv; Rothwell, p. 353–54; Powicke and Cheney, I, 198–99; R. H. Helmholz, 'Bastardy Litigation in Medieval England,' in R. H. Helmholz, *Canon Law and the Law of England* (London: Hambledon, 1987), pp. 187–210 (pp. 203, 208) (first published in *American Journal of Legal History* 13 (1969), 360–83).
[87] *Bracton*, ed. Woodbine, trans. Thorne, III, 294, 295, 298.
[88] *Britton*, ed. Nichols, I, 341–42.
[89] Pollock and Maitland, II, 375–77.
[90] Powicke and Cheney, I, 89–90, 376–77.
[91] Pollock and Maitland, II, 377 and note 3.

wife or an infant less than one year old. Even if the husband acknowledges such a child, it will not be judged legitimate. But in other circumstances, supposititious children, once acknowledged by the father, may not subsequently be disowned, and are legitimate.[92] An example of a child being disowned appears in the *Paston Letters*:

> Heydonnis wyffe had chyld on Sent Petyr day. I herde seyne that herre husbond wille nowt of here, nerre of here chyld that sche had last nowdyre. I herd seyn þat he seyd 3yf sche come in hesse precence to make her exkewce þat he xuld kyt of her nose to makyn her to be know wat sche is, and yf here chyld come in hesse presence he seyd he wyld kyllyn. He wolle nowt be intretid to haue her ay[e]n in no wysse, os I herd seyn.[93]

Marriage as property: Wardship

The property of underage heirs was taken in wardship by the lords from whom it was held to their own profit. Furthermore, the wardship of the heir's body carried with it the right to arrange the heir's marriage. The type of tenure determined who the guardian of the heir's body would be, and hence to whom the right to arrange the marriage belonged. For socage tenure, for example, the right to wardship varied according to local custom, and belonged either to the chief lord, or to a near kinsman who had no claim on the inheritance.[94] For a military tenure, however, the marriage belonged to the chief lord. As *Bracton* states, both male and female heirs who are under twenty-one may be given or sold in marriage, provided they are not disparaged through marriage to their social inferiors. The right to arrange the marriage may be sold on, and the right to marry the heir need not be exercised only once, but may be used several times, as long as the heir is unmarried and underage.[95] This is marriage itself treated as a piece of property: so much so that the right to arrange a marriage was a chattel that could be devised to others by testament.[96]

Sue Sheridan Walker notes that the right to arrange a ward's marriage is contrary to the canon law of free consent in marriage, and notes also that ecclesiastical courts could annul forced marriages.[97] She suggests that the laws relating to

---

[92] *Bracton*, ed. Woodbine, trans. Thorne, II, 186–87; *Britton*, ed. Nichols, II, 18.

[93] Davis, I, 220.

[94] *Bracton*, ed. Woodbine, trans. Thorne, II, 263. *OED* defines *socage* as 'the tenure of land by certain determinate services other than knight service'; the name of the tenure seems to derive from *soke*, defined by *MED* as a right of jurisdiction, and *sokeland*, land located within a lord's *soke*.

[95] *Bracton*, ed. Woodbine, trans. Thorne, II, 257.

[96] *Britton*, ed. Nichols, II, 6.

[97] Sue Sheridan Walker, 'Free Consent and the Marriage of Feudal Wards in Medieval England,' *Journal of Medieval History* 8 (1982), 123–34 (pp. 123, 125).

wardship translated in practice into a form of taxation.[98] This analysis would agree with S. F. C. Milsom's point that the decline of the feudal relationship reduces the lord's interests in a tenure to a collection of economic rights, one of which was wardship.[99] *Britton* expressly forbids lords to force their wards (male or female) to marry.[100] The Statute of Merton (1236) provides a means for the ward to choose freely and for the lord to maintain his economic rights, stating that heirs in wardship are not to be compelled to marry, but must compensate their lord for the maximum amount he might have sold the marriage for.[101] All of this evidence tends to support Walker's argument for wardship as effectively a form of taxation. But there is one reference in *Bracton* which seems to undermine this interpretation, and this is a reference to the ability of parents, still living, to sell the marriage of their heir.[102] No doubt such 'sales' have more to do with dotal transfers than with the circumstances that we have just discussed relating to wardship, but *Bracton* does discuss them in the context of a discussion of wardship, and they seem to leave little room for free consent. *Bracton* further comments that if heirs under the *potestas* of their parents marry without their consent they are not to be disinherited because of this, but punished in another manner if that is the wish of the parents.[103] Again this reference undermines the notion that heirs were free to contract marriages as they wished when property was concerned. Noël James Menuge argues that Walker's evidence for wards marrying as they chose does not constitute a norm, and cites several cases where wards are forced into marriages.[104] It may not be possible to construct a norm for the experience of wards: it is possible that both Menuge and Sheridan are right in that there may have been a wide divergence of experience for individual wards. Some may indeed have experienced wardship as effectively a form of taxation on their freely chosen marriages. Others are likely to have experienced severe pressure to marry against their wishes. The legislation relating to marriage and wardship seems to create the potential for either to happen in practice. A similar argument exists regarding the question of *merchet*, the fine exacted by lords from their peasants for freedom to marry as they chose. Again, there is an argument that this is effectively a form of taxation,[105] but we do see peasants not only paying for the right to marry, but also paying fines in order to avoid marriages proposed for them.[106]

---

[98]   Walker, 'Free Consent,' p. 123.

[99]   Milsom, pp. 109–10.

[100] *Britton*, ed. Nichols, II, 24.

[101] Rothwell, p. 353.

[102] *Bracton*, ed. Woodbine, trans. Thorne, II, 263.

[103] *Bracton*, ed. Woodbine, trans. Thorne, II, 264.

[104] Menuge, p. 83 n.7 and pp. 82–100.

[105] Hanawalt, *The Ties that Bound*, p. 201, argues that 'the merchet was a combination of a marriage tax and land transfer fee.'

[106] For the role of *merchet*, see Eleanor Searle, 'Seigneurial Control of Women's Marriage: The Antecedents and Functions of Merchet in England,' *Past and Present* 82 (1979) 3–43, P. A. Brand, P. R. Hyams, R. Faith and E. Searle, 'Debate: Seigneurial Control of Women's

Satirical treatments of marriage for money

If financial matters are of practical consequence to marriage, almost without exception, the contrast between marriage's spiritual status as a sacrament freely contracted
between two individuals, and its secular status as a means of property transfer, did
not go unnoticed by contemporaries: the financial motivations that might underlie
marriage were much satirised in later medieval England. This sermon passage is
scathing about the alleged motivations of contemporaries in marrying:

> But mony wedd hem wyvys for her worldly goodes, for her grete
> kynne, other for ther fleschely lust; as, be a woman a pore wenche, and
> ther-wyth well condiciond, abell of person, and have no worldly
> goodes and be come of sympell kynne the whiche may not avaunce
> here, full few men covetyn suche on. Some had lever to take an old
> wedow, though sche be ful lothelyche and never schall have cheldren.
> And, fro the tyme that he hathe the mocke that he wedded her for, and
> felethe her breth foule stynkynge and her eyen blered, scabbed and
> febyll, as old wommen buthe, then they spend a-pon strompettes
> that evyll-getyn goodes. And sche shall sytt at home wyth sorowe,
> hungry and thrusty. And thus levethe they in a-vowtry, peraventure
> all her lif tyme. If a mayde be to wedde, the furste thynge that a man
> woll aske – what her frendes woll ȝeve to mary her wyth: and but
> they acorde ther in, . . . they kepe not of here. It semeth, then, they
> wedden the goodes more than the womman. For, had not the goodes
> be, sche schuld goo unwedded, as all day is seyne.[107]

The motif of the young man marrying the unappealing elderly woman for her
property is a common strain in antividual satire,[108] and we can see an equally
graphic description of the unattractiveness of an elderly husband in Chaucer's
Merchant's Tale. The reference at the end of the quotation above, though, in
appealing to the experience of the sermon audience concerning the difficulties
that poor women found in marrying suggests that the satire, indebted to fabliau
antifeminism as it might be, is nonetheless addressing a real issue rather than an
abstract one in discussing the financial motivations for contemporary marriages.
That is an issue discussed in great detail and at substantial length in William
Langland's fourteenth-century allegorical poem, *Piers Plowman*.

There are three major discussions of marriage in *Piers Plowman*: the first
concerning the proposed marriages of Mede, first to False, and subsequently to

---

Marriage,' *Past and Present* 99 (1983), 123–60; for cases, see *Select Cases in Manorial Courts,
1250–1550: Property and Family Law*, ed. and trans. L. R. Poos and Lloyd Bonfield (London:
Selden Society, 1998).

[107] G. R. Owst, *Literature and Pulpit in Medieval England*, 2nd ed. (Oxford: Blackwell, 1961, repr.
1966), p. 381, quoting ms. Bodley 95 fol. 12 et seq.

[108] On which see chapter seven.

Conscience (Passus 2, 3, and 4 in the A, B and C texts), the second in Wit's speech (Passus 10 in A, Passus 9 in B, Passus 10 in C), and the third in the representation of the Tree of Charity (Passus 16 in B, Passus 18 in C).[109] Here I want to investigate the first of these discussions of marriage in the poem, and to argue that Langland's representation of the proposed marriage of the allegorical figures of Mede and False concentrates on the financial aspects of the proposed union in order to attack the financial motivation of contemporary marriage practice. This satire of marriage for money is given greater seriousness by the poem's ultimate concern with the possibility of salvation.

The first matter to be decided in discussion of Passus 2 of Langland's poem is the question of what exactly is taking place. The lines echoing the marriage liturgy that appear at lines A. 2. 49–53 would suggest that what is taking place here is a marriage ceremony.[110] The A text lines echoing the liturgy do not appear in B or C, but many other details of the description of events in A remain unchanged. I would argue that if A. 2 represents a marriage ceremony, then so do B. 2 and C. 2. The ceremony is interrupted in all three texts, but Langland's omission of the lines suggestive of the marriage liturgy from the B and C texts concentrates attention completely on the financial basis of the union. In B and C the enfeoffment which takes place at the truncated marriage ceremony dominates to the exclusion of any spiritual aspect.[111]

The central element in the representation of the marriage ceremony between Mede and False in all three texts is the enfeoffment. The B and C texts explicitly state:

> That Mede is ymaried moore for hire goodes
> Than for any vertue or fairnesse or any free kynde.
> Falsnesse is fayn of hire for he woot hire riche.
>
> (B. 2. 76–78; cf. C. 2. 79–82)[112]

---

[109] All quotations from and references to *Piers Plowman* are to the following editions unless otherwise stated: William Langland, *Piers Plowman: The A Version*, ed. George Kane, revised edn. (London: Athlone, 1988); William Langland, *The Vision of Piers Plowman: A Critical Edition of the B Text*, ed. A. V. C. Schmidt, revised edn. (London: Dent, 1987); William Langland, *Piers Plowman: The C Text*, ed. Derek Pearsall (York, 1988, repr. Exeter: University of Exeter Press, 1994). In drawing on the A, B, and C texts for discussion, I have followed the argument of Tavormina, Preface, p. xv, that 'Langland's changes in the marriage and family materials of Piers are most often shifts of emphasis, rather than downright repudiation of cancelled material.'

[110] For medieval marriage liturgies, see Tavormina, pp. 15–16. In the Sarum Missal, the formula for the man is 'I, N., take the, N., to my wedded wif, to have and to holde fro this day forward, for bettere for wers, for richere for pouerer, in syknesse and in hele; tyl dethe vs departe, if holy churche it woll ordeyne, and therto y plight the my trouthe.' The woman also promised 'to be bonere and buxum in bedde and atte borde': *Manuale et Processionale ad Usum Insignis Ecclesiae Eboracensis*, Surtees Society vol. 63 (London, 1875), Appendix 1, p. 19*.

[111] Tavormina, p. 16 n. 36, suggests that as well as the constitution of dower by a husband for his wife, which had to take place at the church door in order to be legally valid, other transfers of property pertaining to marriage probably took place during the marriage ceremony also. As will be discussed below, the enfeoffment of Mede and False is a jointure.

[112] These words are spoken by Liar, but as Gerald Morgan points out: 'It is to be noted that the words of the charter are not such as a liar would utter, for they state the sinful reality that a

It was necessary for the constitution of dower by a husband for a wife to take place at the church door (i.e. as part of the marriage ceremony). This is not an endowment, however, but an enfeoffment of both False and Mede:

> And Favel with his fikel speche feffeth by this chartre
>
> (B. 2. 79)[113]

and, in the A and B texts, their heirs:

> And thei to have and to holde, and hire heires after
>
> (B. 2. 102; cf. A. 2. 67).

Tavormina comments: 'Whether or not it qualifies as such, Favel's enfeoffment of False and Meed certainly has the flavor of an old fashioned *maritagium* in land or the more modern jointure.'[114] The marriage charter explicitly enfeoffs False and Mede with the land, which will then pass to their heirs. There is no mention of *maritagium*, which did not become a fee until the entry of the third heir, reverting to the donor if the direct line of inheritance failed before that.[115] Furthermore, a *maritagium*, according to *Bracton*, was always given by the wife's family.[116] This enfeoffment is made by Favel, who is more closely associated with False than with Mede.[117] Hence it seems clear that the enfeoffment that the poem describes is a jointure, land held in joint tenancy by the spouses and by the survivor alone after the death of one spouse, a straightforward enfeoffment without the conditions attached to *maritagium*, a gift which could be made by anyone, and not simply by or on behalf of the wife's family.[118]

The transfer of property is the focus of the action in all three texts. In the A text, not only are there references to the enfeoffment of Mede with property at the marriage (A. 2. 37, 47), as well as the reading of the charter itself, but the granting of False to Mede is also expressed as an enfeoffment, in lines that contain a parody of the marriage liturgy (in line 59):

> Wyten & wytnessen þat wonen vpon erþe,
> Þat I, fauel, feffe falsnesse to mede,
> To be present in pride for pouere [or for] riche.   (A. 2. 57–59)

The A text also contains lines echoing the marriage liturgy which appear to portray an exchange of consent between False and Mede, which was all that was necessary

---

liar would aim to conceal': Gerald Morgan, 'Langland's Conception of Favel, Guile, Liar and False in the First Vision of *Piers Plowman*,' *Neophilologus* 71 (1987), 626–33 (p. 630).

113   Cf. A. 2. 37, 58, 62, 63, 66–67, B. 2. 73, 79, 102, C. 2. 73, 83.
114   Tavormina, p. 83; cf. Anna P. Baldwin, *The Theme of Government in Piers Plowman* (Cambridge: Brewer, 1981), p. 32; Elizabeth Fowler, 'Civil Death and the Maiden: Agency and the Conditions of Contract in *Piers Plowman*,' *Speculum* 70 (1995), 760–92 (p. 776).
115   *Bracton*, ed. Woodbine, trans. Thorne, II, 77–79.
116   *Bracton*, ed. Woodbine, trans. Thorne, II, 79.
117   Morgan, 'Langland's Conception,' p. 627.
118   Cf. McFarlane, p. 65.

to create a valid and binding marriage under the Church's consensual model. Such consent may be represented by the word *foreward*, 'agreement,' at A. 2. 50:

> Þanne fauel fettiþ hire forþ & to fals takiþ
> In foreward þat falshed shal fynde hire for euere,
> And he[o] be bou[n] at his bode his bidding to fulfille,
> At bedde & at boord buxum and hende,
> And as syre symonye wile segge to sewen his wille.   (A. 2. 49–53)

The question here is whether the agreement is between Favel and False (in which case this does not represent the exchange of agreement between spouses) or between Mede and False (in which case Mede and False are married). If A. 2. 50 does represent an exchange of consent between Mede and False, then how is it possible to explain the phrasing of Theology's interruption of the ceremony, which suggests that the marriage has not yet taken place? Theology warns:

> [And] er þis weddyng be wrou3t wo þe betide!   (A. 2. 82)

Theology's interruption carries the literal sense in all three texts of a marriage which has not yet occurred (A. 2. 82, B. 2. 118, C. 2. 119). Furthermore, how can the king subsequently offer Mede in marriage to Conscience if she is already married to False? On the other hand, if the agreement made at A. 2. 50 is between Favel and False, why do the following lines echo the marriage liturgy? Perhaps the intention is to emphasize that the agreement is between Favel and False where it should be between False and Mede. Holy Church, in describing to the dreamer the way in which the marriage of Mede and False would take place, emphasizes the deception inherent in the impending marriage. It is clear from A. 2. 24 that the victim of the deception is Mede, and it is clear from the passage as a whole that her free choice is undermined by the schemings of others:

> Tomorewe worþ þe mariage mad of mede & of fals;
> Fauel wiþ fair speche haþ forgid hem togidere;
> Gile haþ begon hire so heo grauntiþ alle his wille;
> And al is li3eris ledyng þat hy li3en togideris.
> Tomorewe worth þe mariage ymad as I þe telle.   (A. 2. 22–26)

In the B text, in contrast, Holy Church has Mercy as a dowry so she can marry as she chooses (B. 2. 31).[119]

---

[119] This is the interpretation of B. 2. 31 favoured by Tavormina, p. 12 and n. 26; cf. William Langland, *Piers Plowman: The Prologue and Passus I–VII of the B Text as found in Bodleian MS. Laud Misc. 581*, ed. J. A. W. Bennett (Oxford: Oxford University Press, 1972–76), p. 121. For the alternative interpretation of Mercy as Holy Church's husband, see Fowler, p. 776 and Colette Murphy, 'Lady Holy Church and Meed the Maid: Re-envisioning Female Personifications in *Piers Plowman*,' in *Feminist Readings in Middle English Literature: The Wife of Bath and All Her Sect*, ed. Ruth Evans and Lesley Johnson (London: Routledge, 1994), pp. 140–64 (pp. 150–52).

In the B and C texts, the marriage of Mede and False is incomplete because there is no exchange of consent: both texts omit the lines seen at A. 2. 49–53. There is a description of the conditions necessary for the creation of a marriage in Passus 9 of the B text, lines not present in A:[120]

> And thus was wedlok ywrought with a mene persone –
> First by the fadres wille and the frendes conseille,
> And sithenes by assent of hemself, as thei two myght acorde;
> And thus was wedlok ywroght, and God hymself it made.
>
> (B. 9. 114–17)

The emphasis here on 'assent of hemself' as creating the marriage bond accords with the consensual model of marriage, but, while Will states in both the B and C texts that he dreams of how Mede was married (B. 2. 53, C. 2. 54), neither text includes a description of an exchange of mutual consent.

Tavormina does suggest that the exchange of consent necessary to create a marriage is present at B. 2. 67–68 and C. 2. 67–68:[121]

> Whan Symonye and Cyvylle seighe hir bother wille,
> Thei assented for silver to seye as bothe wolde.   (B. 2. 67–68)

> When Symonye and Syuile ysey þer bothe wille
> Thei assentede hit were so at sylueres preyere.   (C. 2. 67–68)

What do Civil and Simony represent here? Derek Pearsall suggests that simony may be defined as the sale or purchase of ecclesiastical office, but is here used to personify the practice of canon law in the ecclesiastical courts.[122] Certainly simony can be understood in a broader sense than simply the sale or purchase of ecclesiastical office. Hugh of Saint Victor defines simony as the desire to procure spiritual grace by money.[123] Jean Dauviller makes it clear that the demanding of money for the administration of the sacraments, including the sacrament of marriage, was regarded as simony in canon law.[124] Such an interpretation as applied to the character Simony might support Tavormina's interpretation of B. 2. 67–68 and C. 2. 67–68. It is possible, however, to define simony in a yet broader sense – as the sale or purchase of anything spiritual.

---

[120] A. 2. 22–26, omitted from the B and C texts, might be interpreted as representing a three-stage creation of the bond through betrothal (A. 2. 23), consent (A. 2. 24) and consummation (A. 2. 25). Such a three-step model of marriage appears in English ecclesiastical statutes such as 2 Exeter 7 (Powicke and Cheney, II, 996), but it is still consent to the bond, and not the other two steps, which creates the marriage in canon law.

[121] Tavormina, p. 13; Fowler, p. 777 agrees, but suggests that the reference to the will of both could be to either False and Mede or False and Favel.

[122] Pearsall, p. 58.

[123] Hugh of Saint Victor, *On the Sacraments of the Christian Faith*, trans. Roy J. Deferrari (Cambridge, MA: Medieval Academy of America, 1951), p. 322.

[124] Dauviller, p. 117.

Such an interpretation of the meaning of simony might be taken from Chaucer's *Parson's Tale*: 'And therefore understoond that bothe he that selleth and he that beyeth thinges espirituels been cleped symonyals' (X. 784). The possibility of sale or purchase of the sacraments, moreover, may not be confined to those responsible for their administration. Such activities could also take place in the ecclesiastical courts, as the appearance of Simony and Civil later in the B text makes clear. Alexandra Barratt, arguing that the character of Civil represents the academic study of the civil law, suggests that canon law was largely based upon civil law.[125] Simony certainly represents the sale of ecclesiastical office when he appears with Coveitise ('Covetousness') in Passus 20 of the B text (B. 20. 126–28), but, a few lines later, Civil is turned into Simony by Coveitise (B. 20. 137), and then 'the Official' (B. 20. 137), presumably of the ecclesiastical court divorces them:

> For a menever mantle he made lele matrymoyne
> Departen er deeth cam, and a devors shapte.   (B. 20. 138–39)

'Departen er deeth' is a parodic reversal of the marriage liturgy. Simony would not seem to be the practice of canon law in the ecclesiastical courts, then, as Pearsall suggests, but the corruption of Civil which enables that practice. Such practice is simoniacal not in the sense of the sale or purchase of ecclesiastical office or payment for the administration of a sacrament, but in the broader sense of the sale or purchase of anything spiritual. But if Simony and Civil are corruptions of law which make possible the malpractice of the ecclesiastical courts, it does not seem valid to see them, as Tavormina does, 'as allegorical equivalents to the local priest,'[126] for Langland elsewhere emphasizes a slothful parish priest's ignorance of canon law:

> I have be preest and person passnge thritty wynter [. . .]
> Ac in Canoun nor in Decretals I kan noght rede a lyne.   (B. 5. 416, 422)[127]

Given Langland's emphasis on the ignorance of canon law on the part of parish priests, it does not seem valid to see Simony and Civil as the equivalent of local clergy observing the exchange of consent between Mede and False leading to the creation of the marriage bond. It would seem more valid to see them as representations of an ecclesiastical court who have to be bribed to allow the marriage to proceed despite an impediment which should prevent it from taking place.

---

[125] Alexandra Barratt, 'The Characters "Civil" and "Theology" in *Piers Plowman*,' *Traditio* 38 (1982), 352–64 (p. 356); cf. F. R. H. DuBoulay, *The England of Piers Plowman: William Langland and His Vision of the Fourteenth Century* (Cambridge: Brewer, 1991), p. 98.

[126] Tavormina, p. 13 n. 28.

[127] Barratt, p. 356, suggests that 'Canoun' here is Gratian's *Concordance of Discordant Canons*, or *Decretum*, and that 'Decretals' is the *Decretals of Gregory IX*, the two books that make up the canon law.

What might that impediment be? Consanguinity and affinity were impediments to marriage if the parties to be married had a common ancestor or had ancestors who were married in the previous four generations.[128] There are suggestions of incest in Mede's proposed marriage to False in both the B and C texts. In B, False is both Mede's father and the intended bridegroom:

> For Fals was hire fader that hath a fikel tonge   (B. 2. 25)
> And now worth this Mede ymaried to a mansed sherewe
> To oon Fals Fikel-tonge, a fendes biyete.   (B. 2. 40–41)

The situation in the C text is more complex. As E. Talbot Donaldson states, 'C changes Meed's father's name from False to Favel in the line where her father is first named. But having apparently amended the mix-up, he reverts to B and gives it upon a second occasion as False.'[129] Hence Meed is still to marry False (C. 2. 41–42), but her father's name is given as Favel by Holy Church (C. 2. 25) and as False by Theology (C. 2. 121). Gerald Morgan argues that 'False [. . .] is the outward effect of Favel which is brought into being by means of Guile and Liar.'[130] Donaldson also argues for a close relationship between these characters in the C text, arguing that 'all these w- and f- alliterating personages are of exactly the same sort, indistinguishable in their common desire to make money by misuse of the law.'[131] It seems reasonable to agree, then, with Tavormina's argument that 'Guile, flattery, lying, fickle tongues and faithlessness are close kin, morally speaking, so close that they cannot be fully distinguished. [. . .] Whether or not Langland intended to suggest father-daughter incest in B or C, the similarities in False, Favel and Wrong in these texts do leave the impression that Mede is marrying back into her potential kindred much too closely.'[132] Such a marriage should have been prevented by canon law, although dispensations were available. I would suggest that what is taking place at B. 2. 67–68 and C. 2. 67–68, when Simony and Civil are bribed, is the bribery of representatives of the ecclesiastical courts in order to obtain such a dispensation to marry, not the exchange of mutual consent by False and Mede in front of a parish priest, as suggested by Tavormina.

Why is the transfer of property focused on in the description of the marriage ceremony, to the exclusion of the exchange of consent in the B and C texts? As Lavinia Griffiths puts it, 'It is a problem of *meaning* rather than law that is brought by Mede to Westminster. The dramatic concern becomes the issue of the semantic domain of *mede*.'[133] This is a semantic domain which is set up in

---

[128] Cf. Powicke and Cheney, I, 89.

[129] E. Talbot Donaldson, *Piers Plowman: The C-Text and Its Poet* (London, 1949, repr. Cass: 1966), p. 69.

[130] Morgan, 'Langland's Conception,' p. 632.

[131] Donaldson, p. 70.

[132] Tavormina, p. 9.

[133] Lavina Griffiths, *Personification in Piers Plowman* (Cambridge: Brewer, 1985), p. 31.

the first place by the differing genealogies constructed around Mede by Holy Church and by Theology,[134] on the basis of which differing arguments as to whom Mede should marry are advanced. I would argue that there is also a sense to be investigated here in which this is a representation of a marriage motivated by financial considerations.[135] Such marriages are later condemned by Wit in all three texts.[136]

If property is the focus of the marriage ceremony between Mede and False, it is also the reason (on the literal level) that the decision on Mede's marriage should be referred to the king's court rather than the ecclesiastical court. As Tavormina states, 'The Church had always acknowledged the Crown's jurisdiction over matrimonial cases without spiritual content: cases concerning property, feudal obligations, and other secular aspects of marriage.'[137] Certainly the case is not referred to the secular courts simply because of the corruption of the ecclesiastical courts. That the poem views the ecclesiastical courts as corrupt is clear.[138] B. 15. 235, in contrast, praises the king's court, but the following line immediately qualifies that praise:

> In kynges court he cometh ofte, ther the counseil is trewe;
> Ac if coveitise be of the counseil he wol noght come therinne.
>
> (B. 15. 235–36)

And the C text emphasizes the conditional nature of charity's presence more strongly still:

> In kynges court a cometh, yf his consaile be trewe,
> Ac yf couetyse be of his consaile a wol nat com þerynne.
>
> (C. 16. 357–58).

We have already seen that it is Coveitise that turns Civil into Simony (B. 20. 137): it is clear that he also has the potential to be a corrupting power in the king's court. While Theology demands that the case be sent to London for judgment, he also acknowledges the possibility that the secular courts may provide an incorrect decision.[139] Other explanations have been advanced concerning sending the case to London. Bennett's suggestion is that Mede is treated like a ward in chancery who has been led astray: Tavormina acknowledges such a characterization as useful, but notes that Mede does not qualify as such a ward under a rigorously legal and literal definition.[140] Fowler suggests that Theology's

---

[134] A. 2. 19–21, 83–85, B. 2. 24–27a, B. 2. 116–24, C. 2. 24–29a, C. 2. 118–26.
[135] B. 2. 76–78, C. 2. 79–82.
[136] A. 10. 182–201, B. 9. 156–78, C. 10. 250–80.
[137] Tavormina, pp. 23–30.
[138] See B. 2. 67–68, B. 15. 239–43, B. 20. 138–39, C. 2. 67–68, C. 16. 361–62.
[139] A. 2. 101–2, B. 2. 137–38, C. 2. 150–51.
[140] Bennett, p. 135, Tavormina, pp. 31, 33.

argument is that Mede is being disparaged by the union. This is not, she notes, an impediment under canon law, but as Tavormina observes, it does contravene secular law.[141] Baldwin suggests that the king's involvement is based on Mede's kinship with the king (A. 2. 97, B. 2. 133, C. 2. 146), which would presumably make her heiress to one of the king's tenancies in chief, for which she would require the king's permission to marry.[142] *Bracton* is explicit on the point that female heirs, even women whose parents are living, may not marry without the permission of their chief lords, for fear that, if the woman married the lord's enemy, the lord would be forced to accept that enemy's homage.[143] If we accept the argument of S. F. C. Milsom that with the decline of the feudal relationship the lord's interests in a tenure were primarily economic,[144] it seems likely that the king would have extracted a payment in exchange for granting permission to marry to one of his tenants. That an ideal king's court[145] acts very differently here may be seen as further condemnation by Langland of the extraction of profit from marriage: it is only through the absence of Coveitise ('Covetousness') from the king's court that Charity may enter (B. 15. 235–36, C. 16. 357–38), but, in reality, all of the secular jurisdiction's authority over marriage was related to property issues.

As already mentioned, Langland's attack on financially motivated marriages in Passus 2 to 4 is picked up subsequently in the poem. In Wit's speech, the marriages between Seth's offspring and Cain's offspring have been forbidden by God:[146] these marriages are compared to contemporary marriages for worldly gain in all three texts.[147] He also attacks cross-generational marriages at A. 10. 186–88 and B. 9. 162–64. His comment that many such couples have married since the plague is not in agreement with the demographic evidence,[148] but the intended meaning may be more general: that many couples have married for financial reasons since the plague. The C text omits A. 10. 186–88 / B. 9. 162–64, but retains the comment that many such couples have married since the plague (C. 10. 270), here clearly referring to marriages made for worldly gain. That cross-generational marriages were seen as being financially motivated by Langland's contemporaries is clear from John Wyclif's comments on such marriages:

---

[141] Fowler, p. 777; Tavormina, p. 27 and n. 54.

[142] Baldwin, p. 33.

[143] *Bracton*, ed. Woodbridge, trans. Thorne, II, 255; cf. Pollock and Maitland, I, 320.

[144] Milsom, pp. 109–10.

[145] As Bennett, p. 135, describes it.

[146] A. 10. 158, B. 9. 124–26, C. 10. 247–49.

[147] A. 10. 175–85, B. 9. 153–59, C.10. 250–53.

[148] Tavormina, p. 96, Zvi Razi, *Life, Marriage and Death in a Medieval Parish: Economy, Society and Demography in Halesowen, 1270–1400* (Cambridge: Cambridge University Press, 1980), p. 138, Jack Ravensdale, 'Population Changes and the Transfer of Customary Land on a Cambridgeshire Manor in the Fourteenth Century,' in *Land, Kinship and Life Cycle*, ed. Richard M. Smith (Cambridge: Cambridge University Press, 1984), pp. 197–226 (pp. 209–10).

> Also this contract shulde not be maade bitwixe a yonge man and an
> alde bareyne widewe, passid child-berynge, for love of worldly muk,
> as men ful of coveitise usen sum-tyme – for than cometh soone debat
> and avoutrie and enemyte, and wast of goodis, and sorewe and care
> ynough.[149]

Subsequently in the poem, marriage is represented in potentially problematic terms: as the lowest of the three grades of chastity (although good nevertheless – C. 18.87), and as a potential obstacle to salvation in the representation of Haukyn the active man (e.g. C. 7. 299–304a). The identification of the Father with matrimony (B. 61. 211–13), subsequent to the Father's defence of the fruit on the tree of Charity against the attacks of *Coveitise* (B. 16. 27–30, C. 18. 31–34), implies that marriage can overcome the worldly sin of covetousness, and hence prove an aid to salvation, the poem's ultimate concern. Langland's attack on marriages made for financial gain in the Mede episode, however, draws this aspect of the spiritual value of the marriage sacrament for his contemporaries into question.

The accommodation that exists between ecclesiastical and secular law regarding marriage, then, disguises a fundamental divergence in their respective attitudes to marriage. The State's jurisdiction is interested in marriage only as the location of transfers of property, whereas the Church's jurisdiction is primarily interested in marriage as it pertains to the salvation of the individual. This fundamental ideological divergence concerning marriage sometimes leads to conflict between the two jurisdictions, as in the disputes concerning legitimacy and women's testamentary rights. Elsewhere, it leads to practical contradictions: however much secular law attempts to present wardship as something that does not interfere with free consent, Menuge's evidence would suggest that it could. Such stark contradictions between ecclesiastical and secular interests in marriage are brought into focus in Langland's poem which asks how, for Christians uncertain of salvation, marriage might relate to their ultimate end, especially if tainted by monetary concerns.

Apart from the different interests of the ecclesiastical and secular jurisdictions, there are also contradictions within the secular law, as when the common law and customary law contradict each other. The secular law as it relates to marriage and property, then, is diverse and fragmented: so much so, that it might seem better to refer to secular laws rather than law. Further to that, practice seems at times at least to operate one step ahead of the law, as families put their own interests ahead of sticking to the rules. Barbara A. Hanawalt has suggested that peasants only resorted to rules and customs where internal family arrangements had not been made or had not been successful.[150] We can see

---

[149] John Wyclif, *Select English Writings of John Wyclif*, ed. Thomas Arnold, 3 vols (Oxford: Macmillan, 1869–71), III, 191.

[150] Hanawalt, *The Ties that Bound*, p. 73.

contemporaries using what means they could to get around restrictions in the sale of *maritagia* and the employment of the jointure and the use to get around inheritance rules. It is the interests of families in another function of marriage – the possibility of using marriage to forge alliances – that is the focus of the next chapter.

3

Marriage as Alliance

Beowulf

As is well known, the notion of marriage as an alliance between families, or as a means of cementing peace treaties and settling feuds, is implicit in several passages in *Beowulf*. In the description of the building of the hall of Heorot near the poem's beginning, the poet juxtaposes a description of the hall's construction with an account of its eventual destruction. That destruction comes about because of a feud between relations by marriage: the Danish king Hrothgar, the builder of Heorot, and his son in law, Ingeld:

> Sele hlifade
> heah ond horngeap: heaðowylma bad,
> laðan liges.   Ne waes hit lenge þa gen,
> þæt se ecghete   aþumswerian
> æfter wælniðe   wæcnan scolde.   (lines 81b–85)

The hall rose up high, lofty and wide-gabled: awaited the furious surge of hostile flames. The day was not yet near when violent hatred between son-in-law and father-in-law should be born of deadly malice.[1]

Later in the poem, we are given a glimpse of an earlier part of the story of Ingeld when Beowulf is retelling his adventures in Denmark to his lord, Hygelac, the Geatish king. Here we learn that Hrothgar's daughter, Freawaru, has been promised in marriage to Ingeld as a means of settling a feud between the Danes and the Heathobards. Beowulf comments:

> Sio gehaten is
> geong, goldhroden,   gladum suna Frodan.
> Hafað þæs geworden   wine Scyldinga,
> rices hyrde,   ond þæt ræd talað

---

[1]   *Beowulf*, ed. and trans. by Michael Swanton (Manchester: Manchester University Press, 1978), pp. 38, 39.

78

> þæt he mid ðy wife   wælfæða dæl,
> sæcca gesette.   Oft seldan hwær
> æfter leodhryre   lytle hwile
> bongar bugeð,   þeah seo bryd duge! (20246–31)

Young, adorned with gold, she is promised to the gracious son of Froda. That has been agreed upon by the Scyldings' friend, the guardian of the kingdom, and he considers it good advice that, by means of this woman, he should settle their share of slaughterous feuds, of conflicts. It seldom happens after the fall of a prince that the deadly spear rests for even a little while – worthy though the bride may be![2]

Beowulf's last words here suggest that he has little faith in this marriage of Freawaru and Ingeld as a solution to the feud between the Danes and the Heathobards. This is something that we already know to be well-founded, since it is the resumption of the feud that will lead to the eventual destruction of Heorot. Beowulf's description in the following lines of the way that resentments among the defeated may cause feuds to be rekindled seems to echo the story of Finnsburh, told earlier in the poem by Hrothgar's *scop* (lines 1068–1159). This story, about the collapse of a peace agreement between the Danish kin of Hildeburh and her husband, the Frisian king Finn, may also originate in a marriage between Frisian and Dane to cement a peace agreement.[3]

All of these examples from *Beowulf* emphasize the problems inherent in using marriages to settle feuds, to make alliances, to cement peace treaties between kin groups. But while emphasizing the difficulties, they also testify to the existence of the idea of marriage as peace treaty in early medieval Germanic culture.

Alliance, consent, and kin

Implicit in this idea of marriage as a peace treaty between kin groups is a particular view of family. James A. Brundage argues for the importance of the broader kin group in European kinship structures after the collapse of the Roman empire:

> The extended kinship group was prominent in archaic Germanic society and remained fundamental to Germanic institutions for generations following the invasions. The kindred bore responsibility for fulfilling the obligations incurred by any of its members and for seeing to it that each member both paid what he owed and received what he had a right to. The group also tried to protect the peace and security of its members against outside interference. Reciprocal revenge meant in effect that wrongs were avenged by inflicting injury upon

---

[2]   *Beowulf*, ed. and trans. Swanton, pp. 130, 131.
[3]   *Beowulf*, ed. and trans. Swanton, n. to lines 1068–1159.

> the person responsible for the damage, or, failing that, upon some other member of his or her household, or their kin.[4]

There are two reasons why we might expect a change in this notion of kinship, and the notion of marriage as alliance, in the later Middle Ages. The first is the Church's exclusive jurisdiction over marriage as a spiritual matter in the later medieval period, and its formulation of marriage as something brought about through the consent of the individuals to be married. Jack Goody has argued that there is a long-standing tension between the Church and the power of family ties: pointing out that the Gospels provide the scriptural basis for an elevation of the sectarian community over ties of kin.[5] The consensual model has the effect of giving new freedoms to individuals, but also replaces the domination of the family in questions of marriage with the authority of the Church.[6] The second reason that we might expect a change is that the nuclear family, which is the standard throughout medieval Europe, might be felt to be incompatible with a wider sense of kin. In the sixth century, we do not find families forming households in the sense of a couple and their offspring. By the ninth century, however, as Brundage puts it, 'the Western family has taken the shape that has characterized it ever since that time.'[7]

But in fact, the idea of marriage as alliance persists into the later medieval period: our modern notions of personal consent and the nuclear family as being progressive, and hence likely to replace outmoded ways of thinking involving broad kinship groups and family input into the arranging of marriages, implies some sort of evolutionary model of history. In fact, contradictory as arranged marriages and personal choice might seem to be, these things coexist. The notion of consent as an important factor in the making of marriages is not an altogether new one when the Church formulates its consensual model of marriage, as we saw in chapter one. Similarly, the nuclear family – perhaps more about household organization than a wider sense of kin structure? – is in evidence long before the end of the Anglo-Saxon era, and long before the development of the ecclesiastical model of marital consent.

We can see evidence for the conception of marriages as peace treaties in later medieval England in contemporary texts. A statute that the canonist William Lyndwood attributes to 'Edmundus' (Edmund Rich, the archbishop of Canterbury) in his *Provinciale*, forbids the marriage of minors, but makes an exception if the marriage is made for the purposes of establishing peace.[8] Prohibition of the marriage of minors with the same exception is found in the *Decretals*.[9] A petition of

---

[4]   Brundage, *Law, Sex and Christian Society*, p. 125.

[5]   Goody, pp. 87–90.

[6]   Noonan, 'Power to Choose,' p. 433.

[7]   Brundage, *Law, Sex and Christian Society*, p. 135; these questions are discussed further at the beginning of chapter 6.

[8]   William Lyndwood, *Provincialis Wilhelmi Lyndewode* (Paris, 1501), fol. cxlviii[r]. None of the statutes that Lyndwood attributes to 'Edmundus' are his, all are from other sources: Cheney, 'Legislation,' pp. 400–2.

[9]   Friedberg, II, 673.

1348 from the lord of Hoerne and the lord of Arkel to the pope asks that a dispensation may be granted for the lord of Hoerne to marry the lord of Arkel's eleven-year-old daughter in order to end the conflict between them. The petition was granted on the condition that the facts were accurate.[10] Another petition, this one from the earl of Lancaster in 1349, asks a dispensation for the children of two lords (related in the fourth degree of kindred) to intermarry in order to bring peace.[11] Two similar petitions of 1343 come from Scotland and Ireland.[12] It might be argued that the motivation of peace is being put forward duplicitously here in order to persuade the pope to approve such marriages. The Church's history of attempting to take a role in creating peace between lay factions extends back to the Peace of God and Truce of God movements of the eleventh century.[13] Nonetheless, the concept of peace through marriage must have been quite well founded among the laity in order for appeals to be made on these grounds, and the granting of a dispensation subject to the accuracy of the petition subverts such possibilities.

The Knight's Tale

In her book *Chaucer's Sexual Poetics*, Carolyn Dinshaw draws upon Claude Levi-Strauss's work *The Elementary Structures of Kinship*, arguing that Lévi-Strauss (read in the light of criticisms offered by Gayle Rubin) usefully informs discussion of medieval hermeneutics because both modern and medieval theorists participate in the same kind of patriarchal thinking.[14] She argues that:

> Lévi-Strauss, in *The Elementary Structures of Kinship*, follows and extends Mauss's analysis: society depends not only on linguistic and commercial exchange but on the exchange of women. Women are the most precious of gifts – 'the supreme gift': accordingly, the regulation of the exchange of women between families and groups is the very basis of social organization. The rule of exogamy is 'at the center of an agreement to control warfare among men'; rules governing the exchange of women are the 'most basic peace treaty'.[15]

---

[10] *Calendar of Entries in the Papal Registers Relating to Great Britain and Ireland. Petitions to the Pope. Vol. I. AD 1342–1419*, ed. W. H. Bliss (London: HMSO, 1896), p. 132.

[11] Bliss, p. 151.

[12] Bliss, pp. 15, 27–28.

[13] Carl Erdmann, *The Origin of the Idea of Crusade*, trans. by Marshall W. Baldwin and Walter Goffart (Princeton, NJ: Princeton University Press, 1977), pp. 59–62.

[14] Dinshaw, *Chaucer's Sexual Poetics*, p. 16; Gayle Rubin, 'The Traffic in Women: Notes on the "Political Economy" of Sex,' in *Towards an Anthropology of Women*, ed. by Rayna R. Reiter (New York: Monthly Review Press, 1975), pp. 157–210; Claude Levi-Strauss, *The Elementary Structures of Kinship*, ed. and trans. by James Harle Bell, John Richard von Sturmer and Rodney Needham, revised ed. (Boston: Beacon Press, 1969).

[15] Dinshaw, *Chaucer's Sexual Poetics*, p. 57.

The relevance of Lévi-Strauss's work to later medieval England is difficult to judge. In his preface to the first edition of *The Elementary Structures of Kinship*, he writes:

> Elementary structures of kinship are those systems in which the nomenclature permits the immediate determination of the circle of kin and that of affines, that is, those systems which prescribe marriage with a certain type of relative, or, alternatively, those which, while defining all members of the society as relatives, divide them into two categories, viz., possible spouses and prohibited spouses. The term 'complex structures' is reserved for systems which limit themselves to defining the circle of relatives and leave the determination of the spouse to other mechanisms, economic or psychological. In this work, then, the term 'elementary structures' corresponds to what sociologists call preferential marriage.[16]

By this definition, the kinship structures that we are dealing with in discussing marriage in medieval England are, undeniably, 'complex.' Although Lévi-Strauss attempts to suggest that his analysis of elementary structures may be used as the basis for a general theory of kinship which would also include complex structures, no concrete analysis is undertaken.[17] On the other hand, as we have seen, marriages as peace treaties are found in later medieval England.

Dinshaw uses the model of exchange of women for an analysis of two of Chaucer's *Canterbury Tales*: the *Man of Law's Tale*, and the *Wife of Bath's Prologue*.[18] Here I want to look at marriage in the *Knight's Tale*, not a tale that belongs to Kittredge's traditional 'marriage group,'[19] but one which has a great deal to say about marriages as peace treaties. The plot is essentially that of a love triangle: two young Thebans, Palamon and Arcite, vie for the affections of Emelye, an Amazon princess. But it is a love triangle with a political twist, for Emelye's marriage depends upon the choice of Theseus, the Athenian king, who is the enemy of the Thebans, and holds them in prison.

That Palamon and Arcite are Theseus's enemies is not in doubt. The condition of Arcite's release from Theseus's captivity is that he never returns to Athens, on pain of death:

> This was the forward, pleynly for t'endite,
> Bitwixen Theseus and hym Arcite:
> That if so were that Arcite were yfounde
> Evere in his lif, by day or nyght, oo stounde
> In any contree of this Theseus,

---

[16] Levi-Strauss, Preface, xxxiii.

[17] Levi-Strauss, Preface, xxxiv, pp. 471–75.

[18] Dinshaw, *Chaucer's Sexual Poetics*, pp. 96–97, 114; there is a brief mention of the *Knight's Tale* in these terms in Carolyn Dinshaw, 'The Law of Man and its "Abhomynacions"', *Exemplaria* 1 (1989), 117–48 (pp. 135–36).

[19] On which see Kittredge, 130–58.

And he were caught, it was accorded thus,
That with a swerd he sholde lese his heed.   (1. 1209–15)

Palamon, lamenting Arcite's freedom, supposes that he will make war on Theseus:

Thou mayst, syn thou hast wisdom and manhede,
Assemblen alle the folk of oure kynrede,
And make a werre so sharp on this citee
That by som aventure or some tretee
Thow mayst have hire to lady and to wyf
For whom that I moste nedes lese my lyf.   (1. 1285–90)

The possibility of Arcite's gaining Emelye as a wife by 'tretee' appears here in line 1288, but this is not the route pursued by Arcite. Instead, he returns to Athens disguised as a servant, in order to be close to Emelye. In his description of his situation as a servant, however, Arcite still refers to the enmity between Theseus and himself:

That he that is my mortal enemy,
I serve hym as his squier povrely.   (1. 1553–54)

When (after Palamon's escape from prison) Theseus subsequently stumbles across the infiltrator Arcite and the escapee Palamon, Palamon's appeal to Theseus to kill them both states openly:

This is thy mortal foe, this is Arcite   (1. 1724)

And, speaking for himself:

I am thy mortal foo, [. . .].   (1. 1736)

Theseus's decision to have mercy on them, at the request of the female members of the company, is followed by a pledge by Palamon and Arcite not to act against Theseus (1.1821–27). That there is a conflict requiring settlement, then, is clear.

Theseus states that he forgives them at the request of the queen and of Emelye, 'my suster deere' (1. 1820), and in arranging the contest to determine who shall marry Emelye, he says 'I speke as for my suster Emelye' (1. 1833). The twin references to Emelye as his sister invoke the medieval Church's regulations of affinity, for Emelye is his wife's sister, not his. The Church's insistence on freedom of choice of marriage partner, however, is not echoed here, for Theseus gives Emelye in marriage:

Thanne shal I yeve Emelya to wyve
To whom that Fortune yeveth so fair a grace.   (1. 1860–61)

The Knight's Tale, then, seems to illustrate the situation that Carolyn Dinshaw describes in Lévi-Strauss: the giving of a woman as a gift as part of an agreement to control warfare among men.

All of this, however, is not the first intrusion of the topic of marriage into the tale, for Theseus himself marries at the beginning of the tale, and his marriage too represents a peace treaty. Elaine Tuttle Hansen, commenting on the 'regne of

Femenye' that Theseus has conquered, argues that it equates Amazons with women in general, and with Woman as an idea and a territory. She suggests further that the appearance of the Theban widows immediately afterwards embodies the success of Theseus's taming strategy.[20] I would suggest, however, that the act of supplication by the Theban widows is intended to act as a contrast to the Amazons' act of war, which Chaucer describes in saying that he will pass over narrating:

> [. . .] the grete bataille for the nones
> Bitwixen Atthenes and Amazones;
> And how asseged was Ypolita,
> The faire, hardy queene of Scithia;
> And of the feste that was at hir weddynge,
> And of the tempest at hir hoom-comynge;   (1. 879–84)

This description emphasizes the alteration in the attitudes of the Amazons later in the tale, when Hippolyta and Emelye re-enact the supplication of the Theban widows when they plead with Theseus to spare the lives of Palamon and Arcite:[21]

> The queene anon, for verray wommanhede,
> Gan for to wepe, and so dide Emelye,
> And alle the ladyes in the compaignye.   (1. 1748–50)

Later, in Emelye's plea to Diana, we see her appeal for chastity:

> Chaste goddess, wel wostow that I
> Desire to ben a mayden al my lyf,
> Ne nevere wol I be no love ne wyf.
> I am, thow woost, yet of thy compaignye,
> A mayde, and love huntynge and venerye,
> And for to walken in the wodes wilde,
> And noght to ben a wyf and be with childe.
> Noght wol I knowe compaignye of man.   (1. 2304–11)

The appeal is later modified to a request that if she has to have either Palamon or Arcite, it should be the one that most desires her (1. 2322–25). Her plea to retain her chastity is phrased in terms that we might still consider Amazonian: she wishes to continue to hunt and serve Diana, and she is 'yet' one of her company. But this is the role in which the reader has seen Theseus represented earlier in the tale (1. 1673–82), and we are told that '[. . .] after Mars he serveth now

---

[20]   Hansen, pp. 217–18.

[21]   In Boccaccio's *Teseida*, Chaucer's source for the *Knight's Tale*, Teseo's decision to spare Palamon and Arcite is not based on any request from his wife and sister-in-law: *Chaucer's Boccaccio: Sources of* Troilus *and the* Knight's *and* Franklin's Tales, ed. and trans. by N. R. Havely (Cambridge: Brewer, 1980), p. 121; *Sources and Analogues of Chaucer's Canterbury Tales*, ed. W. F. Bryan and Germaine Dempster (Chicago: University of Chicago Press, 1941), p. 98.

Dyane' (1. 1682). Emelye's supplication to Diana is a challenge to Theseus's authority, and hence is modified and refused. The passive role allocated to women in the tale is explicitly articulated when Arcite looks at Emelye:

> And she agayn hym caste a freendlich ye
> (For wommen, as to speken in comune,
> Thei folwen alle the favour of Fortune.)   (1. 2680–82)[22]

Hence the refusal to articulate Emelye's feelings at Arcite's funeral. Chaucer (or the narrator) will not tell:

> [. . .] how that Emelye, as was the gyse,
> Putte in the fyr of funeral servyse;
> Ne how she swowned whan men made the fyr,
> Ne what she spak, ne what was hir desir;   (1. 2941–44)

Although Arcite's dying wish that Emelye should marry Palamon is addressed directly to her (1. 2783–97), the decision is not hers. Theseus and his parliament decide for her:

> 'Suster,' quod he, 'this is my fulle assent,
> With al th'avys heere of my parlement,
> That gentil Palamon, youre owene knyght,
> That serveth yow with wylle, herte, and myght,
> And ever hath doon syn ye first hym knewe,
> That ye shul of youre grace upon hym rewe,
> And taken hym for housbonde and for lord.
> Lene me youre hond, for this is oure accord.   (1. 3075–82)

Palamon, too, was Theseus's enemy, and so 'accord' here can mean either 'decision' (by agreement of Theseus and his parliament) or 'agreement' (between Theseus and Palamon).[23] In any case, Emelye is once again a gift, and although her opinion is not expressed, it is notable that Theseus spends fifteen lines informing Emelye that she is to marry Palamon and describing his merits, whereas Palamon is informed in three, because Theseus feels he needs little persuasion (1. 3091–93).

Palamon's marriage to Emelye is somewhat problematic, given that she has already married Arcite, his cousin (1. 1018–19): Arcite is clearly referred to as her husband at 1. 2823.[24] Theseus's constant references to Emelye as his sister

---

[22] The lines in parentheses are omitted from some manuscripts.

[23] *MED* gives the following readings (among others) for 'accorden': '2(a) To reconcile (persons}; make friends of; setten accord(ed; ~ in pes; to bring about reconciliation (between persons).'

[24] In the *Teseida*, Arcita and Emilia are married, but their marriage is not consummated: Havely, pp. 141–42, Bryan and Dempster, p. 102. However, consummation was not necessary for a marriage to be canonically valid. Gratian's *Decretum* specifically forbids a brother from marrying his brother's widow, even if consummation of the first marriage did not occur: Friedberg, I, 1065. The text reads: 'Frater sponsam fratris post mortem eius non potest ducere. Si quis desponsaverit sibi aliquam et preveniente mortis articulo eam cognoscere not potuit, frater eius

foregrounds the existence of impediments of affinity, and if affinity makes her Theseus's sister, it also makes her Palamon's cousin through her marriage to Arcite. But the problem of incest is not mentioned in the description of her marriage to Palamon, for it is necessary for her to marry Palamon in order for the alliance to hold. An actual case that offers a parallel may be seen in a papal letter of 1354 to the duke of Brittany, allowing his eldest son John to marry the king Edward's daughter Margaret, or, if Margaret died, another daughter Mary, or, if John died, that the duke's second son might marry Mary, despite an impediment in the third and fourth degrees of consanguinity.[25] It is obvious that it does not matter who marries whom in this case: what matters is the alliance. It is this ideology of alliance with which the aristocracy invest the practice of matrimony, made acceptable to the Church by its peacemaking role but at odds with the canon law's insistence on the right of free consent, and frequently also in violation of impediments to matrimony on grounds of consanguinity, affinity, or age, that is present in the *Knight's Tale*.

The Paston Letters

The fifteenth-century Paston correspondence has a great deal to say about the marriages and marriage negotiations of members of the Paston family. In a 1973 article, Ann S. Haskell argued that freedom of choice in marriage for members of the family, or the lack of it, seemed to depend upon gender. Commenting on the family's opposition to the clandestine marriage between Margery Paston and a servant, Richard Calle, Haskell writes:

> In addition to their objections in Margery's case, the Pastons also successfully destroyed the love match of another daughter, Anne, and negotiated for her a marriage of their own choice. Events in the lives of the Paston sons, John II and John III, offer a distinct contrast. The younger John married for love, not, it is true, without some difficulties in the marriage arrangements, but his own mother intervened to smooth things over. More remarkable is the course of marital misadventures in John II's life. This John was head of the family and to him were tied the major Paston properties, including the castle, yet the family did not even suggest whom he should wed. Far from trying to negotiate a match for him, his mother asked him at one point if the rumor she heard of an impending marriage were true. This John,

non potest eam in uxorem ducere.' Palamon and Arcite are cousins (1. 1019), but they are referred to repeatedly as sworn brothers (1. 1131, 1135, 1147, 1161, 1181, 1652). In any case, as the children of two sisters (1. 1019), Palamon's marriage to Arcite's wife is still incestuous. The regulations on the impediment of affinity are set out in canon 50 of the Fourth Lateran Council (1215): *Decrees of the Ecumenical Councils*, ed. N. P. Tanner (London: Sheed and Ward, 1990), p. 257; cf. discussion of the affinity regulations in Pollock and Maitland, II, 405.

[25] Bliss and Johnson, p. 615.

called 'the best cheser of a gentell woman', was engaged in a number of alliances, including the one that produced a daughter out of wedlock, whom Margaret Paston recognized by leaving a modest dowry.[26]

Haskell's comments on the family's subversion of the desires of their female members is accurate, but John II and John III did not have the free hand they appear to have at first glance.[27] It is John Paston II's marriage that is relevant to the discussion of marriage as alliance, but it is perhaps worth commenting on the circumstances of both brothers. While Haskell argues that John III's marriage to Margery Brews was a love-match, John III in fact employed his brother in interviewing a long list of potential candidates for marriage, beginning with Alice Boleyn in 1467.[28] We can see in the extended negotiations between the Paston family and the family of Margery Brews why family support was essential, for John III required financial support from his family in order to successfully conclude the negotiations. He is refused assistance by his elder brother, and it is implied that this is because he has not been involved in the negotiations:

> Iffe I weere att the begynnyng off suche a mater, I wolde have hopyd to have made a bettyr conclusyon, iff they mokke yow notte. Thys mater is drevyn thus ferforthe wyth-owte my cowncell; I praye yow make an ende wyth-owte my cowncell. Iffe it be weell, I wolde be glad; iff it be oderwyse, it is pité. I praye yow troble me no moore in thys mater.[29]

Instead, as Haskell observes, John III receives the financial help that he requires from his mother, the widowed Margaret Paston, who is in dispute with John II over the potential loss of part of the family's lands through the marriage of John III. Colin Richmond notes that the birth of male issue to John III and Margery meant that the manor of Sparham, settled jointly on the couple and their issue (rather than their male issue) by Margaret Paston, would not now pass out of the hands of the Paston family, although it did leave the main branch of the family, represented by John II.[30] John II's concerns about this grant appear clearly in a letter to his mother: he refuses to ratify the grant but agrees not to dispute it.[31] John II did play a role in the eventual marriage agreement, though, conferring the manor of Swainsthorp on John III and Margery Brews (with Sir Thomas Brews, Margery's

---

[26] Ann S. Haskell, 'The Paston Women on Marriage in Fifteenth Century England,' *Viator* 4 (1973), 459–84.

[27] John and Margaret Paston had two sons named John: the elder is usually referred to by modern writers as John Paston II, the younger as John Paston III.

[28] *Paston Letters and Papers of the Fifteenth Century*, ed. Norman Davis (Oxford: Oxford University Press, 1971–76), I, 396.

[29] Davis, I, 503.

[30] Colin Richmond, 'The Pastons Revisited: Marriage and the Family in Fifteenth-Century England,' *Bulletin of the Institute of Historical Research* 58 (1985), 25–36 (p. 30).

[31] Davis, I, 500–1.

father, lending John III the money to get the manor out of mortgage as part of the marriage settlement, as well as granting a marriage portion of 400 marks).[32] But to state that John III marries purely for love is to ignore the fact that he keeps his options open during negotiations with Sir Thomas Brews. In a letter of 9 March 1477, John II states that he has gone to see a 'Mestresse Barly', whom he considers an unsuitable match for his brother, and enquires how things are progressing with 'Mestresse Brewys'.[33] This takes place in the same month that Margaret agrees to grant Sparham to John III and Margery Brews (although the matter has still not been settled by June). This might simply indicate that John III is keeping his brother in the dark about how far things have progressed in his negotiations with Sir Thomas Brews. Alternatively, it might indicate that he is not taking the success of those negotiations for granted, and is still exploring alternative possibilities. John III is quite duplicitous with all parties in the marriage negotiations: in a letter probably written on 28 June 1477 to his mother, he encloses two other letters written by him but purportedly written by his mother to be sent, having been copied 'of some other manys hand,' one to Elizabeth Brews, Margery's mother, and the other to John III himself, that he can show to his potential in-laws.[34] A memorandum of John III's relating to the marriage negotiations, probably slightly earlier than the letter just mentioned, shows that he intends to 'kepe secret fro my moder that the bargayn is full concludyd.'[35] John III's marriage agreement, then, is very much dependent upon managing relations with the property holding members of his family. Although (unlike his aunt Elizabeth and sister Anne) he is the instigator of negotiations concerning his marriage, and it is he who influences their direction, it is clear that without the assistance of the property holding members of his family, he would have been unable to conclude the negotiations successfully.

Haskell's suggestion that it is gender (rather than property) which confers the freedom to choose is based largely upon the negotiations for the marriage of John II. The family as a whole are not involved in these negotiations. Margaret, his mother, writes to him of his 'ensuraunce' (i.e. his engagement) in the following terms in 1469:

> I have non very knowleche of your ensuraunce, but if ye be ensured I
> pray God send you joy and wurchep to-geder, and so I trost ye shull
> haue if it be as it is reported of here.[36]

As Haskell notes, then, the family were barely informed of John II's marital negotiations, much less involved. John II was in a position to negotiate his own marriage because, subsequent to the death of his father, he was not in need of assistance

---

[32] Davis, I, 607; cf. Richmond, p. 30.
[33] Davis, I, 499.
[34] Davis, I, 608–10.
[35] Davis, I, 608.
[36] Davis, I, 338.

from other members of his family in order to agree a financial settlement to accompany his marriage. There is another reason for the family's lack of involvement in the affairs of John II, however. Several letters give evidence of a dispute between John II and his father.[37] In a letter of 8 April 1465, Margaret Paston writes to her husband:

> Item, I vnderstand be John Pampyng that ye wolle not þat your sone be take in-to your hows nor holp be you tylle suche tyme of yere as he was put owt thereof, the wiche shalle be a-bowght Seynt Thomas messe. For Godys sake, ser, a pety on hym and remembre yow it hathe be a long season syn he had owt of you to helpe hym wyth, and he hathe obeyed hym to yow and wolle do at all tymis, and wolle do that he can or may to have your good faderhod. And at þe reuerence of God, be ye hys good fader and have a faderly hert to hym.[38]

This sundering between John II and the rest of the household endured subsequent to his father's death, and, in April 1467, John III writes to him that he has not come home in seven years.[39] The family's absence from the marriage negotiations seem to be a single symptom of this larger breach, rather than evidence of abstention on the part of the Pastons from interference in the premarital negotiations of male family members.

Furthermore, although the rest of the family were not involved in the negotiations of John II's engagement to Anne Haute, Colin Richmond suggests that the engagement was entered into for the benefit of the family rather than for the personal benefit of John II (although, as he observes, those interests might be identical, given John II's position as the head of the family).[40] Anne Haute was a relative of the queen, Elizabeth Woodvill, and such an alliance seemed certain to have benefits for the family. Richmond points to a letter of April 1469 (the month after the engagement) from the queen's brother to a member of the duke of Norfolk's council, indicating his support for John II in the dispute between the Pastons and the duke, and clearly mentioning the marriage as the reason for his support.[41] Although the family as a whole do not take part in the negotiations, then, once again this looks like marriage as a political alliance.

Richmond also argues, however, that the risings of 1469–71 altered the political situation to make the union an unattractive one for both sides: the potential benefits to the Paston family never occurred.[42] But the union proved a difficult one to disengage from, and this raises the question of what sort of consent to

---

[37] Davis, I, 126–31, 287–88.
[38] Davis, I, 293.
[39] Davis, I, 535.
[40] Richmond, p. 28.
[41] Richmond, p. 27; Davis, II, 571–72.
[42] Richmond, pp. 27–28.

marry passed between John Paston II and Anne Haute? John II's mother, Margaret, writes in her letter to him on hearing of his 'ensuraunce':

> And a-nemps God ye arn as gretly bownd to here as ye were maried;[. . .].[43]

Margaret Paston's statement here that the engagement binds John II as strongly as a marriage brings to mind R. H. Helmholz's argument for a difference between popular conception and canon law on what was meant by consent to marry: Helmholz argues that many people regarded as mere betrothal the exchange of consent that the Church regarded as marriage.[44] If John II's agreement to marry Anne Haute was expressed in the present tense, then it would have been a clandestine marriage rather than a betrothal, whatever the intent of the persons concerned. The letters do not specify the nature of the consent exchanged. In the letters which the queen's brother, Anthony Woodvill, Lord Scales, writes in support of John II against the duke of Norfolk, he states that the marriage is fully concluded:

> And for asmoch as maryage ys fully concluded by-twyx the seyd Ser John Paston and oon of my nerrest kynneswomen [. . .].[45]

> And for asmoch as a maryage ys fully concluded bytwyx Ser John Paston and my ryght ner kynneswoman Anne Hawte [. . .].[46]

'Fully concluded' might mean 'fully agreed', but four years later, the attempt to abandon the agreement has ended up in Rome. John Paston II writes to John Paston III:

> Ye prayed me also to sende yow tydynges how I spedde in my materis, and in cheff of Mestresse Anne Hault. I haue answere ageyn froo Roome that there is the welle off grace and salve sufficiaunt fore suche a soore, and that I may be dyspencyd with.[47]

I find it difficult to accept H. S. Bennett's assertion that it was necessary to apply to Rome for dispensation of an espousal:[48] he may be confusing betrothal and clandestine marriage here, as he does in his discussion of the clandestine union of John's sister, Margery Paston, with the family's bailiff, Richard Calle. In canon law, the exchange of future consent between a couple was invalidated if both agreed, if one party entered religion, or of one party exchanged words of present consent with a third party.[49] Subsequently unfulfilled marriage agreements do appear elsewhere in

---

[43] Davis, I, 338.

[44] Helmholz, *Marriage Litigation*, p. 31.

[45] Davis, II, 571.

[46] Davis, II, 572.

[47] Davis, I, 471.

[48] H. S. Bennett, *The Pastons and their England: Studies in an Age of Transition* (Cambridge: Cambridge University Press, 1922), p. 38.

[49] Dauviller, pp. 40–41, 130–33; cf. Friedberg, II, 661.

the *Paston Letters*.[50] Colin Richmond suggests that the exchange of consent between John Paston II and Anne Haute was a betrothal, but that it was followed by, and probably preceded by, sexual relations.[51] I cannot find any evidence for this in the letters, but it is as plausible as my own speculation that they might have exchanged present rather than future consent. In any case, the result is the same: canon law was clear that future consent (i.e. a betrothal) followed by intercourse made marriage. Most important for this discussion, though, is Richmond's suggestion that the change of political climate rendered the political advantages of the marriage useless for both sides. Hence the need to dissolve the union, whatever sort of union it was. Once any political advantage in the alliance had gone, there was no point in maintaining the marriage.

Despite the Church's proposition of a model of marriage which emphasized the free consent of the individuals to be married in the creation of the marriage bond, then, the idea of marriage as an alliance between families persists into the later Middle Ages, where we can find traces of it both in literature and in practice.

---

[50] For example, between William Clopton and Agnes Paston for the marriage of Elizabeth Paston: *The Paston Letters*, ed. James Gairdner, 6 vols (1904; repr. Stroud: Sutton, 1983), II, 661. There is no evidence of an exchange of consent between William and Elizabeth.

[51] Richmond, p. 28.

4

Love and Marriage

C. S. Lewis and marital love

In his 1936 book, *The Allegory of Love*, C. S. Lewis argued that a new form of love had found expression in the French troubadour poetry of the central Middle Ages, and that this new form of love exercised a fundamental influence on the literature of the later medieval period, in France, but also in England. He argued further that this new form of love with which medieval literature was concerned had nothing to do with marriage, and was in fact an idealization of adultery. For Lewis, marriage from the medieval aristocracy's viewpoint had nothing to do with sentiment, and everything to do with the ideology of marriage as alliance discussed in the previous chapter. He also argued that the medieval Church's theory of marriage excluded any possibility of love being important in the making of medieval marriages. If we consider Georges Duby's notion of two models of marriage, one aristocratic and one ecclesiastical, existing in France in the central Middle Ages, it will be clear that, for Lewis, the marriage ideologies of both groups are seen as hostile to the idea of love as something compatible with marriage:

> Marriages had nothing to do with love, and no 'nonsense' about marriage was tolerated. All matches were matches of interest, and, worse still, of an interest which was continually changing. When the alliance which had answered would answer no longer, the husband's object was to get rid of the lady as quickly as possible. Marriages were frequently dissolved. The same woman who was the lady and 'the dearest dread' of her vassals was often little better than a piece of property to her husband. He was master in his own house. So far from being a channel for the new kind of love, marriage was rather the drab background against which that love stood out in all the contrast of its new tenderness and delicacy. The situation is indeed a very simple one, and not peculiar to the Middle Ages. Any idealization of sexual love, in a society where marriage is purely utilitarian, must begin by being an idealization of adultery.

The second factor is the medieval theory of marriage – what may be called, by a convenient modern barbarism, the 'sexology' of the medieval church. A nineteenth-century Englishman felt that same passion – romantic love – could be either virtuous or vicious according as it was directed towards marriage or not. But according to the medieval view passionate love itself was wicked, and did not cease to be wicked if the object of it were your wife. If a man had once yielded to this emotion he had no choice between 'guilty' and 'innocent' love before him: he had only the choice, either of repentance, or else of different forms of guilt.[1]

Lewis's formulation of 'courtly love' has been both influential and much criticized: its broader implications are not really of concern to us here, and it is the assertion of the incompatibility of love and marriage that I wish to address.[2]

There are two basic points to be made against Lewis's argument that love and marriage are incompatible in the central Middle Ages. Firstly, although the interests of kin, property, and alliance were of great importance in the making of marriages, the consensual model of marriage promoted and enforced by the Church courts did allow individuals to marry one another simply on the basis of a willingness to do so, and in spite of all other obstacles. Couples could simply marry for love (any sort of love) if they wished, and while those marriages might have difficult consequences for the persons concerned, they would be valid. An example might be the clandestine marriage between Margery Paston and one of the family's servants, the bailiff, Richard Calle. The pair are separated by the family until it is clear that they have in fact contracted marriage, and Calle writes to his wife during this period of separation about 'the gret bonde of matrymonye that is made betwix vs, and also the greete loue that hath be, and as I truste yet is, be-twix vs, and as on my parte neuer gretter.'[3] This letter tends to support H. S. Bennett's argument that the pair married for love.[4] The marriage had to be upheld: Lewis's argument that marriages were easily dissolved is not an accurate one. It came at a price, however. Richard Calle was kept on in his job as bailiff, but Margery was cast out of the family. Marriage for love might run against family interests, and it might have family consequences, but it was entirely possible.

The second point to be made against Lewis's argument is that love and marriage were not incompatible in the view of the medieval Church. The Church's encouragement of marital love goes back to St Paul, and the easiest method of disproving Lewis's assertion that love and marriage were incompatible in the eyes of the medieval Church is perhaps to quote a thirteenth-century French marriage sermon that cites Paul in its encouragement of love between spouses:

[1]   Lewis, pp. 13–14.
[2]   For a critique of Lewis's arguments, see Kelly, pp. 19–26; for a recent reappraisal of *The Allegory of Love*, see Colin Burrow, 'C. S. Lewis and *The Allegory of Love*,' *Essays in Criticism* 53 (2003), 284–94.
[3]   Davis, I, 498.
[4]   Bennett, *The Pastons*, p. 42.

Amare etiam debet vir uxorem. Eph. v [25]: Diligite uxores vestras sicut Christus dilexit ecclesiam, et tradidit semetipsum pro ea. Et potest attendi hec similitudo in duobus. Primo in hoc ut zelet pro salute uxoris. Christus etiam pro salute ecclesie mortuus est. Secundo in hoc quod si adulterat et post peniteat a viro misericorditer recipiatur. Osee iii. [i]: Diligite mulierem dilectam ab amico et adulteriam, sicut diligit dominus filios Israel, et ipsi respiciunt ad deos alienos. Item Eph. v [28]: Viri debent diligere uxores suas ut corpora sua. Ibidem: Qui suam uxorem diligit, seipsum diligit. Item in eodem [v. 33]: Unusquisque uxorem suam sicut seipsum diligat. . . .

Furthermore a man ought to love his wife. *Ephesians*, v: 'Love your wives as Christ loved the Church, and gave himself up for it'. And we may note two things from this analogy. Firstly, that he should long ardently for the salvation of his wife. For Christ died for the salvation of the Church. Secondly, that if she commits adultery, and should afterwards repent, she should be received with mercy by her husband. *Hosea*, iii: 'Love the woman who has been loved by the friend and committed adultery, just as the Lord loves the sons of Israel, and they look to alien gods'. Again, *Ephesians*, v: 'A husband ought to love his wife as his own flesh'. Likewise: 'He who loves his wife, loves himself'. Again, in the same, 'Everyone should love his wife as he loves himself'. . . .[5]

The medieval Church, then, did indeed encourage couples to love one another: D. L. D'Avray argues that the encouragement of marital love is a prominent theme in later medieval marriage sermons.[6] Another example is the sermon of Gérard de Mailly which suggests that husband and wife should have 'an intimate or deep-seated love of the heart,' *intima vel interna cordium dilectione*.[7]

Nor is the Church's discussion of marital love restricted to its popular pronouncements. The theologian Hugh of St Victor emphasizes love, *dilectio*, between spouses as an important part of the sacrament of marriage, arguing in his discussion of the sacraments that the substance of the sacrament is the mutual love of souls, guarded by the bond of conjugal society and agreement, which symbolizes the love of God for the soul.[8] Erik Kooper argues that the major influence on Hugh's thought is Augustine: that both Augustine and Hugh agree that the essence of marriage lies in the personal relationship between the spouses, and that

---

[5] Sermon by Guillaume Peyraut, O. P., cited in David D'Avray, 'The Gospel of the Marriage Feast of Cana and Marriage Preaching in France,' in *The Bible in the Medieval World: Essays in Memory of Beryl Smalley*, ed. Katherine Walsh and Diana Wood (Oxford: Blackwell, 1985), pp. 207–24 (p. 215).

[6] D. L. D'Avray, *Medieval Marriage Sermons: Mass Communication in a Culture without Print* (Oxford: Oxford University Press, 2001), Preface, p. vii.

[7] D'Avray, *Medieval Marriage Sermons*, pp. 256, 257.

[8] Hugh of Saint Victor, trans. Deferrari, p. 326; cf. also the passage from Hugh's *De virginitate B. Mariae* quoted by Brooke, pp. 278–79; Elliott, pp. 138–39 and n. 21 observes the influence of Hugh on Peter Lombard's thinking on the sacramentality of marriage, but notes that Peter Lombard omits Hugh's emphasis on married love.

this emphasis on marital love is a natural consequence of Augustine's suspicion of sexuality.[9] Kooper distinguishes this tradition of thinking about the relationship between spouses, which he characterizes as monastic and Augustinian, from a philosophical and Aristotelian tradition which he associates with Thomas Aquinas's writings on the friendship (*amicitia*) that should exist between married couples.[10] Several major medieval theologians, then, theorize the marital relationship in terms of love or friendship between spouses.

When canon law texts concern themselves with the relationship between spouses, they do so by discussing *maritalis affectio* as the appropriate bond between spouses. *Maritalis affectio*, 'marital affection,' is a legal term, one that Gratian derives from Roman law, where it meant an habitual attitude of respect, deference, and consideration towards one's spouse that differentiated a marital relationship from carnal cohabitation. Gratian uses the term several times in key passages on marriage, but nowhere defines it. As used by Gratian, it seems to mean consent to have another as a spouse, and, as in Roman law, distinguishes lawful marriage from mere cohabitation. The concept was developed under Alexander III who uses it to refer not to consent to marry but to postnuptial affection, and it was subsequently used both in the sense in which it appears in Gratian and in this new sense.[11]

When it came to enforcing postnuptial affection, the phrase was usually used in cases where estranged couples were to be reunited, and ordered to treat one another with marital affection. Spouses were effectively commanded to love one another.[12] But, as Michael M. Sheehan argues, when it came to legal enforcement, it was not the presence of emotional attachment, but external appearances that the courts usually concerned themselves with.[13] This is true in cases from later medieval England that are concerned with marital affection. A papal letter of 1354 to the bishop of Winchester instructs the bishop to compel John, earl of Warenne, to receive and treat with marital affection his wife, Joan de Barre, who married him having obtained a dispensation to overcome an impediment. John alleged, after many years of marriage, that the dispensation was surreptitious (a new impediment

[9] Erik Kooper, 'Loving the Unequal Equal: Medieval Theologians and Marital Affection,' in *The Olde Daunce: Love, Friendship, Sex, and Marriage in the Medieval World*, ed. Robert R. Edwards and Stephen Spector (New York: the State University of New York Press, 1991), pp. 44–56 (p. 46); Ecclesiastical suspicion of even marital sex is discussed in chapter five, below.

[10] Kooper, pp. 49–51; cf. Lewis, p. 16; on OE *freondscype* (whose meaning differs slightly from MnE 'friendship') as a description of the relationship of lovers or spouses, see Fell, pp. 68–69.

[11] Noonan, 'Marital Affection in the Canonists,' 479–509; for the concept of marital affection in Roman law, see Corbett, p. 92; Michael M. Sheehan, '*Maritalis Affectio* Revisited,' in *The Olde Daunce: Love, Friendship, Sex and Marriage in the Medieval World*, ed. Robert R. Edwards and Stephen Spector (Albany: the State University of New York Press, 1991), pp. 34–44 (pp. 36–38) (reprinted in Michael M. Sheehan, *Marriage, Family and Law in Medieval Europe: Collected Studies*, ed. James K. Farge (Toronto: University of Toronto Press, 1996), pp. 262–77) offers an account of the term's development similar to Noonan's.

[12] Noonan, 'Marital Affection,' pp. 500–4.

[13] Sheehan, '*Maritalis Affectio* revisited,' pp. 36–38.

may have appeared), but the papal letter declares that the marriage holds.[14] In another case, which occurs in London in 1496, Nicholas Elyott is charged with failing to treat his wife with marital affection. Many of their neighbours appear and confirm the charge, and he agrees to take her back.[15] As well as intervening in cases where spouses no longer cohabited, certainly the courts also punished visible manifestations of a lack of marital affection such as violence towards a spouse: in 1300, for example, Thomas Louchard of Droitwich, Worcestershire, was whipped by order of an ecclesiastical court for beating his wife with a stick.[16] While canon law may have developed a notion of marital affection as a postnuptial emotional bond between spouses that could be enforced in practice by the ecclesiastical courts, it is understandable that the courts for the most part focused reactively on visible manifestations of affection's absence.

Marital and extramarital love

If the Church did promote love within marriage, however, this does not mean that it promoted all love within marriage. Love incorporates a broad range of human feelings, and medieval discussions of love saw some of these feelings as good and appropriate within marriage, but not so others. Sometimes the distinction may turn on the question of terminology. When St Paul recommends love to the married in Ephesians 5, he is discussing *dilectio*, which may indeed be translated as 'love.' But when C. S. Lewis talks about 'sexual love,' 'passionate love' or 'romantic love', he is referring to *amor*. And we can see some medieval writers arguing, as Lewis does, that *amor* is a sort of love distinct from that which can occur within marriage. This is the twelfth-century writer Andreas Capellanus, whose *De Amore* is important to Lewis's argument:

> Vehementer tamen admiror quod maritalem affectionem quidem, quam quilibet inter se coniugati adinvicem post matrimonii copulam tenentur habere, vos vultis amoris sibi vocabulum usurpare, quum liquide constet inter virum et uxorem amorem sibi locum vindicare non posse. Licet enim nimia et immoderata affectione coniugantur, eorum tamen affectus amoris non potest vice potiri, quia nec sub amoris verae definitionis potest ratione comprehendi.

> I am mightily surprised that you consent to allow marital affection, which any couple is allowed to have after being joined in matrimony, to appropriate the name of love, for it is clearly known that love cannot claim a place between husband and wife. Although they may be united in great and boundless affection, their feelings cannot attain

---

[14] *Papal Letters. Vol. III*, ed. Bliss and Johnson, p. 116.
[15] Hair, p. 117.
[16] Hair, p. 44.

the status of love because they cannot be gathered under the heading of any true definition of love.[17]

Andreas refers to the sort of affection that can occur within marriage as *maritalis affectio*, but distinguishes this from the sort of love called *amor*, which is the sort of love his treatise is discussing. His argument is that marital and extramarital love are fundamentally different.[18] Philippe Ariés argues that this was a common pre-modern distinction:

> Nowadays we tend to forget an absolutely basic phenomenon in the history of sexual behaviour, which remained quite unchanged from the earliest times up to the eighteenth century [. . .] – the distinction that men of nearly all societies and ages, except our own, have drawn between love within and love outside marriage.[19]

But the distinctions between the variety of Latin terms which may be translated by the English word 'love' – *affectio*, *amicitia* and *caritas* among others – are not necessarily hard and fast in the eyes of all medieval writers. In his *City of God*, St Augustine has an interesting mini-essay on the Latin terms used for 'love' in the Bible, where he notes the interchangeability of the terms *amor*, 'love', *dilectio*, 'fondness', and *caritas*, 'charity' in the Scriptures. He observes that quite a number of people imagine that *dilectio* and *caritas* are something different from *amor*, and that perhaps *amor* is used in a bad sense where the other two are used positively, but he shows that in the Scriptures they are not distinguished from one another. All of these terms, he says, can be used in a good or a bad sense.[20] Likewise, in the sermon quoted earlier, Guillaume Peyraut uses *amor* and *dilectio* interchangeably in discussing married love, saying *Amare etiam debet vir uxorem*, and then quoting Ephesians in support: *Diligite uxores vestras sicut Christus dilexit ecclesiam, et tradidit semetipsum pro ea*. St Thomas Aquinas also discusses the relationship between *amor*, *amicitia*, *dilectio* and *caritas* in his *Summa Theologiae*. Aquinas concludes that the different terms are alike, but not interchangeable. For Aquinas, *amor* incorporates the senses of *dilectio* and *caritas*, but not vice versa:

> Dicendum quod quatuor nomina inveniuntur ad idem quodammodo pertinentia: scilicet amor, dilectio, caritas et amicitia. Differunt tamen in hoc, quod amicitia, secundum Philosophum, est quasi habitus; amor autem est dilectio significantur per modum actus vel passionis; caritas autem utroque modo accipi potest.

[17] Andreas Capellanus, *On Love*, ed. and trans. P. G. Walsh (London: Duckworth, 1982), p. 147; for a differing interpretation of Andreas's meaning in this passage, see Cartlidge, pp. 27–31.

[18] Cf. Lewis, pp. 36–37.

[19] Philippe Ariès, 'Love in Married Life,' in *Western Sexuality: Practice and Precept in Past and Present Times*, ed. Philippe Ariès and André Bejin, trans. Anthony Forster (Oxford: Blackwell, 1985), p. 130.

[20] St Augustine, *The City of God against the Pagans*, ed. and trans. T. E. Page et al., Loeb Classics, 7 vols (London: Heinemann, 1966), IV, 186–93.

> Differenter tamen significatur actus per ista tria. Nam amor commu-
> nius est inter ea: omnis enim dilectio vel caritas est amor, sed non e
> converso. Addit enim dilectio supra amorem electionem præceden-
> tem, ut ipsum nomen sonat. Unde dilectio non est in concupiscibili,
> sed in voluntati tantum, et est in sola rationali natura. Caritas autem
> addit supra amorem, perfectionem quandam amoris, inquantum id
> quod amator magni pretii æstimatur, ut ipsum nomen designat.

> There are four words whose meanings are very much alike: *amor*,
> *dilectio*, *caritas*, and *amicita*: still, they are not interchangeable. For
> *amicitia*, as Aristotle remarks, is dispositional, whereas *amor* and
> *dilectio* are episodic; and *caritas* may be either.

> Furthermore, these last three terms refer to acts in different ways.
> *Amor* has the widest reference of the three; every instance of *dilectio*
> or *caritas* is an instance of *amor*, but not vice versa. *Dilectio*, as the
> word itself suggests, adds to the notion of *amor* an implicit reference
> to antecedent *electio* or choice; it is therefore not seated in the affec-
> tive orexis, but in the will, and so is confined to rational natures.
> *Caritas* adds to the notion of *amor* the note of a certain perfection in
> that *amor*, the suggestion that the object loved is highly prized: as the
> very word *caritas* suggests.[21]

Aquinas' interpretation of the word *amor* would seem to differ significantly from
the way in which we have just seen Andreas use it. For while Andreas uses *amor* to
mean a specific sort of love which excludes certain types of human affection (such
as *maritalis affectio*), Aquinas uses *amor* to mean love in a very broad sense, which
is inclusive of many other sorts of love.[22] For both Augustine and Aquinas, then,
although nuances are acknowledged in the Latin terminology used to describe
various sorts of love, their use of *amor* and related terms seems to differ from that
of Andreas, and *amor* and *affectio* are not necessarily terms that are to be placed
in opposition to one another.

That Aquinas uses *amor* in a very wide sense is not to say, however, that he
regards all forms of love as essentially identical, for he too recognizes that love
incorporates a wide spectrum of human feeling. Gerald Morgan writes that the
most lucid account of the nature of love by a medieval poet is that given by Dante
in *Purgatorio* xvii. 91–105 and xviii. 19–75, and that Dante's account of love in
these passages introduces us to a distinction between natural and rational love
fundamental to Aquinas's thought.[23] Dante writes:

> 'Nè creator nè creatura mai,'
> cominciò el, 'figliuol, fu sanza amore,
> o naturale o d'animo; e tu 'l sai.

---

[21] Aquinas, XIX, pp. 68, 70 (Latin text), 69, 71 (English translation).

[22] See Aquinas, XIX, 63, 65.

[23] Gerald Morgan, 'Natural and Rational Love in Medieval Literature,' *Yearbook of English Studies* 7 (1978), 43–52.

Lo naturale è sempre sanza errore,
ma l'altro puote errar per malo obietto
o per troppo o per poco di vigore.' (xvii. 91–96)

He began: 'Neither Creator nor creature, my son, was ever without
love, either natural or of the mind, and this you know. The natural is
always without error; but the other may err through an evil object, or
through too much or too little vigor.'[24]

What Dante describes here is the distinction between natural and rational love,
the former the unerring and instinctive urge of all created things directing them
towards God, the latter the very human love that involves fallible choices. Rational
love can be good or bad depending on whether or not it is in accord with the
judgment of the intellect, which should judge all desired goods in relation to the
ultimate good of man's real objective, union with God.[25] As Augustine puts it,
Recta itaque voluntas est bonus amor et voluntas perversa malus amor, 'A right will
therefore is good love and a wrong will is bad love.'[26] For Aquinas, then, human
loves do not exist in a vacuum but as part of wider moral scheme, and love can
err, as Dante puts it above, through choosing an evil object, or through too much
or too little feeling. In a marital context, this sense of it being possible to love
someone or something too much, and for love therefore to be bad where it might
have been good, meant that, while it was good to love your wife and children, it
was possible to love them excessively, if, for instance, you loved your spouse and
family more than you loved God.[27] Marital love is good, but it is distinguished
from excessive (and hence bad) love by the exercise of appropriate restraint.

The notion of different loves finding their place within a greater order is one
common in medieval thought. David Herlihy discusses the notion of the *ordo caritatis*, the scheme which prescribed degrees of affection, and its influence on
medieval Christian thought on the subject of love.[28] The notion originates with
Origen, who suggested that, firstly, we should love God, followed by our parents, our
children, our 'domestics,' and our neighbours. Origen did not mention spouse
or siblings in this scheme, but elsewhere he proposed a parallel order of affection
relating to women: here the order is mothers, sisters, wives, and then all other
women. Origen's notion of an *ordo caritatis* was subsequently taken up by Augustine
and later writers, persisting into the later Middle Ages.[29] Herlihy suggests that the
notion of an *ordo caritatis* also helps to dispel some apparently antifamilial comments in the Gospels, at Matthew 10:37 and Luke 14:26, for example. Herlihy notes
that Biblical commentators could now gloss these passages not as a condemnation

---

[24] Dante Alighieri, *The Divine Comedy of Dante Alighieri*, trans. Charles S. Singleton, Bollingen
Series LXXX, 3 vols (Princeton, NJ: Princeton University Press, 1973), II, 184, 185.

[25] Morgan, 'Natural and Rational Love,' p. 47.

[26] Augustine, *City of God*, ed. and trans. Page et al., IV, 290, 291.

[27] Chaucer's *Parson's Tale* discusses excessive love for a wife or a child at X. 376 and 860.

[28] Herlihy, 'Family', pp. 121–32.

[29] Herlihy, 'Family,' pp. 122–23.

of familial love or self-love, but rather of disordered love. Love of self and family was not condemned, but should be superseded by love of God.[30]

If there was an appropriate order for love, there was also a notion of excessive or disordered love. Disordered love and its consequences receive a good deal of attention in medieval thinking about love. A Middle English lyric describes inordinate love as follows:

> I shall say what inordinate love is:
> The furiosite and wodness of minde,
> A instinguible brenning fawting blis,
> A gret hungre, insaciat to finde,
> A dowcet ille, a ivell swetness blinde,
> A right wonderfulle, sugred, swete errour,
> Withoute labour rest, contrary to kinde,
> Or withoute quiete to have huge labour.[31]

The comparison of excessive love to madness, *wodness*, and the suggestion of a parallel with physical sensations such as inextinguishable burning and insatiable hunger, is something that we also find in medical texts, which define *eros* as an illness akin to melancholy, caused by a defect in the estimative faculty of the brain, which causes the sufferer to overvalue the object of their desire, and to become obsessed with them.[32]

Marital and extramarital love: Two Canterbury Tales

Disordered love is also a common literary subject, and at this point I want to turn to two poems from Chaucer's *Canterbury Tales* which seem to turn, in part at least, on the distinctions between different sorts of love: between the love that is appropriate between spouses within a marriage, and the love which is not. In the *Merchant's Tale*, January has constantly engaged in fornication prior to his marriage (IV. 1248–51), and he now sees marriage as a legitimate way to continue his previous lustful behaviour. The tale, drawing on January's opinion of marriage as simply a legitimation of the activities that he has engaged in outside of marriage, seems to explore the similarities and differences that exist between married and unmarried love. The distinction between *maritalis affectio* and a love more usually found outside of marriage may be relevant to the tale. January is allegedly concerned to beget children in order to pass on his property (IV. 1437–40), but this is simply an excuse for demanding a young wife (IV. 1415–18).[33] In the event, all of

---

[30] Herlihy, 'Family,' pp. 123–24.

[31] *Medieval English Lyrics*, ed. R. T. Davies (London: Faber, 1963), p. 195.

[32] On lovesickness, see Mary Frances Wack, *Lovesickness in the Middle Ages: The Viaticum and its Commentaries* (Philadelphia: University of Pennsylvania Press, 1990).

[33] The Wife of Bath similarly justifies her behaviour in terms of offspring: 'God bad us for to wexe and multiplye' (III. 28). D. W. Robertson, Jr., *A Preface to Chaucer* (Princeton, NJ: Princeton University Press, 1962), p. 322, points out that 'the Wife is obviously not interested

his property goes to May (IV. 2172–74), even though May hints that she is pregnant (IV. 2335–37). Gifts between spouses, however, were not legally valid under the common law.[34] Explaining why this is so, the legal manual *Bracton* refers to the feelings of love that might motivate such gifts:

> Et si tales fieri possent donationes ob amorem inter virum et uxorem habitum, posset alter ipsorum egestate et inopia consumi, quod non est sustinendum.

> And if such gifts could be made because of love between husband and wife, one of them might be destroyed by want and poverty, which cannot be tolerated.[35]

Marital affection, however, is described earlier as being a more praiseworthy motivation:

> Simplices etenim donationes non propter nuptias fiunt, sed propter nuptias vetitae sunt, et propter alias causas, propter libidinem forte, vel unius partis egestatem, et non propter ipsorum nuptiorum affectionem efficiuntur, secundum quod superius tactum est.

> For simple gifts are not made because of marriage, but forbidden because of it, being made for other reasons, because of lust, perhaps, or the poverty of one of the parties, and not because of the affection growing out of the marriage itself, as was touched upon above.[36]

Amor here seems closer to lust than to marital affection, and indeed it is precisely January's lust for his wife which causes him to hand over all of his property to May.[37]

If this might lead us to think that January's feelings for his wife are not those appropriate to marriage, then there is evidence elsewhere to support this. To return to the subject of the appropriate place of intercourse within marriage, we might note St Jerome's statement in his *Adversus Jovinianum* that there is nothing worse than to love a wife as if she were an adulteress.[38] Chaucer might have had this quotation in mind when he characterized January as a subject of Venus:

> And Venus laugheth upon every wight,
> For Januarie was bicome hir knyght
> And wolde bothe assayen his corage
> In libertee, and eek in mariage;   (IV. 1723–26)

in generating children but simply in the pleasure of the process involved,' and points to the same joke being used in a fifteenth-century paraphrase of the Ten Commandments.
[34] *Bracton*, ed. Woodbine, trans. Thorne, II, 97–99; *Britton*, ed. and trans. Nichols, I, 223, 227, 234.
[35] *Bracton*, ed. Woodbine, trans. Thorne, II, 99.
[36] *Bracton*, ed. Woodbine, trans. Thorne, II, 98–99.
[37] I owe this point to Alcuin Blamires.
[38] Jerome, trans. Fremantle, p. 386.

Just as Damian, who cuckolds January at the tale's end, is a subject of the same goddess:

> This sike Damyan in Venus fyr
> So brenneth that he dyeth for desyr.   (IV. 1875–76)

Both January's foolish self-impoverishment, and his similarity to Damian in his love for May, tend to highlight the differences between what January feels for his wife and what prescriptive texts about marriage suggest is appropriate.

Although Kittredge's reading of the 'Marriage Debate' in the *Canterbury Tales* presented an influential view of the *Franklin's Tale* as a representation of an ideal marriage which resolves the debate by presenting a model of equality between spouses,[39] it is possible to read the tale as echoing the difficulties presented in the other tales of the 'Marriage Group,' rather than resolving them. Here I want to argue that the *Franklin's Tale* seems to echo the way in which the *Merchant's Tale* draws a distinction between love within marriage and love outside of marriage. That the marriage agreement between Dorigen and Arveragus presents an interpretative difficulty has long been acknowledged by critics. The poem's description of their marriage agreement:

> Heere may men seen an humble, wys accord;
> Thus hath she take hir servant and hir lord –
> Servant in love, and lord in mariage.   (V. 791–93)

sets up a servant/lord opposition which makes the reader aware of an inherent contradiction in the marriage relationship agreed between Dorigen and Arveragus that requires resolution. Dorigen offers obedience to Arveragus in taking him as her husband:

> That pryvely she fil of his accord
> To take him for hir housbonde and hir lord,
> Of swich lordshipe as men han over hir wyves. (V. 741–43)

There is nothing unusual in this. In medieval English marriage formulas, women promise obedience in marriage, and men do not. In the Sarum missal, the formula that the man recites is:

> I, N., take the, N., to my wedded wif, to have and to holde fro this day
> forward, for bettere for wers, for richere for pouerer, in sykenesse and
> in hele; tyl dethe vs depart, if holy churche it woll ordeyne, and therto
> y plight the my trouthe [. . .].[40]

The woman, however, also promises 'to be bonere and buxum in bedde and at borde.' In the *Franklin's Tale*, instead of exercising this right to his wife's obedience

---

[39] Kittredge, pp. 130–58.
[40] *Manuale et Processionale*, Appendix I, p. 19*.

that marriage gives him, Arveragus promises at the tale's outset to act within marriage as a lover does outside it, and to obey his lady, Dorigen (V. 745–50). Hence Arveragus is both her servant and her lord, and hence the difficulty of this marriage agreement, which as David Aers says, 'tries to graft the language of courtly male service of women onto the conventional language of male domination in marriage.'[41] The tensions within this agreement are clear when Arveragus modifies his pledge by reserving to himself the title of sovereignty 'for shame of his degree' (V. 751–52): 'degree' here must refer to his status as a husband, as Dorigen is of 'heigh kynrede' (V. 735), which rules out any other issues of status.

If the *Franklin's Tale* seems to concern itself with the difference between marital and extramarital love here at the beginning of the tale in the formulation of the marriage agreement between Dorigen and Arveragus, this is also the case elsewhere within the narrative. In particular, the description of Dorigen's lovesickness would seem to show another example of a love unusual and perhaps inappropriate within marriage. Dorigen suffers from lovesickness when Arveragus departs for England for the sake of his honour:[42]

> For his absence wepeth she and siketh,
> As doon thise noble wyves whan hem liketh.
> She moorneth, waketh, wayleth, fasteth, pleyneth;
> Desir of his presence hire so destreyneth
> That al this wyde world she sette at noght.   (V. 817–21)

Lovesickness is something that we see a lot of in *The Canterbury Tales*: other sufferers are Arcite, the falcon in the *Squire's Tale*, and another of the characters of the *Franklin's Tale*, Aurelius. The clerks of the *Miller's Tale* pretend to be lovesick, but one of them discovers that a more direct approach results in more success in his wooing of Alisoun. In Chaucer's other writings, Troilus is the most distinguished example of 'the loveris maladye of Hereos.' But Dorigen is an unusual member of this company in that she is married to the object of her desire, the man who is the source of her love-melancholy.

Mary Frances Wack notes the absence of discussions of female lovesickness from the academic medical tradition which derives from the discussion of lovesickness in Constantine the African's *Viaticum*. The exception is the discussion of Peter of Spain (later pope John XXI).[43] There are resonances between Peter's description of lovesickness and Chaucer's description of Dorigen's love-melancholy. In a discussion of how lovesickness affects men and women differently, Peter states that

---

[41] David Aers, *Chaucer, Langland, and the Creative Imagination* (London: Routledge, 1980), p. 163.

[42] Mourning for an absent husband is something that can be seen elsewhere in Middle English literature: e.g. *The Owl and the Nightingale*, lines 1583–1602. But what distinguishes Dorigen's mourning is its excessive nature, demonstrated by her display of the medical symptoms of lovesickness.

[43] Wack, pp. 121–23, 175.

weakness of hope is the cause of lovesickness,[44] and that lovesickness is more easily cured in women than in men:

> Dicendum quod amor hereos cicius et frequencius generatur in mulieribus propter debilitatem spei in eis et quia frequencius stimulantur ad coitum, licet non ita fortiter. Sed in viris est difficilioris cure, eo quod inpressio alicuius forme dilecte in cerebro viri est fortior et difficilioris irradicacionis quam inpressio forme in cerebro mulieris, eo quod vir habet cerebrum siccius quam mulier et inpressio facta in sicco est difficilioris eradationis quam facta in humido. Per hoc patet solutio rationum.

> It must be said that lovesickness is more quickly and frequently generated in women on account of their weak hope and because they are more frequently stimulated to intercourse, although not so strongly. But in men it is more difficult to cure, because the impression of any desired form in the brain of a man is stronger and harder to erase than the impression of a form in the brain of a woman, because a man has a drier brain than a woman, and an impression made in the dry is harder to erase than that made in the moist. In this the answer to the arguments is evident.[45]

Dorigen's friends attempt to cure her of her lovesickness 'by hope and by resoun' (V. 833). They try, furthermore, to cure her through the impression of consolation, which succe initially at least (V. 834–36). Dorigen proves easier to cure than does Aurelius, who suffers hopelessly for two years (V. 1101–4). Constantine the African suggests various distractions for the lovesick, to prevent them from sinking into excessive thoughts,[46] and following Dorigen's relapse into lovesickness, a relapse prompted by seeing the rocks along the shoreline which she fears may cause Arveragus's death (V. 847–93), her friends this time take her by rivers and wells (V. 898) and to a garden full of flowers (V. 902) to distract her. Chaucer's familiarity with medieval medical views on lovesickness is clear from his rather technical discussion of the illness in the *Knight's Tale* (I. 1373–76).[47] His description of Dorigen's lovesickness would seem similarly indebted to the medical texts.

It is Dorigen's lovesickness which causes her to make her pledge to her suitor, Aurelius. As the poem states earlier:

> Ire, siknesse, or constellacioun,
> Wyn, wo, or chaungynge of complexioun
> Causeth ful ofte to doon amys or speken.
> On every wrong a man may nat be wreken. (V. 781–84)

---

[44] Wack, pp. 222 (Latin text), 223 (English translation).

[45] Wack, pp. 222, 223.

[46] Wack, pp. 190, 191.

[47] Chaucer's familiarity with 'the cursed monk, daun Constantyn,' if not specifically with the *Viaticum*, can be seen from the two references to him in the *Canterbury Tales*, at I. 433 and IV. 1810.

Dorigen's agreement to grant Aurelius her love is conditional, and the impossible condition is not simply to be taken as an emphatic restatement of the refusal of Aurelius that she has already made, but also a reflection of her fidelity to and love for Arveragus, for the rocks that she asks Aurelius to remove are also the obstacles that she fears may impede her husband's return. In Boccaccio, a possible source for Chaucer here, the task is a very different one: to make a garden flower in winter.[48]

But while it is clear that Dorigen's promise to Aurelius is in fact a refusal of his proposition of adultery, and it is clear also that the formulation of that promise in fact expresses her loyalty to her husband, it is still the case nonetheless that she should not have made the pledge. When, towards the end of the tale, Aurelius releases Dorigen from that promise, he does so, as Gerald Morgan notes, by using the formal legal language of a quitclaim:[49]

> I yow relesse, madame, into youre hond
> Quyt every serement and every bond
> That ye han maad to me as heerbiforn.   (V. 1533–35)

Under the common law, wives were unable to make contracts because they had no rights over property,[50] but the legal disabilities of married women under the common law owed a great deal to antifeminist statements in canon law, and Gratian's statement in *Decretum* c. 33 q. 5 c. 17, where he forbids women from making promises, derives the wife's legal disability from her subjection to her husband:

> Nulla est mulieris potestas, sed in omnibus uiri dominio subsit. Item Ambrosius in libro questionum Veteris Testamenti: Mulierem constat subiectam dominio uiri esse, et nullam auctoritatem habere; nec docere potest, nec testis esse, neque fidem dare, nec iudicare.

> A woman has no power but in all things may be subject to the power of a man. From Ambrose, in his Book of Questions on the Old Testament: It is agreed that a woman is subject to the power of a man, and has no authority; nor is she able to instruct nor to be a witness nor to make a promise nor to make a legal judgment.[51]

This was an influential passage in later medieval law, and it finds an echo in Chaucer's *Parson's Tale*:

> And eek, as seith the decree, a womman that is wyf, as longe as she is a wyf, she hath noon auctoritee to swere ne to bere witnesse withoute

---

[48]   The relevant episode from *Il Filocolo* is printed in Bryan and Dempster, pp. 379–81.

[49]   Geoffrey Chaucer, *The Franklin's Tale from the Canterbury Tales*, ed. Gerald Morgan (Dublin: Irish Academic Press, 1980, repr. 1992), p. 114.

[50]   Holdsworth, III, 411; Pollock and Maitland, II, 405.

[51]   Latin text in *Corpus Iuris Canonici*, I, 1255; the English translation given here is from Blamires, p. 86 – as Blamires notes, the quotation is from Ambrosiaster, not Ambrose; for the legal influence of *Decretum* c. 33 q. 5, see Elliott, pp. 155–56.

leve of hir housbonde, that is hire lord; algate, he sholde be so by resoun.(X. 931)

The suggestion that Chaucer is making in having Aurelius use legal language in releasing Dorigen from her promise is obviously not that the pledge was in any way legally enforceable. It is, I think, to suggest that Dorigen ought not to have made a promise because of her legal disabilities as a wife. Her subjection to her husband should have prevented her from taking oaths. Viewed in this way, the problem of the validity of Dorigen's promise derives in part from the problem of sovereignty in marriage posed at the tale's outset.[52] If Dorigen was subject to her husband, as was the norm, her promise would have no validity. But at the beginning of the tale, Arveragus vowed not to exercise 'maistrie' over his wife, and, as Richard Firth Green has shown, this gives her the freedom to enter into contracts without her husband's consent.[53] When Arveragus does order Dorigen to keep her word, it is clear that he *is* exercising his sovereignty over her. In the lines where Aurelius asks Dorigen where she is going, and Dorigen replies:

> 'Unto the gardyn, as myn housbonde bad,
> My trouthe for to holde – allas, allas!'   (V. 1512–13)

it is clear here that she is going because Arveragus instructed her to, rather than of her own free will. But paradoxically, Arveragus's exercising of sovereignty over Dorigen in ordering her to fulfil her promise simultaneously relinquishes his sovereignty over her in affirming that her word, given independently of him, holds.

The *Franklin's Tale*, then, would seem to be engaging with the discussions of marriage in some of the other tales normally included in the 'Marriage Group' for its representation of the marriage of Dorigen and Arveragus, but rather than resolving the difficulties posed in previous tales, it seems rather to amplify them. The *Franklin's Tale*, like the Merchant's, seems to explore the difficulties of marital love by showing that the sorts of love more often found outside of marriage can be potentially disastrous within it.

---

[52] For a similar argument, on different evidence, see Angela M. Lucas and Peter J. Lucas, 'The Presentation of Marriage and Love in Chaucer's *Franklin's Tale*,' *English Studies* 72 (1991), 501–12; cf. Timothy H. Flake, 'Love, *Trouthe*, and the Happy Ending of the *Franklin's Tale*,' *English Studies* 77 (1996), 209–16.

[53] Richard Firth Green, *A Crisis of Truth: Literature and Law in Ricardian England* (Philadelphia: University of Pennsylvania Press, 1999), pp. 310–11.

5

Marital Sex

There are some obvious difficulties in attempting to write about marital sex in the Middle Ages. For the most part, the texts that provide us with evidence about medieval social practices were written by clerics. These texts are necessarily problematic, in that they were written by clergy who should have been unmarried and celibate, and who were often either uneasy or hostile to all forms of sexual behaviour. They do not provide us with firsthand evidence of the experience of married people themselves. But the medieval Church's prolonged attempts to govern the sexual behaviour of the married laity nonetheless provides us with a great deal of evidence, about the nature of ecclesiastical intervention, and about actual practice.

The medieval Church's unease about sexual intercourse extended to marital as well as extramarital sex. Indeed, from a theoretical point of view, the position of extramarital intercourse was fairly straightforward for the Church, in that it was always sinful. The only things in question were the seriousness of the sin, and the measures that needed to be taken to combat it (this latter question, of course, providing significant practical difficulties for the Church). The role of marital intercourse was more complicated, for marriage was licit for Christians, and the married were obliged to accede to the sexual demands of their partners – to render the marital debt, as St Paul put it. But could they commit sin in doing so? Anxiety about marital intercourse, and the possibility of sin within it, troubled ecclesiastical commentators throughout the medieval period.

Augustine, Jerome, and the debate on Jovinian

The most influential writer on marriage among the Church fathers was St Augustine, who returned to the subject of marriage repeatedly across his large body of writings. In *De bono coniugali* he discusses marriage positively, arguing that it contains three goods within it: fidelity, offspring, and the sacrament. As already discussed (p. 13, above), in writing *De bono coniugali* Augustine is intervening in a controversy begun by another Christian writer, Jovinian, who argued in the 390s that marriage and virginity were of equal merit. Jovinian's opinions were condemned as heretical, and provoked an antimatrimonial backlash in the form of St Jerome's text *Adversus Jovinianum*,[1] seen by contemporaries as going too far in attacking not only Jovinian, but the institution of marriage itself. Its influence on the mainstream of ecclesiastical thinking on marriage was outweighed by the more moderate approach of Augustine, but Jerome's text nonetheless extended a long reach, influencing antimatrimonial writing throughout the Middle Ages, and famously providing much of the source material for Chaucer's *Wife of Bath's Prologue*.

Jerome's text attacks Jovinian by emphasizing the model of the three grades of chastity, which placed virginity, widowhood, and marriage in that order of merit, and so placed marriage in a position greatly inferior to that of virginity. Augustine's intervention in the debate also draws upon the model of the three grades of chastity, and his treatise *De bono coniugali* is accompanied by two companion pieces on the other two grades. Augustine is concerned in these works to establish the merits of marriage (in contrast with Jerome), but as a relative rather than an absolute good (unlike Jovinian). He writes:

> Non ergo duo mala sunt conubium et fornicatio, quorum alterum peius, sed duo bona sunt, conubium et continentia, quorum alterum est melius; [. . .].

> So marriage and fornication are not two evils, of which the second is the worse; rather, marriage and continence are two goods, of which the second is the better; [. . .].[2]

In praising marriage, and particularly in praising the procreation of offspring within marriage as good, Augustine is also writing in reaction to the views of the heretical Manichaean sect, of which he had once been a member. The Manichaeans were dualists who believed the spirit was good, but the body and the world were evil. They consequently opposed procreation. Augustine, in contrast, praises the raising of offspring as one of the three goods of marriage.[3] But the question of lust within marriage troubled him. As he writes in chapter six of *De bono coniugali*:

> Iam in ipsa quoque immoderatiore exactione debiti carnalis, quam eis non secundum imperium praecipit sed secundum ueniam concedit apostolus, ut etiam praeter causam procreandi sibi misceantur, etsi eos praui mores ad talem concubitum impellunt, nuptiae tamen

---

[1]   For the context of Augustine's writing on marriage, see Peter Brown, *The Body and Society: Men, Women and Sexual Renunciation in Early Christianity* (New York: Columbia University Press, 1988); Brundage, *Law, Sex and Christian Society*, chapter 3; *Saint Augustine on Marriage and Sexuality*, ed. Elizabeth A. Clark (Washington: Catholic University of America Press, 1996); For a defence of Jerome, see John Oppel, 'Saint Jerome and the History of Sex,' *Viator* 24 (1993), 1–22.

[2]   Augustine, ed. and trans. Walsh, pp. 18, 19.

[3]   Augustine consequently opposes the use of contraception: on which see John T. Noonan, *Contraception: A History of its Treatment by the Catholic Theologians and Canonists*, enlarged ed. (Cambridge, MA: Belknap, 1986), chapter four.

ab adulterio seu fornicatione defendunt. Neque enim illud propter nuptias admittitur, sed propter nuptias ignoscitur.

Even when such physical debts are demanded intemperately (which the Apostle permits in married couples as pardonable, allowing them to indulge in sex beyond the the purpose of procreation, rather than laying down the law as command), and though debased habits impel partners to such intercourse, marriage is none the less a safeguard against adultery or fornication. Nor is marriage the cause of such behaviour, but marriage makes it pardonable.[4]

He then argues that while intercourse for procreation is blameless,[5] intercourse for lustful purposes is sinful, but only venially. Adultery and fornication, however, he regards as mortally sinful. He also emphasizes that abstention from all sexual intercourse is better than sex, even if that sex takes place within marriage for the purpose of procreation.[6] But if this discussion of sex within marriage might seem to clearly distinguish between marital sex, which could at most be venially sinful, and extramarital sex, which was always mortally sinful, this proves not to be the case. Returning to the topic later in the treatise, Augustine comments that failing to abstain from sex on appropriate days and engaging in unnatural intercourse are mortally sinful within marriage.[7]

P. G. Walsh argues that in taking the position that lustful behaviour within marriage is 'pardonable', Augustine is implicitly 'rejecting the insulting claim made by Jerome and others that a husband or wife can be an adulterer in marriage.'[8] But James Brundage argues that 'up to a point Augustine agreed with Jerome's strictures against 'excessive' marital sex.' Brundage suggests that what Jerome has in mind in his condemnation of 'excessive' sex are things such as inappropriate coital techniques as well as excessive ardour, and these are things which, of course, Augustine disapproves of as well.[9] The differences between Augustine and Jerome are significant, but they are questions of emphasis. Fundamentally, both agree that sin, even mortal sin, is possible within marital intercourse.

---

[4] Augustine, ed. and trans. Walsh, pp. 12–15.
[5] Later in his career, Augustine would argue in *City of God* 14.23 ff. that sexual intercourse would have occurred in Paradise without sin, had Adam and Eve not sinned and been expelled from Eden: Augustine, *City of God*, ed. and trans. Page et al., IV, 378 ff.
[6] Augustine, ed. Walsh, p. 15.
[7] Augustine, ed. Walsh, p. 25.
[8] Augustine, ed. Walsh, Introduction, xxi; Jerome, trans Fremantle, p. 386; the expression that the too ardent lover of his wife is an adulterer is attributed to Sextus. Pierre J. Payer, *The Bridling of Desire: Views of Sex in the Later Middle Ages* (Toronto: University of Toronto Press, 1993), pp. 7, 120–24, argues that 'adulterer' here is not to be understood literally. As we saw in the previous chapter, medieval thinkers often distinguished between marital love, which exercised restraint, and extramarital love. Unrestrained sexual intercourse, then, is like adultery in that it fails to exercise the restraint which distinguishes marital love and marital sex from such actions outside of marriage.
[9] Brundage, *Law, Sex and Christian Society*, p. 91.

Sex, marriage, and the Anglo-Saxons

Two sources of interest for the understanding of the regulation of sexual behaviour in Anglo-Saxon England are the penitentials produced by the Anglo-Saxon Church, and the law codes produced by the Anglo-Saxon kings. In Anglo-Saxon England, the Church did not enjoy exclusive jurisdiction over marriage as it did in the later Middle Ages, and Germanic marriage practices which existed prior to Christianity and which might have been at odds with its teachings–on subjects such as concubinage and divorce, for example–may have survived into the conversion period and afterwards.[10]

If the writings of the Church fathers, such as Augustine and Jerome, provide evidence of the early Christian theological debate on the nature of marriage and the role of sexual behaviour within it, these later texts provide evidence of the actual implementation among the laity of the ethical positions that the theological writers had formulated centuries earlier. As Pierre J. Payer comments:

> Taken together, the early penitentials provide a comprehensive treatment of the heterosexual life of the married. It is unlikely that a confessor familiar with these works would encounter instances of sexual behaviour not covered by them. While not creative of a sexual ethic *ex nihilo*, they specified the consequences implied by the previous patristic teaching on the legitimacy of sexual intercourse and are important witnesses of the penitential practice for dealing with marital sexual offences. Because they were intended to be practical handbooks, they must also have served an important instructional function, educating confessors and, through them, the faithful.[11]

The penitentials covered topics relevant to marital sexuality such as sexual abstinence, proper forms of sexual intercourse, the use of aphrodisiacs and contraception, as well as adultery. The latter is the most discussed sexual offence in the penitentials, as it is in the Anglo-Saxon laws.[12] Payer suggests that *adulterium* as used in the penitentials has a wider application than the modern English word 'adultery', including sex with another's wife or fiancée, sex with a nun, bestiality, or sex between a priest and his spiritual daughter.[13] They also covered a much

---

[10] Brundage, *Law, Sex and Christian Society*, pp. 143–45; Goody, pp. 75–76; Angela M. Lucas, *Women in the Middle Ages*, p. 68; Clunies Ross, 3–34.

[11] Pierre J. Payer, *Sex and the Penitentials: The Development of a Sexual Code, 550–1150* (Toronto: University of Toronto Press, 1984), p. 34.

[12] Frantzen, p. 145.

[13] Payer, *Sex and the Penitentials*, p. 21; for the use of the terms 'fornication' and 'adultery' in very broad senses in medieval canon law from Gratian onwards, see James A. Brundage, 'Adultery and Fornication: A Study in Legal Theology,' in *Sexual Practices and the Medieval Church*, ed. Vern L. Bullough and James A. Brundage (Buffalo and New York, 1982), pp. 129–34.

wider range of sexual offences, not necessarily applicable to married people, which included bestiality, incest, homosexuality, masturbation, and so on.

Two sections of the *Penitential of Theodore*, a collection associated with Theodore of Tarsus, archbishop of Canterbury (668–690) (but not assembled by Theodore himself), deal specifically with marriage. Book one section fourteen prescribes penances to be performed after the marriage ceremony (greater if the persons have been married before). It prescribes penances for a husband who has marital relations with his adulterous wife, for one who puts away his wife and marries another, and for one who commits adultery with his neighbour's wife, or with a virgin, or with his slave. It provides different penances for female adultery.[14] It forbids the tasting of blood or semen as an aphrodisiac (oral sex is also forbidden elsewhere in the penitential as 'the worst of evils,' attracting penances from seven years in length to life, but possibly in the context of male-male sex rather than marital intercourse). It forbids women from entering church at a time of impurity, or after childbirth.[15] It also forbids intercourse at these times, or on the Lord's day, or more generally at what is described as 'the improper season.' It forbids sexual intercourse from behind, which attracts a penance of forty days for the first offence, and anal intercourse, which carries the same penance as bestiality. In discussing abortion it distinguishes between a period up to forty days after the conception, 'before the foetus has life,' and the period after that where the offence is compared to murder.[16] The second discussion of marital sex takes place alongside the discussion of other issues relating to marriage (such as the taking of religious vows and when separated spouses may remarry) in book two section twelve of the penitential. This prescribes various times at which the married should abstain from intercourse: for three nights before communion, for forty days before Easter, for three months before birth and forty days afterwards. It states that impotence is a cause for separation, that a husband should wash himself before he goes to a church after sex with his wife, and that a husband should not see his wife nude.[17]

The penitentials, then, cover a very broad range of topics relating to sexual behaviour in general, including sex within marriage. The Anglo-Saxon laws, in contrast, are far from comprehensive in their treatment of sexual behaviour: they

---

[14] But as noted by Frantzen, p. 153, even within a single penitential text, multiple and perhaps contradictory options are offered for penances. He argues that this could mean that confessors were offered leeway regarding penances to be imposed.

[15] As Payer notes (*Sex and the Penitentials*, p. 36) Bede's account of Pope Gregory's correspondence with St Augustine of Canterbury differs from the penitential on this topic. On 'churching' – the ceremony of purification after childbirth – in the later Middle Ages, see Paula M. Rieder, 'Insecure Borders: Symbols of Clerical Privilege and Gender Ambiguity in the Liturgy of Churching,' in *The Material Culture of Sex, Procreation, and Marriage in Premodern Europe*, ed. Anne L. McClanan and Karen Roscoff Encarnación (New York and Basingstoke: Palgrave, 2002), pp. 93–113.

[16] McNeill and Gamer, pp. 195–97.

[17] McNeill and Gamer, pp. 208–11. The taboo against nudity seems to have endured through most of the medieval period: Brundage, *Law, Sex and Christian Society*, pp. 424–25.

do not concern themselves with marital sex to any great extent, except in the context of adultery. James Brundage argues that:

> Adultery in early Germanic society was an exclusively female crime, although a few codes also penalized men for adultery under some circumstances. Adultery was far more serious than fornication, since the adulteress cast doubt upon the legitimacy of her husband's descendants as well as offending his honor and pride.[18]

Allen J. Frantzen argues that this 'also suits the Anglo-Saxon legal evidence.'[19] Adultery is treated as an offence against property, and the compensation is usually financial. The Laws of King Alfred state that if anyone has sex with the wife of a man whose *wergeld* (a compensation price that varied with status) is 1200 shillings, he must pay 120 shillings compensation to the husband; likewise, to a husband whose *wergeld* is 600 shillings, he must pay 100 shillings compensation; and to a commoner he must pay 40 shillings compensation. Similarly, if a young woman who is betrothed commits fornication, she must pay compensation relative to her *wergeld*.[20] An exception to this treatment of adultery as an offence with financial penalties comes in the Laws of Cnut, which prescribes that an adulterous woman brings disgrace upon herself, loses all that she possesses to her wronged husband, and must lose both her nose and her ears.[21]

The much narrower focus of the Anglo-Saxon legal texts, in contrast to the broad scope adopted by the penitentials, might seem to offer us much less evidence. On the other hand, depending on how we interpret the legal texts' silence on these issues, they may offer a greater insight into lay mindsets as they concern marriage. The relative lack of interest in marital sexual offences except where adultery (and hence inheritance and property) is concerned may indicate a limited scope on the part of Anglo-Saxon law, a tendency to leave the regulation of such matters to the Church. Alternatively, it may indicate a relatively relaxed set of sexual ethics in contrast to that displayed by the compilers of the penitentials.

Sex, the canonists, and vernacular literature

The canon law texts of the central Middle Ages and their subsequent commentators devoted a great deal of attention to marriage and sexuality.[22] But their conclusions

[18] Brundage, *Law, Sex and Christian Society*, p. 132.
[19] Frantzen, p. 142.
[20] Attenborough.
[21] *The Laws of the Kings of England from Edmund to Henry I*, ed. and trans. A. J. Robertson (Cambridge: Cambridge University Press, 1925); Frantzen, p. 143, comments that this penalty was new to Anglo-Saxon law, and that other evidence suggests that financial penalties were normal for adultery.
[22] On which see Brundage, *Law, Sex and Christian Society*, chapters 5 to 9.

on the status of marital sex embody an ambiguity like that observed earlier in the writings of Augustine. As James A. Brundage writes of the thirteenth and fourteenth centuries, 'all the major theologians and canonists of the period taught that marital relations were free from sin under some circumstances, although they failed to agree just what those circumstances might be.'[23] The four legitimate reasons usually given for marital intercourse were payment of the marital debt, procreation, preventing incontinence for oneself, and preventing incontinence for one's spouse. But although these may be legitimate, that is not to say that they do not involve sin: the canonist Huguccio argued that if they involved pleasure, they were sinful, while later commentators disagreed.[24] Chaucer's *Parson's Tale* lists these four reasons, and comments (gloomily echoing Huguccio) that 'scarsly may ther any of thise be withoute venial synne, for the corrupcion and for the delit' (*Canterbury Tales*, X. 942).

Some of the continuing ambiguities concerning the status of marriage in later medieval ecclesiastical thinking are visible in references to the institution and sacramentality of marriage. Marriage was regarded as a sacrament in the later Middle Ages, but its position as a sacrament was a problematic one. In the English statute 1 Salisbury 82, priests are urged to commend to the laity the dignity and goods of marriage, and to make the embraces of fornicators repulsive by contrast, by stressing that marriage was first amongst the sacraments, instituted by God in Paradise.[25] This is a reference to the blessing of marriage in Genesis 1.28, *crescite et multiplicamini*. But another Salisbury statute, 1 Salisbury 15, distinguishes marriage (and holy orders) from the other sacraments in that marriage is for the avoidance of the sin of fornication.[26] Aquinas likewise places marriage last amongst the sacraments because it pertains less to the spiritual than the other sacraments.[27] The interpretation of marriage as a remedy for lust refers to Paul's statement to that effect in 1 Cor. 7. And so the English statute 2 Exeter 7 highlights the dual institution of matrimony, distinguishing between the prelapsarian institution of marriage (described in Genesis), where marriage is a duty, and its postlapsarian concession (by Paul), where it is a remedy for lust.[28]

Marital sex continues to come under scrutiny in confession: if anything, penitential practice becomes more important after the Fourth Lateran Council of 1215 declared that every Christian should confess at least once a year. Penitentials again inquired into a broad range of potential sexual offences: as a tract on confession and penance included with the statutes of Coventry stated, all emission of

---

[23] Brundage, *Law, Sex and Christian Society*, p. 448.

[24] Brundage, *Law, Sex and Christian Society*, pp. 281–83, 44–53.

[25] Powicke and Cheney, I, 86–87.

[26] Powicke and Cheney, I, 65; echoed in subsequent statutes: Powicke and Cheney, I, 232, 367–68, 634. Other statutes that state that marriage is for the avoidance of fornication are in Powicke and Cheney, I, 165–67, 201, 440, II, 987.

[27] Aquinas, LVI, 149.

[28] Powicke and Cheney, II, 996; on the dual institution of matrimony, see Payer, *Bridling of Desire*, pp. 63–65, 185–89.

semen was mortally sinful unless it happened while asleep or with one's own wife, lawfully, and in accordance with the marital debt.[29] Further to that, they enquired about any possible sexual activities by marital partners outside of marriage. Penances for such offences varied depending on whether or not the offence was public knowledge. Public offences were to be atoned for with public penance, but private sins obtained private redress. 1 Salisbury 34 reads:

> (De confessione coniugatorum)
> Mulieribus autem coniugatis talis iniungatur penitentia unde non reddantur maritis suis suspecte de aliquo occulto crimine et enormi. Idem de viris uxoratis observetur, dummodo sufficientur puniatur delictum et condigna sit satisfactio.[30]

> (Concerning the confession of married persons)
> But such penance is enjoined on married women that they are not returned thereafter to their husbands suspected of any secret offence and wickedness. The same procedure is to be carried out concerning married men, providing that the fault is sufficiently punished and appropriate redress is made.

1 Winchester 58 states similarly that secret fornicators should be punished through secret correction.[31] Sexual offences that appear publicly, in court, were treated very differently, and people could suffer public corporal punishment as part of their penance. The same rules did not hold for all. The records of the episcopal visitation of Canterbury diocese from 1292 to 1294 record a judgment in a case where a knight committed adultery which states that it was not appropriate for a knight to do public penance for his adultery. A money fine was levied instead (it was usually, but not always, possible to commute penance for money). The woman that he committed adultery with, presumably of lower social status, was whipped five times around the church, despite being pregnant.[32]

But, paradoxically, despite clerical suspicion of marital sex, ecclesiastical courts also seem to have enforced it. The marriage vows for English women saw them promise 'to be bonere and buxum in bedde and atte borde' in addition to the common promise of both spouses to have and to hold, for better for worse, for richer and poorer, in sickness and in health.[33] This pledge to be obedient in bed and at the table was the subject of a Durham case in 1451 where a wife is accused of disobedience at bed and table. Presumably the husband is suing for the payment of the marital debt as part of his grievance.[34] A papal letter of 1344 to the

---

[29] Powicke and Cheney, I, 222–23.
[30] Powicke and Cheney, I, 71.
[31] Powicke and Cheney, I, 135.
[32] Rothwell, p. 718.
[33] *Manuale et Processionale*, Appendix 1, p. 19*.
[34] Hair, p. 35.

bishop of Lincoln shows the enforcement of marital intercourse quite clearly: in a previous decision, Isabella le Foxle was not bound to pay the conjugal debt to her husband, Thomas; this letter declares that as Isabella is too modest to exact the conjugal debt, it may be exacted by Thomas, her husband.[35]

The ambiguities of ecclesiastical writers concerning marital sex finds echoes in later medieval vernacular literature. Some of Chaucer's *fabliaux* seem to parody well-known ecclesiastical positions: in the *Merchant's Tale*, January's descriptions of marriage as a 'paradys terrestre' and his assertion that no sin is possible in marital intercourse (*Canterbury Tales*, 4. 1836–41) seem perhaps parodic of Augustine's position in *City of God* 14.23 ff. that marital intercourse in Eden would have taken place without the sin of lust, and consequently without sin. The parody, of course, comes from the fact that January is living in a decidedly post-lapsarian *fabliau* world, which is very different from the prelapsarian Eden he paints it as. A much broader parody of ecclesiastical thinking on marriage appears in the *Wife of Bath's Prologue*. Other vernacular literary texts which deal extensively and seriously with the question of the role of sex within marriage, such as Langland's *Piers Plowman* and Gower's *Confessio Amantis*, tend to stress a basic obedience to the precepts of the Church. Langland's Wit stresses obedience to the law on a basic level,[36] and Gower's text promotes 'honeste love,' also asserting that it is enough to obey the law. But both texts show a nervous awareness that these positions are, at best, relatively good, echoing the ambiguity of the Church's own position on the status of marriage and the role of intercourse within it.[37]

Chaste marriage

The ambiguities and contradictions in the Church's teaching on marriage and the role of sex within it led to practical possibilities which it found uncomfortable. An example was chaste marriage, where the Church's ambiguity about the role of sex within marriage led in some cases, ironically, to female empowerment. Ambivalence about marital sex led the Church to sanction a model of marriage based on consent which could accommodate chaste marriages with the partners remaining in the world, rather than leaving it to enter monastic life. The possibility of persons remaining married but abstaining from sexual intercourse appears early in Christian writing. In *De bono coniugali*, Augustine suggested that sexual intercourse within marriage, although pardonable in youth, was something that should pass with age:

> Nunc uero in bono licet annoso coniugio, etsi emarcuit ardor aetatis inter masculum et feminam, uiget tamen ordo caritatis inter maritum

---

[35] Bliss and Johnson, pp. 167–68.

[36] James Simpson, *Piers Plowman: An Introduction to the B Text* (London: Longman, 1990), p. 112.

[37] As I argue elsewhere: 'Love and Marriage in the *Confessio Amantis*,' *Neophilologus* 84 (2000), 485–99.

et uxorem, qui quanto meliores sunt tanto maturius a commixtione carnis suae pari consensu se continere coeperunt, non ut necessitas esset postea non posse quod uellent, sed ut laudis esset primum noluisse quod possent.

But as things stand, in a good marriage between elderly partners, though the youthful passion between male and female has withered, the ordered love between husband and wife remains strong. The better the couple are, the earlier they have begun by mutual consent to abstain from sexual intercourse–not because it had become physically impossible for them to carry out their wishes, but so that they could merit praise by prior refusal to do what they were capable of doing.[38]

The model of Christ's parents was an important one for the Church's theory of chaste marriage: as we have seen, the consensual theory of marriage allowed the justification of the marriage of Christ's parents as being fully complete despite nonconsummation. But although the Church allowed marital chastity, it did not necessarily encourage it in practice.

Gratian outlined in the *Decretum* the conditions under which it was possible for a married person to take a vow of continence (sexual abstention) as opposed to a vow of abstinence (other forms of self-denial):

Ex premissis apparet, quod continentiae uota nec mulier sine uiri consensu, nec uir sine mulieris consensu Deo reddere potest. Si autem consensu alterius eorum ab altero promisso fuerit, et si postmodum in irritum deducere uoluerit qui permisit, non tamen valet, quia in debito coniugii eque mulier habet potestam uiri, sicut et uir mulieris; atque ideo, si quilibet eorum alterum a suo iure absoluerit, ad preteritam seruitutem ipsum reuocare non poterit. Quia uero in ceteris uir est caput mulieris, et mulier corpus uiri, ita uota abstinentiae uiro permittente mulier potest promittere, ut tamen eodem prohibente repromissa non ualeat inplere, et hoc, ut diximus, propter condicionem seruitutis, qua uiro in omnibus debet subesse.

From what has been described previously, it is apparent that neither a woman without the agreement of a man, nor a man without the consent of a woman, is able to enact before God vows of *continence*. If, however, it shall be promised by one with the consent of the other, and if afterwards he who allowed it shall wish to set aside the vow of continence, nevertheless, it is not possible, because in fulfilling the sexual obligation of marriage, the woman holds power equally with the man. Thus if either one of them shall release the other from the marriage right, he or she is not then able to recall the other to the former servitude. But, since in other respects the man is the head of the woman and the woman is the body of the man, a woman is able to make vows of *abstinence*, with the man's permission: but if he prohibits her, she may not fulfil her

---

[38] Augustine, ed. Walsh, pp. 6, 7.

promises, and this, as we have said, is because of the condition of servitude by which she ought to be subject to the man in all things.[39]

English statutes echoing Gratian clearly envisage that such vows will be taken in the context of one party or another entering religion. 1 Salisbury 89 reads:

> De transitu coniugatorum ad religionem.
> Item, doceant sacerdotes frequenter populum et prohibeant sub anethmati ne alter coniugum transeat ad religionem, nec recipiatur, nisi per nos aud nostram licentiam. Item, moneant mulieres ne faciant vota nisi cum magna deliberatione et cum consensu virorum suorum et consilio sacerdotum.

> Concerning the transition of married persons towards religion. Likewise, priests should often teach the people and prohibit under anathema that one party in a married couple should take up the religious life, nor be received into it except through our offices and with our permission. Similarly, they should command women not to make vows except after great deliberation and with the consent of their husbands and on the advice of their priest.[40]

1 Chichester 30, similarly, reads:

> Moneantur coniugate ne voveant nisi de consensu virorum et consilio sacerdotum. Non transeat ad religionem alter coniugatorum nisi de licentia episcopi.

> Married women must be warned not to take vows except with the consent of their husbands and on the advice of a priest. One of the spouses must not adopt the religious life without the licence of the bishop.[41]

It was, however, possible to take a vow of chastity and remain in the world. Dyan Elliott notes a distinction between the solemn vow, made in front of a church official, and usually including an entrance into religion for both parties, and the simple vow, equally binding, but made without formalities, and usually made by those who wished to remain in the world.[42]

Elliott suggests that the marriage of Mary and Joseph might have inspired those who wished to remain in the world but nevertheless preserve chastity in marriage, but she notes that the clergy did its best to limit such an effect by emphasizing Mary's singularity.[43] We can see something similar in hagiographical accounts of

---

[39] Gratian, *Decretum* c. 33 q. 5 c. 11, in Friedberg, I, 1254; English translation in Blamires, p. 84. This passage forms part of a more general discussion of the legal dominance of men in marriage, which Elliott, p. 156, notes had influence in civil as well as canon law: Friedberg, I, 1253–56; English translation in Blamires, pp. 83–87

[40] Powicke and Cheney, I, 89.

[41] Powicke and Cheney, I, 457.

[42] Elliott, pp. 159–62.

[43] Elliott, pp. 177–78.

the chaste marriages of Mary of Oignies and St Bridget of Sweden. Jacques de Vitry, the author of the *life* of Mary of Oignies (1215), emphasizes that Mary's mortification of her flesh is exceptional, and is to be revered, but not to be imitated. The Middle English translation of her *vita* reads:

> I seye not þis, preisynge þe exces, but tellynge þe feruoure. In þis and many oþer þat she wroghte by priuelege of grace, lat þe discrete reder take hede that priuelege of a few makiþ not a commun lawe. Folowe wee hir vertues; (þe werkes of hir vertues) wiþ-outen specyal priuelege folowe maye wee not.[44]

He also stresses that Mary does not persuade her husband John to agree to a vow of chastity. Rather, John is inspired to take the vow, and he retains his authority over her:

> And whan she so a good while had lyued wiþ John, hir spouse, in matrymoyne, oure lorde byhelde the meeknes of his mayden and gracyously herde hir prayers: for John was enspyred to haue Mary as taken to kepe, whom he hadde firste as wife. Hee made þe chast man tutour of his mayden, þat she shulde haue solas of hir keper, and lafte to hir a trewe puruyour, þat sche myȝhte more frely serue oure lorde.[45]

Elliott notes that de Vitry's assertion that Mary was returned to the hundredfold reward of virginity has led some to assert that she remained a virgin throughout her marriage,[46] thus absorbing her into a more conventional category of spirituality. Something similar seems to happen with St Bridget of Sweden (c. 1303–73).[47] In a fifteenth-century poem, 'A Salutation to St Birgitta', by John Audelay, a monastery chaplain, Bridget is praised as a virgin. The poem opens by praising her chaste marriage:

> Hayle! maydyn & wyfe. hayle! wedow brygytt.
> Hayle! þu chese to be chast & kepe charyte,
> Hayle! þu special spouse, kyndle to þe knyt;
> Hayle! he consentyd to the same by concel of the
> To be relegyous.   (lines 1–5)[48]

---

[44] C. Horstmann, 'Prosalegenden: Die Legenden des ms. Douce 114,' *Anglia* 8 (1885), 102–96 (p. 136).

[45] Horstmann, p. 136.

[46] Elliott, p. 239; the equation of the hundredfold/sixtyfold/thirtyfold reward with the three grades of chastity is from St Jerome, p. 347.

[47] For the influence of Bridget in England, see Roger Ellis, ' "Flores ad fabricandam . . . coronam": An Investigation into the Uses of the Revelations of St Bridget of Sweden in Fifteenth Century England,' *Medium Aevum* 51 (1982), 163–86.

[48] Audelay's poem is printed in *The Revelations of Saint Birgitta*, ed. William Patterson Cumming, EETS o.s. no. 178 (London: Oxford University Press, 1929), Introduction, xxxi–xxxvii.

Line 48 seems to state explicitly that she remained a virgin:

> Haile! he grounded þe in grace in þi vergenete   (line 48)

The end of the poem seems to state the same thing at line 204:

> Al þat redis reuerenly þis remyssioune
> Prays to blisful Bregit, þat merceful may,
> Fore hem þat med this mater with dewocion
> þat is boþ blind & def, þe synful Audelay.
> I pray ȝoue specialy,
> Fore I mad þis with good entent
> In þe reuerens of þis vergyn verement,
> Heo graunt ȝoue grace that beþ present
> To haue ioy & blis perpetualy.   (lines 198–206)

As is clear from the Middle English *Life* attached to Roger Ellis's edition of Bridget's *Revelations*, she was not a 'vergyn verement,' but had several children with her husband before their vows of chastity and his subsequent death.[49] Such accounts seem designed to discourage pious laywomen from imitating models such as Mary and Bridget.

But in fact we can see examples of English laywomen attempting to imitate the models that hagiographical accounts of narrative chastity have offered them. For example in the *Life* of Christina of Markyate, Christina's parents have her married to a man named Burthred at the instigation of Ralph, the bishop of Durham, who had previously tried to seduce her.[50] Christina, however, had previously taken a vow of chastity that betrothed her to God, and refused to live with her husband. Her frustrated parents let Burthred into her bedroom at night in secret in the hope that this would resolve matters. Christina took this opportunity to propose to Burthred that they should live together in a chaste marriage, telling him the story of St Cecilia as an example:

> Historiam ordine retexuit illi beate Cecilie et sponsi sui Valeriani. qualiter illibate pudicicie coronas eciam morituri meruerunt accipere

---

[49] *The Liber Celestis of St Bridget of Sweden*, ed. Roger Ellis (Oxford: Oxford University Press, 1987), pp. 1–2.

[50] *The Life of Christina of Markyate: A Twelfth Century Recluse*, ed. and trans. by C. H. Talbot (Oxford: Clarendon, 1959). On Christina's marriage, it is difficult to determine the nature of the contract that occurs between Christina and Burthred. Thomas Head, 'The Marriages of Christina of Markyate,' *Viator* 21 (1990), 75–101 (p. 89 and n. 53) argues that in the twelfth century there was little linguistic precision in the distinction between betrothal and marriage. He argues (p. 92) that Christina's life is contemporary with the evolution of the canonical theory of marriage, and that consequently there was no normative understanding of marriage during this period of debate and development. Hence the author of Christina's *vita* uses words for both betrothal and marriage in describing the ceremony that has taken place. In the description of the ceremony, we are told it is a betrothal: 'et eadem hora Burthredus illam in coniugem sibi desponsavit' (Talbot, p. 46). And we are later told that her parents wish

de manu angeli. [. . .]. Et nos inquid quantum possumus sequamur illorum exempla. ut consortes efficiamur in eorum perhenni gloria. Quia si compatimur: et coregnabimus. Non pudeat te repudiari scilicet ne tui concives improperent tibi quasi a me repudiato viliter ingrediar in domum tuam. et cohabitemus in ea aliquanto tempore. specietenus quidem coniuges. in conspectu Domini continentes.

She recounted to him in detail the story of St Cecilia and her husband Valerian, telling how, at their death they were accounted worthy to receive crowns of unsullied chastity from the hands of an angel. [. . .]. Let us therefore,' she exhorted him, 'follow their example, so that we may become their companions in eternal glory. Because if we suffer with them, we shall also reign with them. Do not take it amiss that I have declined your embraces. In order that your friends may not reproach you with being rejected by me, I will go home with you: and let us live together there for some time, ostensibly as husband and wife, but in reality living chastely in the sight of the Lord.[51]

Christina's attempts to persuade Burthred (and her parents) do not succeed, and she eventually has to take other measures to preserve her chastity. But it is clear that the availability of the model of St Cecilia assists her in making her case for marital chastity.

The marriage of Margery Kempe

The story of St Cecilia may also find an echo in the attempt of another Englishwoman to live chastely within marriage. The fifteenth-century *Book of Margery Kempe* might, perhaps, be labelled the earliest surviving autobiographical writing in English.[52] While trying to persuade her husband to agree to a vow of chastity, Kempe has a vision in which Jesus tells her:

Þow must fastyn þe Fryday boþen fro mete & drynke, and þow schalt haue þi desyr er Whitsonday, for I schal sodeynly sle þin husbonde.[53]

---

to arrange the wedding (Talbot, p. 54). But it is also referred to as a *coniugium*, a marriage (Talbot, p. 112).

[51] Talbot, pp. 50, 51.

[52] As it is described in *The Book of Margery Kempe*, trans. B. A. Windeatt (Harmondsworth: Penguin, 1985), Introduction, p. 9. The term has its difficulties. Kempe did not intend to write an autobiography, but, as Stephen Medcalf points out, a saint's life: Stephen Medcalf, 'Inner and Outer,' in *The Later Middle Ages*, ed. Stephen Medcalf (London: Methuen, 1981), pp. 108–71 (p. 113). Kempe's authorship of the text is complicated by the role of her two amanuenses, on which see Lynn Staley Johnson, 'The Trope of the Scribe and the Question of Literary Authority in the Works of Julian of Norwich and Margery Kempe,' *Speculum* 66 (1991), 810–38. The label 'autobiographical' has a certain appropriateness nonetheless.

[53] Margery Kempe, *The Book of Margery Kempe*, ed. Sanford Brown Meech and Hope Emily Allen, EETS, o.s. no. 212 (London: Oxford University Press, 1940), p. 21. All further references are to

David Aers observes a parallel here with the story of St Cecilia, who tells her husband on their wedding night that, if he attempts to have intercourse with her, an angel will kill him.[54] This is Chaucer's retelling of the relevant part of the Cecilia story in his *Second Nun's Tale*, where Cecilia tells her new husband:

'I have an aungel which that loveth me,
That with greet love, wher so I wake or sleepe
Is redy ay my body for to kepe.
And if that he may feelen, out of drede,
That ye me touche, or love in vileynye,
He right anon wol sle yow with the dede,
And in youre yowthe thus ye shullen dye;
And if that ye in clene love me gye,
He wol yow loven as me, for youre clennesse,
And shewen yow his joye and his brightnesse.'

(*Canterbury Tales*, 8. 152–61)

If this possible echo means that Cecilia is a potential influence on Kempe, then Mary of Oignies and Bridget of Sweden are much more concrete presences in her text, despite the attempts that we have already seen to contain their narratives and make them less likely models for imitation.[55]

As we saw in Gratian and in the English statutes, one party to a marriage cannot take a vow of chastity without the consent of the other, and so Kempe, despite her wish to live chastely, is obliged to continue to render the marital debt:

And aftyr þis tyme sche had neuyr desyr to komown fleschly wyth hyre husbonde, for þe dette of matrimony was so abhominabyl to hir þat sche had leuar, hir thowt, etyn or drynkyn þe wose, þe mukke in þe chanel, þan to consentyn to any fleschly comownyng saf only for obedyens. & so sche seyd to hir husbond, 'I may not deny ȝow my body, but þe lofe of myn hert & myn affeccyon is drawyn fro alle erdly

---

this edition. A late fifteenth-century annotator of the manuscript has altered the passage in a marginal note to read 'I schal sodeynly sle the flesshely lust in thin husbonde' (p. 21 n. 2).

[54] David Aers, *Community, Gender and Individual Identity: English Writing, 1360–1430* (London: Routledge, 1988), p. 93.

[55] For the influence of hagiographical narrative on Kempe and her text, see Elliott, pp. 20–7; Kempe's text explicitly compares her to Bridget (p. 47) and on a pilgrimage to Rome, Kempe speaks with one of the saint's servants, visits the room in which she died, and hears a sermon about her (p. 95); Kempe's text also justifies her weeping by reference to Mary of Oignies (p. 153); Karma Lochrie, *Margery Kempe and Translations of the Flesh* (Philadelphia: University of Pennsylvania Press, 1991), p. 118, suggests that the allusion to Mary here is that of Kempe's amanuensis and not her own, but cf. the comparisons drawn in Ute Stargardt, 'The Beguines of Belgium, the Dominican Nuns of Germany and Margery Kempe,' in *The Popular Literature of Medieval England*, ed. Thomas J. Heffernan (Knoxville: University of Tennessee Press, 1985), pp. 277–313.

creaturys & sett only in God.' He wold haue hys wylle, & sche obeyd
wyth greet wepyng & sorwyng for þat sche mygth not levyn chast.

(pp. 11–12)

Kempe's text shows a clear awareness of the Church's sense of the relationship of
marital sex to sin. She describes marital sex as *leful*, 'lawful' (p. 15), but this does
not mean, of course, that it might not be sinful. Part of her reason for wishing to
live chastely is that she is convinced that the sexual pleasure that she enjoyed with
her husband before her conversion to religion was excessive, and that they had
'dysplesyd God be her inordynat lofe & þe gret delectacyon þat þei haddyn eyþyr
of hem in vsyng of oþer' (p. 12). John Kempe, however, will not agree to the vow
for then he would not be able to have sex with her without committing a mortal
sin (p. 24). The specific reference to 'dedly synne' implies an awareness that marital intercourse can sometimes be regarded as venially sinful. Kempe nevertheless
continues to render the marital debt, as she ought according to ecclesiastical
thinking. Jesus, speaking to her in a vision concerning wives who wish to remain
chaste but are obliged to render the marital debt, indicates that the rendering of
the marital debt for obedience despite a desire to remain chaste is an act of merit,
for he accepts the intention for the deed (p. 212). That Kempe did continue to
have intercourse with her husband is implied by the evidence that when she did
eventually manage to persuade her husband to agree to a vow of chastity, she may
have been pregnant.[56]

Kempe's worldly marriage is replaced by a mystical marriage with God:

> Also þe Fadyr seyd to þis creatur, 'Dowtyr, I wil han þe weddyd to my
> Godhede, for I schal schewyn þe my preuyteys & my cownselys, for þu
> xalt wonyn wyth me wyth-owtyn ende.' (p. 86)

David Herlihy notes that, while saints' lives often express an abhorrence of sexual
relations in reality, descriptions of mystical marriages sometimes contain imagery
that goes beyond the spiritual into the physical, and even the erotic.[57]

This is the case with Kempe. God tells her:

> Þerfore most I nedys be homly wyth þe and lyn in þi bed wyth þe.
> Dowtyr, thow desyrest gretly to se me, & thu mayst boldly, whan þu
> art in þi bed, take me to þe as for þi weddyd husbond, as thy derwor-
> thy derlyng, & as for thy swete sone, for I wyl be louyd as a sone schuld
> be louyd wyth þe modyr & wil þat þu loue me, dowtyr, as a good wife
> owyth to loue hir husbonde. & þerfor þu mayst boldly take me in þe

---

[56] Laura L. Howes, 'On the birth of Margery Kempe's Last Child,' *Modern Philology* 90 (1992),
220–25 (pp. 220–21). Although Kempe tells us that the text is not written in chronological
order (p. 5), she gives birth to a child while on pilgrimage to Jerusalem, and denies the accus-
ations of an anchorite that the child was conceived while abroad (p. 103). It is clear that her
vows of chastity precede the pilgrimage.

[57] Herlihy, *Medieval Households*, p. 118.

armys of þi sowle & kyssen my mowth, myn hed, & my fete as swetly
as thow wylt.   (p. 90)

Kempe's initial pleasure in sex, the 'inordynat lofe & þe gret delectacyon' that she
experienced earlier in her marriage, was later replaced by the sense that she would
prefer to 'etyn or drynkyn þe wose, þe mukke in þe chanel' than have sex with her
husband. That initial pleasure seems resurrected here in her description of the
intimacy of a spiritual sexuality.

Kempe's text records a great deal of hostility to her religious experiences and her
consequent behaviour, from many sources: sceptical clergy, hostile laypersons (men
in particular), and her reluctant husband. Her behaviour is clearly threatening to
many people, and her freedom from the conventional constraints of marriage or
enclosed religious life comes at a significant cost. She was frequently accused of
Lollardy (pp. 28, 111–12, 124, 129, 132–35), partly at least because she was a lay-
woman speaking of religious matters.[58] She was also seen as a threat to the authority
of husbands over their wives (p. 116, 133). Her behaviour, then, was seen as threatening to both husbandly and clerical authority, according to those who accused her.
Ute Stargardt notes that the extent of the hostility of Kempe's contemporaries is
inscribed in her text:[59] hostile behaviour from men is sometimes expressed as the
threat of rape (pp. 14, 133), which Kempe fears even in old age (p. 241).

Kempe nonetheless succeeds to some degree in managing to live a life very
different from that which these people would have preferred for her. She succeeds in doing this, I think, for two reasons. The first is that the Church provided orthodox models with which she could compare her behaviour: Mary of
Oignies, Bridget of Sweden, and St Cecilia are examples. Kempe's work is written in the context of these and other very specific and explicit influences, openly
acknowledged in the text, and her life was probably lived with reference to the
justification of these authoritative models. Although, as we have seen, the
Church attempted to discourage any potential role for these narratives as
models for imitation, given the threat that they posed to masculine construc-
tions of marital and clerical authority, they remained, nonetheless, orthodox
and licit models for Kempe to appeal to. The Church did allow people to live in
chaste marriages in the world, given its nervousness about marital sex and the
need to justify the marriage of Christ's parents. This allows Kempe a model to
live by which liberates her from the authority of her husband without forcing
her into a convent.

The second reason that Kempe is able to succeed in living a religious life in the
world free from her husband's authority is economic. She agrees to pay his debts in
exchange for his agreement to take the vow of chastity (p. 25). It is odd, however,
that Kempe should have any assets with which to pay her husband's debts, when we

---

[58]   For the political context of public hysteria concerning Lollardy, especially in 1417, see
      Anthony Goodman, *Margery Kempe and her World* (London: Longman, 2002), pp. 142–46.
[59]   Stargardt, p. 305.

remember that under the common law all property owned by either husband or wife was under the husband's authority for the duration of the marriage.[60] Furthermore, gifts between spouses were not valid under the common law.[61] It is unlikely that Kempe had independent control over her property throughout her marriage. She certainly refers to businesses that she ran, for example her brewing business (p. 9). References in contemporary documents mention 'Johannes Kemp braceator (brewer)':[62] it seems that the business was her husband's, at least in name, in accordance with the common law's injunction that all property be his. Stephen Medcalf observes that Kempe's father died in the year that she obtained her husband's agreement to a vow of chastity: this is not mentioned in the text. Medcalf suggests that the inheritance of her father's property might have enabled her to pay her husband's debts.[63] If this was the case, then Kempe's payment of her husband's debts might have occurred in one of two ways. If her property was under the control of her husband, then she might have assisted him financially by agreeing to the permanent alienation of property that belonged to her but was under her husband's control. Her consent in the king's court would have been necessary for any property transaction that would endure longer than the lifetime of her husband.[64] Alternatively, if Kempe inherited property from her father held in use (the ancestor of the modern trust), she might have continued to have the inheritance held in that way: i.e. nominally owned by feoffees who controlled the property to her benefit. R. H. Helmholz suggests a rise in the number of married women having property held in use in the fifteenth century, as a way around their proprietary disability under the common law.[65] Ironically, given that the use seems to have been employed by women to achieve financial independence from their husbands, early uses, which had no basis in statute law, seem to have been enforced by the ecclesiastical courts.[66]

Subsequent to their simple vow of chastity, agreed between themselves, John and Margery Kempe subsequently took a solemn vow of chastity before the bishop of Lincoln. At the taking of the vow, Kempe requested that the bishop grant her a mantle and a ring and white clothing as signs of her religious status (p. 34). Kempe is initially reluctant to obey God's command that she wear white clothing, for fear of being slandered (p. 32), and the bishop is reluctant to grant it to her, referring her to the archbishop of Canterbury when pressed (p. 35). She does not seem to have worn white clothing until she was on her pilgrimage to Jerusalem (p. 76). The mayor of Leicester questions her wearing of white clothing (p. 116), as does the archbishop of York, who asks her if she is a maiden. When she

---

[60] *Britton*, ed. Nichols, I, 227.
[61] *Bracton*, ed. Woodbine, trans. Thorne, II, 97–99; *Britton*, ed. Nichols, I, 223, 227, 234.
[62] Meech and Allen, Appendix III, p. 364.
[63] Medcalf, p. 116.
[64] *Bracton*, ed. Woodbine, trans. Thorne, IV, 30–31.
[65] R. H. Helmholz, 'Married Women's Wills in Later Medieval England,' in *Wife and Widow in Later Medieval England*, ed. Sue Sheridan Walker (Ann Arbor: University of Michigan Press, 1993), pp. 165–82 (pp. 173–74).
[66] Helmholz, 'The Early Enforcement of Uses,' pp. 1504, 1507.

replies that she is a wife, he declares her a heretic and orders her to be fettered (p. 124). Kempe's request for white clothing, the symbol of virginity, and the mantle and the ring, symbols of vidual chastity,[67] make clear her ambiguous position with regard to the conventional model of the three grades of chastity after she has taken her vow. In fact, her position as a wife becomes impossible: although she should have remained under her husband's authority following their vows, gossip and slander about their chaste status forced them to separate (pp. 179–80). Her travels on pilgrimages without her husband then caused her difficulties in protesting her married status. Furthermore, when her husband was injured in a fall, she was blamed for neglecting him. She then took him home and cared for him, childish and incontinent, until his death (pp. 179–80).

Kempe's text survives in only a single manuscript, rediscovered in the twentieth century. It was printed in 1501 by Wynkyn de Worde, successor to William Caxton. Lochrie notes that the printed text was entitled 'a shorte treatise of contemplacyon taught by oure lorde Ihesu cryste, or taken out of the boke of Margerie kempe of lynn': the text transformed into an instructional handbook for devotional purposes, the autobiographical element removed.[68] As Meech puts it, 'In no extract is there a single circumstance of the worldly life of Margery.'[69] In 1521, the extracts printed by de Worde were reprinted by Henry Pepwell, with the closing comment: 'Here endeth a shorte treatyse of a deuoute ancres called Margerye kempe of Lynne.'[70] This identification of Kempe as an anchoress, following the removal of all autobiographical elements from her text, falsifies her life just as Audelay's falsifies St Bridget's. These women, whose lives combined marriage with religious experience, are absorbed after their deaths into patterns of religious behaviour that pose less of a threat to masculine authority, clerical and secular. But it is ecclesiastical ambiguity about the role of sex within marriage that allows them to take on these roles in the first place.

---

[67] Stargardt, p. 281.
[68] Lochrie, p. 220; the text of de Worde's edition, with Pepwell's variants, is in Meech and Allen, Appendix II, pp. 353–57.
[69] Meech and Allen, Introduction, xlvi.
[70] Meech and Allen, Introduction, xlvii.

6

Marriage and Family

Family and kinship

Familia, as David Herlihy tells us, comes from the noun *famulus*, 'a slave,' and the original meaning of *familia* was a band of slaves, a meaning that persisted after the decline of slavery to refer to groups of servants or serfs. This meaning of *familia* extended to include all persons placed under the authority of a single person, an authority that could include the *patria potestas* of a man over his wives and children. Hence its modern sense.[1]

It is generally agreed that the medieval family was a nuclear family, essentially based around a core unit of a coresidential couple and its offspring, although it might also include other family members for periods of time, and the household, as opposed to the family, might also include other persons such as domestic servants (or slaves in the early Middle Ages), agricultural labourers, or children from outside the immediate family who were being fostered.[2] Herlihy argues that the rise of the nuclear family comes about with the decline in Europe of large scale farm management by bands of slaves, and the rise in its place of peasant farming, which created farms that could support a small family unit.[3]

In the early Middle Ages, however, it is usually thought that the extended kin group played an important social role, particularly in regard to seeing that obligations by and to other members of kin were kept, and in the obligation to avenge family members killed as a result of feud.[4] The importance of kin and its contribution to individual identity is a prominent theme in Old English literature. In *The Wanderer*, an exile laments his outcast status and his lack of kin:

> Swa ic modsefan   minne sceolde,
> oft earmcearig,   eðle bidæled,

---

[1] Herlihy, 'Family,' pp. 115–16; *Familia* also meant 'property' – Herlihy, 'Family,' pp. 117–18.
[2] See, for example, Sally Crawford, *Childhood in Anglo-Saxon England* (Stroud: Sutton, 1999), p. 10.
[3] Herlihy, *Medieval Households*, p. 5.
[4] Brundage, *Law, Sex and Christian Society*, p. 125.

freomægum feor	feterum sælan,
siþþan geara iu	goldwine minne
hrusan heolstre biwrah,	ond ic hean þonan
wod wintercearig	ofer waþema gebind,
sohte sele dreorig	sinces bryttan,
hwær ic feor oþþe neah	findan meahte
þone þe in meoduhealle	min mine wisse,
oþþe mec freondleasne	frefran wolde,
weman mid wynnum.	(lines 19–29a)

'So I, careworn, deprived of fatherland,
Far from my noble kin, have often had
To tie in fetters my own troubled spirit,
Since long ago I wrapped my lord's remains
In darkness of the earth, and sadly thence
Journeyed by winter over icy waves,
And suffering sought the hall of a new patron,
If I in any land might find one willing
To show me recognition in his mead hall.'[5]

Beowulf likewise makes clear the imperative to avenge kin: the poem portrays two attempts to settle feuds as doomed to failure because of the desire for revenge (1136b–59a, 2041–69a).

Barbara Hanawalt, however, has argued that extended kin are of no more importance at any point in medieval England than they are now, and that Anglo-Saxon social custom did not emphasize obligations to extended kin.[6] Lorraine Lancaster, in her study of Anglo-Saxon kinship, has argued that it is close kin who are most important, but that the extent of broader kinship links may not have been hard and fast: 'that a circle of kinsmen, variable according to many factors, including biological chance, patterns of residence, ease of communication and possibly personal preference, made up the group defined by the recognition of ties of kinship.'[7] The circle of effective kin *may* have been relatively small, but this is not necessarily a universally applicable rule.[8]

Hanawalt also argues for the later medieval period (citing Helmholz) that cases in the ecclesiastical courts demonstrate that people did not know their kinship ties, and were unable to find witnesses or prove to the satisfaction of the courts that they were related to their spouses.[9] There are two comments worth making in relation to this assertion. Firstly, witness evidence in court cases is not necessarily to be taken at face value as absolute truth: that the Church was concerned about manipulation of the courts in cases like these, concerning this sort of evidence, is clear

---

5   *A Choice of Anglo-Saxon Verse*, ed. and trans. Richard Hamer (London: Faber, 1970), pp. 174–77.
6   Hanawalt, *The Ties that Bound*, pp. 80–81.
7   Lancaster, p. 234.
8   Lancaster, p. 371.
9   Hanawalt, *The Ties that Bound*, p. 81.

from 4 Lateran 52, for example. Secondly, while there are of course cases where people were unable to trace relationships, there are also a great many marriage cases where the existence of impediments was discovered: if people were generally entirely ignorant of their wider kinship links, the Church would not have relied so heavily on the announcement of the banns as a reliable protection against incest, and couples would not have married clandestinely to avoid the incest prohibitions, as it is clear many did. As Lancaster comments concerning kinship in the early Middle Ages, individual circumstances might often dictate awareness or lack of it about the wider kin group. And as we saw in chapter three, the notion of marriage as alliance, which might be taken to suggest the existence of a sense of broad kinship groups and their wider interests, persists right up to the end of the medieval period. Some awareness of wider kin, then, and a sense of broader kinship ties, may endure throughout the medieval period, although it is the nuclear family which is the basis of the medieval household, and immediate kin that count most.

The first major change in the structure of the medieval European family comes with the attempts of the Church to impose exogamy upon societies that may previously have practiced in-marriage: as we saw earlier, endogamy persists in Ireland right into the central and later Middle Ages, causing outrage elsewhere. Ecclesiastical attempts to impose exogamy in England are visible from the early seventh century, when St Augustine of Canterbury writes to Pope Gregory asking for guidance on questions relating to the English Church. Augustine's fifth question concerns the degrees within which marriage is permitted. Bede's *Ecclesiastical History* reports Gregory's reply that although Roman law permitted the marriages of first cousins, marriages closer than the third or fourth generation should be forbidden, as should marriage to stepmothers or sisters-in-law. He states that many of the English contracted such marriages while they were still heathen, and states that they are now to be instructed that this is a grave offence.[10] Lorraine Lancaster notes that 'the frequency of defection from ecclesiastical rulings on marriage with near kin was a cause of warning and complaint,' and incest is still being denounced in the eleventh century in Wulfstan's *Sermo Lupi ad Anglos*, the legislation of Cnut (in which Wulfstan had a hand), the Law of the Northumbrian Priests, and *Be wifmannes beweddunge*.[11] In-marriage does persist into the later medieval period, when clandestine unions are a means of avoiding the prohibition, although usually not with very close kin.

The incest prohibition widens and narrows: from the eleventh to the thirteenth centuries it reaches its widest span in prohibiting marriages between anyone related within seven degrees of consanguinity and affinity. A change in the system

---

[10] St Bede, *Ecclesiastical History of the English People*, trans. L. Sherley Price, R. E. Latham, D. H. Farmer, revised ed. (Harmondsworth: Penguin, 1990); the concession of marriage in the fourth degree seems to have caused contemporary controversy, and the authenticity of Gregory's authorship was questioned, but see Goody, p. 35, for the existence of a ms. tradition independent of Bede on the continent.

[11] Lancaster, pp. 240–41.

used for reckoning kin in the eleventh century, from the Roman to the Germanic, also extended the number of prohibited marriages. The Roman system had calculated each degree on the basis of an act of generation – thus, brother and sister are related in the second degree, uncle and niece in the third. In the Germanic system, each degree was equated with a generation, and so a person was prohibited from marrying anyone with whom they had a common ancestor in the previous seven generations.[12] 4 Lateran 50 (1215) narrows the number of grades again: the modified consanguinity regulations meant that any persons with an ancestor in common in the previous four generations were forbidden to marry.[13] The modified rules of affinity meant that anyone whose ancestors had married or had intercourse in the previous four generations could not marry.[14]

Why is the Church so interested in promoting exogamy? Jack Goody has argued that it does so in its own financial interest: that the Church's prohibition on marrying within seven degrees of consanguinity and affinity relates to the fact that Roman law calculated seven degrees of kinship for purposes of inheritance. Goody argues that the Church is ensuring that it was impossible to marry anyone from whom one could formerly have inherited, and that this contributes to breaking up larger kin structures and ensures that land can be bequeathed to the Church.[15] Other historians of marriage have disagreed.[16] David Herlihy offers an alternative argument that the imperative to exogamy should be viewed in tandem with the imperative to monogamy in attempts to prohibit polygyny and concubinage. Herlihy suggests that early medieval aristocratic households practice 'resource polygyny,' where privileged males accumulate women, leading to tensions within houses and across social strata, and promoting marriage through abduction. He therefore puts the case that the Church's imperative to exogamy and monogamy attempts to ensure the circulation of women between households, promoting domestic and social peace.[17]

The second major change in the medieval family in the early Middle Ages is the attempt to impose absolute monogamy within regularized marital unions. The Church attempts to do this first of all by preventing the offspring of irregular

---

[12] Goody, pp. 37, 136–37.

[13] Goody, pp. 136–37.

[14] Pollock and Maitland, II, 405.

[15] Goody, p. 37; on the role of Christianity in breaking up larger kin structures, cf. Crawford, p. 11.

[16] Brundage, *Law, Sex and Christian Society*, pp. 606–7; David Herlihy, 'Making Sense of Incest: Women and the Marriage Rules of the Early Middle Ages,' in David Herlihy, *Women, Family and Society in Medieval Europe: Historical Essays 1978–1991*, ed. A. Molho (Oxford: Berghahn, 1995), pp. 96–109 (pp. 102–4) (first published in *Law, Custom, and the Social Fabric in Medieval Europe: Essays in Honor of Bryce Lyon*, ed. Bernard S. Bachrach and David Nicholas (Kalamazoo, MI, 1990), pp. 1–16).

[17] Herlihy, 'Making Sense of Incest,' pp. 107–9; cf. Lévi-Strauss on exogamy as peace treaty; that the Church's decisions on marriage regulation may sometimes be connected with a desire to promote peace has already been briefly mentioned in the discussion of marriage as alliance, chapter 3, above.

unions from inheriting. In early Germanic law, a man's offspring with his concubine could inherit, whereas his offspring with his slave could not. It was this distinction between free-born and slave-born that the Church attempted to convert into a distinction between legitimate and illegitimate.[18] In the later Middle Ages, the problem of concubinage is problematized by the recognition of clandestine unions, and the policy of the Church towards irregular cohabitations is to attempt to formalize them as marriages where possible.[19] The Church never succeeded completely in wiping out concubinage, however.[20]

The third major alteration in ideologies of the family comes in the central Middle Ages when kinship structures alter somewhat. Anglo-Saxon kinship structures were bilateral, or cognatic: that is to say, descent was traced both through male and female relatives.[21] Property could devolve through either male or female members of the family, whether via inheritance or dotal grants, and responsibility for vengeance also applied both to maternal and paternal kin.[22] Although there was some bias towards the male line, Anglo-Saxon society was not patrilineal. There is, however, an emergence of a tendency towards patrilineal or agnatic lineage, which traces descent exclusively through males, within the European aristocracy in the central Middle Ages.[23] Patrilineality reduces the status of women within the kin group: married women leave the kin group, and their children are members not of their kin, but of their husband's. It also creates a bias away from partible inheritance and towards primogeniture, facilitating the consolidation of wealth within branches of families and the emergence of aristocratic dynasties.[24] This patrilineal view of kinship does not replace bilineal kinship, but is superimposed upon it.[25]

Agnatic lineages and primogeniture never came to absolutely dominate English heirship. Multiple forms of tenure and inheritance persist in later medieval England, and this meant that difficult choices remained with regard to heirship. We find evidence of parents trying to make provision for younger sons against the claims of the eldest son and heir in drafts of the fifteenth-century will of Agnes Paston, where she recalls the death of her husband William many years before, and his attempts to ensure that his youngest sons should not be destitute. In Agnes' retelling, William expresses his will verbally concerning provisions to be

---

18   Clunies Ross, pp. 6, 27–28; Goody, p. 76.
19   Brundage, 'Concubinage and Marriage.'
20   Brundage, *Law, Sex and Christian Society*, pp. 606–7.
21   Lancaster, p. 232.
22   Goody, pp. 18–19.
23   Herlihy, *Medieval Households*, p. 82; David Herlihy, 'The Making of the Medieval Family: Symmetry, Structure, and Sentiment,' in David Herlihy, *Women, Family and Society in Medieval Europe: Historical Essays 1978–1991*, ed. A. Molho (Oxford: Berghahn, 1995), pp. 135–53 (p. 143) (first published in *Journal of Family History* 8 (1983), 116–30).
24   Herlihy, *Medieval Households*, pp. 82–83, 92–98.
25   Herlihy, *Medieval Households*, p. 83, Herlihy, 'The Making of the Medieval Family,' p. 143; Goody, pp. 229–39, argues more generally for the coexistence of agnatic and bilateral kinship.

made for his two youngest sons, and asks his heir, John Paston, if he holds himself content with the provision that has been made for him. In any case, he says, if John is not content, he is, for he will not leave the youngest sons without enough to live on. Following William's death, however, John Paston takes the lands for himself in the absence of a written will.[26]

Naming does not necessarily reflect patrilineal tendencies, as with modern surnames in western societies. Anglo-Saxons did not generally have surnames, as opposed to bye-names that were not passed down, but family members sometimes had names that alliterated: Sally Crawford points to King Alfred, whose father was named Æthelwulf, brothers Æthelred, Æthelbert, and Æthelbald, son Edward, and so on.[27] When surnames do emerge, they do so unevenly. Richard McKinley finds that surnames are rare outside the upper classes in East Anglia prior to 1200, and fairly common by the late thirteenth century: it was not unusual, however, for an individual to have several designations.[28] Surnames also came from several sources: personal names, occupations, places of residence or relevant topographical features, nicknames, and terms for relationship were all common sources of surnames.[29] Furthermore, the way in which surnames passed between people was not entirely regular. Children might have surnames based on their mother's personal name, rather than their father's.[30] Married women did not always take their husband's names, keeping their father's surname instead. There is no uniformity here, however: some women who marry twice continue to use the first husband's surname, and sometimes their second husbands would take that surname too.[31] As an example of the fluidity of surnames, Zvi Razi cites the case of a villager named Alexander on the manor of Halesowen in the late thirteenth century. Alexander was a clerk living in the hamlet of Kenelmstowe, near the Church of St Kenelm. Accordingly, he had three surnames – 'de Kenelmstowe,' 'de St Kenelm' and 'the Clerk.' His son Clements was called 'Clements the son of Alexandre of St Kenelm' and 'Clements Tandi,' until his marriage to Emma de Folfen and his move to her family's property. He then becomes 'Clements de Folfen,' taking her father's name as his own.[32] Surnames do eventually stabilize in a patrilineal direction in the later medieval period – a stabilization that Hanawalt links to the growth of written records[33] – but they remain fluid for quite a long time.

26   *Paston Letters*, ed. Gairdner, iv, 249–51.
27   Crawford, p. 121; Richard McKinley, *Norfolk and Suffolk Surnames in the Middle Ages*, English Surnames Series II (London: Phillimore, 1975), p. 3, Richard McKinley, *The Surnames of Oxfordshire*, English Surnames Series III (London: Leopard's Head, 1977), p. 7, Richard McKinley, *The Surnames of Sussex*, English Surnames Series V (Oxford: Leopard's Head, 1988), p. 29, note the lack of pre-Conquest surnames in the areas surveyed.
28   McKinley, *Norfolk and Suffolk Surnames*, pp. 5, 7, 14, 15.
29   McKinley, *Surnames of Oxfordshire*, pp. 3–4.
30   McKinley, *Norfolk and Suffolk Surnames*, p. 13.
31   McKinley, *Surnames of Oxfordshire*, pp. 181–82, 184, 190.
32   Razi, p. 3.
33   Hanawalt, *The Ties that Bound*, p. 82.

Across the medieval period, then, we can see three major changes taking place in family structures with the rise of exogamy, monogamy, and patrilineage. None of these innovations are absolutely successful, possibly because they interfere with other agendas. Both monogamy and patrilineage can sometimes get in the way of inheritance strategies, which are themselves an important objective of marriage. Similarly exogamy sometimes interferes with marriages made for purposes of alliance – hence the dispensations to marry that we saw in chapter three where alliances needed to be forged through marriages between kin.

Women, work, and gender roles

Much of the work that medieval women did was focused on the household. As Barbara A. Hanawalt observes, 'two areas are traditionally assigned to the wife: the daily running of the household and the raising and training of the next generation.'[34] The work carried out by rural women is described in the late medieval *Ballad of the Tyrannical Husband*, where husband and wife switch places for a day. The husband accuses his wife of either sitting at home idle all day or wandering around tattling. In response, she argues that she has more to do than him, and describes her workload. She stays awake all night caring for a child. She is up milking the cows while he is still asleep. She makes butter and cheese, feeds the fowl, bakes, brews, makes clothing, feeds the animals and makes food for her husband and herself.[35] All this before noon, minding the children at the same time.[36] Women's work in higher social classes was similarly focused on the running of the household, but on a much larger scale, extending to estate management in the absence of a husband on business.

The work that women did outside the home, as Maryanne Kowaleski notes, 'demanded skills they learned informally within the family.'[37] Brewing and the production of cloth were common female occupations. *Spinster* is an occupational bye-name for a female clothworker before it becomes a term for an unmarried woman.[38] Margery Kempe ran a brewing business, and, in *Piers Plowman*, textiles and brewing are the trades of Coueitise's wife, Rose the Regratour, through which she engages in various sharp practices:

---

[34] Barbara A. Hanawalt, 'Peasant Women's Contribution to the Home Economy in Late Medieval England,' in *Women and Work in Preindustrial Europe*, ed. Barbara A. Hanawalt (Bloomington: Indiana University Press, 1986), pp. 3–19 (p. 3).

[35] Hanawalt, 'Peasant Women's Contribution,' p. 8, observes that in practice, weaving, tailoring, brewing and baking might be carried out by specialists in these service occupations, even in village-sized communities.

[36] Larrington, pp. 110–11.

[37] Maryanne Kowaleski, 'Women's Work in a Market Town: Exeter in the Late Fourteenth Century,' in *Women and Work in Preindustrial Europe*, ed. Barbara A. Hanawalt (Bloomington: Indiana University Press, 1986), pp. 145–66 (p. 155).

[38] McKinley, *Surnames of Oxfordshire*, p. 148; *OED* s.v. *spinster*.

My wyf was a wynstere & wollene cloth made,
And spak to the spynstere to spynnen it softe.
The pound that heo [payede] by peisid a quarter more
Thanne [myn owene] aunsel dede, [whanne] I weighede trewethe.
I boughte hire barly; heo breugh it to selle.
Penyale and pilewhey heo pouride togidere.
For laboureris and lough folk that lay be h[y]mselue;
The beste in my bedchaumbre lay be the wough.   (A. 5. 129–36)

Kowaleski's analysis of 435 cases of women who worked for wage or profit in late fourteenth-century Exeter finds 160 servants, 150 brewers and tapsters, 99 retailers and merchants, 55 prostitutes, 17 brothel keepers, and 51 artisans (mostly working in the cloth industry).[39] The 'servants' include wetnurses, midwives, and healers, but are for the most part young unmarried girls.[40] Generally, the work done by the women in Kowaleski's survey was low-status and intermittent, and many of the women worked more than one job.[41]

The wife's other major task was childrearing. Childbirth itself was very dangerous, as stressed by 1 Salisbury 88:

(De provisione mulieris pregnantis)
Item, moneant sacerdotes mulieres pregnantes de parochia sua ut, cum tempus partus instare intelligunt, sibi prospiciant ut aquam promptam habeant et paratam, et propter iminens periculum locute fuerint de confessione cum sacerdote, ne subito preocupate non possint cum voluerint copiam habere sacerdotis.[42]

(Concerning regulations for pregnant women)
Similarly, priests should advise pregnant women of their parish that, when they know that the hour of birth is at hand, they must see that they have water prepared and at hand, and that because of the danger threatening them they must have said confession with a priest, for fear that, in a sudden crisis, when they want to use the services of a priest, they cannot.

The *Book of Margery Kempe* describes the suffering which accompanies childbirth:[43]

And, aftyr that sche had conceyued, sche was labowrd wyth grett accessys tyl the chyld was born & than, what for labowr sche had in

---

[39] Kowaleski, p. 148.
[40] Kowaleski, p. 153.
[41] Kowaleski, pp. 155–57; some professions paired easily – on the association of the profession of tapster with that of prostitute, see Karras, *Common Women*, pp. 71–73.
[42] Powicke and Cheney, I, 89.
[43] Highlighting the dangers of childbirth and the suffering involved is a conventional feature of virginity literature: see for example *Medieval English Prose for Women: Selections from the Katherine Group and Ancrene Wisse*, ed. and trans. Bella Millett and Jocelyn Wogan-Browne (Oxford: Clarendon, 1990), p. 31.

chyldyng & for sekenesse goyng beforn, sche dyspered of hyr lyfe, wenyng sche mygth not leuyn. (p. 6)

Kempe's confession just after childbirth, undertaken when she was in fear of her life, led her to mention a sin that her confessor would not allow her to reveal in full. As a result, Kempe lost her mind, and was restrained to prevent her from injuring herself (pp. 7–8). That this was not an uncommon experience is shown by the description later in the text of another woman suffering similarly after childbirth, and similarly restrained (pp. 177–78). After the birth, women of the peasantry and in the towns by and large suckled their own infants, but noblewomen did not, choosing instead to have their children fed by wetnurses.[44]

Childhood

Research in recent years has argued against previous assumptions that there was no real validity in the notion of medieval childhood.[45] That medieval people had an awareness of the stages of life, and marked off childhood and adolescence as a separate category, is clear from the various schemes of the 'ages of man' current in the Middle Ages, which divided life into schemes of three, four, six, or seven ages.[46] As Sally Crawford points out, Old English not only had words for child (*cild* and *bearn*), but for childhood (*cildhad*), childish (*cildisc*) and childishness (*cildsung*).[47] In response to the suggestion that medieval parents might not have formed strong affective bonds with their children in the way that modern parents do, as a protective measure against the emotional pain of losing many of them given high child mortality rates, we might quote from the fourteenth-century English poem *Pearl*. The poem opens with the narrator beside the grave of his infant child, and these lines describe his grief:

> Bifore that spot my honde I spenned
> For care ful colde that to me caght;
> A devely dele in my hert denned,
> Thagh resoun sette myselven saght.
> I playned my perle that ther was spenned
> Wyth fyrce skylles that faste faght;
> Thagh kynde of Kryst me comfort kenned,
> My wrecched wylle in wo ay wraghte. (*Pearl*, 49–56)[48]

---

[44] Shahar, pp. 59–60.

[45] For an overview of research, see Hanawalt, 'Medievalists and the Study of Childhood.'

[46] J. A. Burrow, *The Ages of Man: A Study in Medieval Writing and Thought* (Oxford: Oxford University Press, 1996), pp. 2, 6, 12–19, 33–35, 72, 80.

[47] Crawford, p. 45.

[48] *Sir Gawain and the Green Knight, Pearl, Cleanness, Patience*, ed. J. J. Anderson (London: Dent, 1996).

However literally or not we might read the opening of *Pearl*, it seems that the poet can expect an audience to recognize a parent's grief on loss of a child.

Although child mortality from natural causes was high in the Middle Ages,[49] there were also, inevitably, unwanted children, or children whose parents were unable to raise them.[50] The Church attempted to enforce the protection of children against infanticide and accidental death, and attempted to prohibit abortion and contraception. The *Penitential of Theodore* prescribes a penance of fifteen years for infanticide, but a lesser penance of either seven or ten years' penance for infanticide by a poor woman.[51] It prescribes penance of one year for the abortion of a child if less than forty days have passed since conception, but abortion following forty days is to be treated as murder. Penances are also prescribed for neglect on the part of parents or others for allowing children to die unbaptized.[52] Contraception was also condemned, most severely in the *Decretals*, which regarded its use as homicide, although this was not the generally accepted position of the Church.[53]

Later medieval English statutes show concern that intercourse too near to childbirth may harm the child.[54] They also warn against the dangers of overlaying infants who share a bed with adults. 3 Worcester 27 states:

> Prohibeanturque singulis diebus dominicis per presbiteros tam matres quam nutrices iuxta se teneros pueros collocare ne forte contingat per earum iniuriam seu incuriam pueros suffocari, set in cunabilis iaceant firmiter fulciendis.[55]

> And it should be prohibited strongly by priests, on each Sunday, for mothers and for nurses to place young children beside them (in bed), lest it should happen through their fault or negligence that the children are suffocated, but they are to lie in cradles with strong supports.

The parents of suffocated infants were liable to prosecution: in a London case of 1496, the couple may have been cleared because the compurgators testified that the child had died of sickness. In another London case, in 1490, Joan Foster was prosecuted for crushing two infants in her bed: one hers, the other belonging to Joan Paris.[56] Helmholz notes that most prosecutions for infanticide in the

---

[49] Shahar, p. 149, suggests that 20% to 30% of infants died in the first year, and only 50% reached the age of five.

[50] J. A. Tasoulias, '*Wulf and Eadwacer* Reconsidered,' *Medium Aevum* 65 (1996), 1–18, suggests that the Old English poem *Wulf and Eadwacer* may be interpreted as representing the distress of a mother whose child born out of wedlock has been subjected to death by exposure by members of her community.

[51] For the influence of this canon, see Noonan, *Contraception*, pp. 159–60.

[52] McNeill and Gamer, pp. 197–98.

[53] Danielle Jacquart and Claude Thomasset, *Sexuality and Medicine in the Middle Ages*, trans. Matthew Adamson (Princeton: Princeton University Press, 1988), p. 93.

[54] Powicke and Cheney, I, 222.

[55] Powicke and Cheney, I, 302.

[56] Hair, pp. 103, 134.

province of Canterbury in the fifteenth century were for suffocation, and he suggests that almost all of these were cases of overlaying.[57]

As Shulamith Shahar notes, a medieval childhood is shorter than a modern one, at least in the sense that entry into the workforce was not delayed for as long as it is nowadays. On the other hand, children might serve long apprenticeships, or wait a long time to achieve financial independence, and so might not be regarded as fully adult by other members of society any earlier than today.[58] Dante, for example, reckons *adolescenza* to last until twenty-five.[59] The experience of preparation for adult roles varied according to social class, and the occupation that the child was preparing for. The heirs of the nobility were raised at home. Other noble boys were sent to court to enter service, becoming pages at quite young ages, perhaps between seven and ten years of age. Serious military training followed at around twelve, and the children became knights between the ages of fifteen and nineteen.[60] Children destined for ecclesiastical life attended school, as did the children of prosperous urban families for a few years at least, prior to leaving home to begin their apprenticeships as merchants or bankers.[61] Peasant children were raised at home, and gradually participated in the labour force.[62]

Children might also be raised in families other than their own. Sally Crawford argues that Anglo-Saxon fosterage fell into three main categories. The most common was where a nurse was brought into an élite household to help in raising the child. A second alternative was the placing of the child in another house, often that of a relative, which Crawford suggests might have been the equivalent of sending a child to school. Finally, there were circumstances in which a child might enter another household, not on a temporary basis, but permanently, giving rights of inheritance.[63] Lorraine Lancaster observes that Anglo-Saxon kinship was extended in various ways through semi-kinship (the existence of 'half' brothers and sisters through remarriage), ritual kinship (godparenting), and quasi-kinship, which applied in particular to fostering. Old English had a wide terminology relating to quasi-kinship through fostering – *foster fæder, fostor modor, foster cild, foster bearn, fosterling, fosterbroðor* and *foster sweostor* are all found.[64] As Crawford observes, extending family ties through fostering might have proved a protection against orphanage in an era of high mortality.[65] Fostering continued through the

---

[57] R. H. Helmholz, 'Infanticide in the Province of Canterbury during the Fifteenth Century,' in R. H. Helmholz, *Canon Law and the Law of England* (London: Hambledon, 1987), pp. 157–68 (p. 160) (first published in *The History of Childhood Quarterly* 2 (1975), 379–90).

[58] Shahar, p. 29.

[59] Burrow, *Ages of Man*, p. 7.

[60] Shahar, pp. 209–11.

[61] Shahar, pp. 225–27.

[62] Shahar, p. 242.

[63] Crawford, pp. 122–26.

[64] Lancaster, p. 239.

[65] Crawford, pp. 129–30.

later medieval period, although formal adoption with inheritance rights was outlawed (with the occasional *de facto* adoption proving the exception).[66] In part, fostering could be a means of preparing a child for adult life. As Barbara A. Hanawalt comments:

> Much rested on adolescent children's placement. It was in those forma-tive years that parents had to think ahead to the formation of advan-tageous marriages, perpetuation of the lineage, and establishment of careers or sufficient landed property. Well-born parents also wanted their children trained in life-skills: manners, languages, ease in social discourse, demeanor, and physical attractiveness were essential to a successful young courtier, male or female.[67]

Placing a child in a well-connected household, then, was providing them with a practical education in the skills they would need later in life. What work a young child might be expected to do in their adoptive household can be guessed at from a late medieval conduct poem for young children, *The Babees Book*, directed at 'yee Babees in housholde that done duelle.'[68] The poem directs children:

> Yif that yee se youre lorde or youre lady
> Touching the housholde speke of any thinge,
> Latt theym alloone, for that is curtesy,
> And entremete yow nouhte of theyre doynge,
> But be Ay Redy withe-oute feynynge
> At hable tyme to done your lorde service,
> So shalle yee gete anoone a name of price.
> Also to brynge drynke, holde lihte whanne tyme ys,
> Or to doo that whiche ouhte forto be done.   (lines 106–14)[69]

Essentially, children seem to be expected to fetch and carry, perform basic house-hold tasks, and to learn manners (particularly when to speak and when not to). Fostering was not always a happy and successful experience for medieval children.[70] But sending their children to be raised in other households does not necessarily indicate a lack of parental concern and affection for the well-being of their offspring. We do sometimes see children exploited in the interests of adults: we have already seen cases of children coerced into marriage, and the practice of wardship places the financial interests of adults above the needs of the ward. We sometimes see exploitation in fostering also, as when the taking of a child into a

---

66 Shahar, pp. 124–25.
67 Barbara A. Hanawalt, 'Female Networks for Fostering Lady Lisle's Daughters,' in *Medieval Mothering*, ed. John Carmi Parsons and Bonnie Wheeler (New York and London: Garland, 1996), pp. 239–58 (p. 241).
68 *The Babees Book*, ed. Frederick J. Furnivall (London: Early English Texts Society, 1868), p. 2.
69 *Babees Book*, ed. Furnivall, p. 5.
70 Hanawalt, 'Female Networks,' p. 254.

household results from hostage-taking as part of a political settlement. But this is not true of the practice in general: there is ample evidence in medieval law, literature, and practice that medieval parents cared for their children. Whatever the differences between medieval and modern families, both are capable of being affectionate.

7

After Marriage

Divorce

Saint Augustine viewed Christian marriage as a lifelong commitment. In his formulation of the three goods of marriage as *fides, proles, et sacramentum*, the sacramentality of marital union referred to the indissolubility of the marital bond. Augustine's model of the indissoluble marriage was influential throughout the Middle Ages, and, in the later Middle Ages, the marriage vow taken in England contains within it an expression of the lifelong nature of the commitment being made. Partners took one another as spouses 'tyll dethe vs departe.'[1] Christian disapproval of divorce was an innovation: divorce was legal in ancient Jewish law, as it was in ancient Rome and in early medieval Germanic law.[2] Consequently it took the medieval Church a long time to succeed in promoting its idea that marriage was an indissoluble union. In early medieval England, we can see Christian moralists permitting divorce on a number of grounds. The *Penitential of Theodore* permits remarriage in a number of circumstances. A man may remarry if his spouse commits fornication (but a woman may not). A woman may remarry if her husband becomes a slave through theft, or fornication, or some other offence, but only if it is her first marriage. A deserted husband may remarry after five years with the bishop's consent if he and his wife have not been reconciled. Men and women whose spouses have been taken into captivity or abducted by enemies may remarry: the regulations vary on the length of time they must wait before remarriage, and on the question of which partner should be recognized if the original spouse returns after remarriage has taken place.[3] These concessions regarding slavery and captivity are perhaps best seen as Christian doctrine adapting itself to the harsh realities of life in Anglo-Saxon England. James A. Brundage argues that divorce by mutual consent was common in seventh- and eighth-century

---

[1] *Manuale et Processionale*, Appendix 1, p. 19*.
[2] Brundage, *Law, Sex, and Christian Society*, pp. 53, 94–96, 114–17, 131.
[3] McNeill and Gamer, pp. 208–10.

Gaul, and probably elsewhere too: divorce for adultery was generally sanctioned, as was remarriage following such separations. But Brundage argues that this changes at the end of the eighth century: adultery remained grounds for separation, but such separations no longer permitted remarriage.[4] As the Middle Ages progressed, and the Church gradually gained control over the jurisdiction of marriage, the notion of marriage as a lifelong commitment, made between two persons joined together by God in a bond not to be undone by man, gained the position of orthodoxy.

In the central and later Middle Ages, divorce remained in two forms. The first, divorce *a vinculo*, was what we would nowadays call an annulment. The second, divorce *a mensa et thoro*, was what we would call a separation. A divorce *a vinculo* was a release from the bond of marriage, granted on the grounds that the marriage had never been valid. Such a divorce could be granted if one of the parties already had an existing spouse, and so was not free to marry, or because of an impediment which meant that the marriage should never have taken place. The list of such potential impediments was a long one: a relationship of consanguinity or affinity might exist between the partners, it might be impossible to consummate the marriage because of impotence, the consent of one of the parties might have been obtained through force or fear. There might exist the 'impediment of crime' (where two adulterers promised to marry while one had a living spouse, or where two adulterers plotted the death of a living spouse). Consent might have been exchanged where one or both of the parties were underage. Error of person or error of condition might have occurred, or solemn religious vows or major holy orders might have been taken by one of the parties before the marriage. Finally, if one of the couple was not a Christian, the marriage might be dissolved.[5] Despite the length of this list of grounds for divorce, R. H. Helmholz's survey of English matrimonial litigation finds that in fact there is very little litigation for divorce in later medieval England on any grounds.[6] All of these reasons for obtaining a divorce *a vinculo* are concerned with the giving of consent at the moment when the marriage is contracted. Even allowing divorce on the grounds of impotence is related to the issue of consent, for impotence is seen as a pre-existing condition which renders the afflicted person permanently unable to consent to marriage. These reasons for divorce in later medieval canon law, then, reflect the law's focus on consent as creating the bond. Marriages can be dissolved, or rather, declared invalid, because of defects in the consent given at the moment when they were contracted. Medieval canon law contrasts with the laws of other societies which allow for the dissolution of marriages not only because of questions regarding the validity of the initial consent, but also because of events that might occur later in a marriage, such as adultery on the part of one of the parties, for example. These were not seen as

4   Brundage, *Law, Sex, and Christian Society*, pp. 143–44.
5   Helmholz, *Marriage Litigation*, pp. 74–100.
6   Helmholz, *Marriage Litigation*, p. 74.

grounds for dissolving a marriage. Rather, an irreconcilable crisis in a marriage could lead to a divorce *a mensa et thoro*, where couples could obtain permission to avoid sharing a bed and table. But although such a separation meant that the married couple no longer had to behave as man and wife towards one another, they remained married, and could not remarry until the death of their spouse. Divorces *a mensa et thoro* could be granted if one of the spouses committed adultery, was an heretic or an apostate, or committed acts of cruelty towards their spouse. Helmholz finds that almost all cases relate to the last of these.[7]

We cannot rely entirely on the ecclesiastical courts for evidence about marital breakdown in later medieval England, however. Many people attempted to regulate their own matrimonial affairs without recourse to the Church courts.[8] An example can be seen in a 1294 document agreeing terms of separation between Edmund, earl of Cornwall, and his wife Margaret, who had been pursuing him in the ecclesiastical courts for the restoration of her conjugal rights. The agreement makes a financial settlement, and both parties agree to abandon litigation.[9] Unsurprisingly, the Church condemned such pacts where both parties agreed not to sue for the restoration of conjugal rights and effected their own separations in so doing.[10] R. H. Helmholz's survey of marriage litigation finds a large number of cases of 'self-divorce,' where people believe that they have a valid canonical reason for divorce, but do not bring the case before the ecclesiastical court, preferring to settle the matter privately, a practice condemned in 1 Winchester 59 (1224).[11] Because of the consent model and the consequent legality of clandestine unions, these cases of self-divorce and remarriage only come to light when the discarded partner sues in the ecclesiastical court for the enforcement of the original marriage contract: Helmholz notes that the allegation of a pre-existing marriage was the most frequent way in which marriages were dissolved in the medieval courts.[12] Again, then, we might argue that the Church's own consensual model of marriage actually hinders it in the implementation of its doctrine.

Insofar as it was determined by the ecclesiastical courts, then, the availability of divorce was severely restricted in later medieval England. In theory, remarriage was for the most part available only on the death of a spouse. But there is some evidence that people also seem to have regulated their matrimonial affairs privately, outside of the jurisdiction of the courts, and that such extra-judicial self-regulation applied to matters such as separation and divorce as well as clandestine marriage. The overall extent of this in practice is difficult to judge.

---

[7] Helmholz, *Marriage Litigation*, pp. 100–101.
[8] Helmholz, *Marriage Litigation*, p. 31.
[9] Rothwell, pp. 832–34.
[10] Helmholz, *Marriage Litigation*, p. 103.
[11] Helmholz, *Marriage Litigation*, p. 58; Powicke and Cheney, I, 135.
[12] Helmholz, *Marriage Litigation*, pp. 57, 64.

Widowhood and bereavement: Ecclesiastical attitudes

In the Middle Ages, as now, men predeceased women on the whole, and so it is widows rather than widowers who are prominent in medieval society. Widows are prominent because of their social status, which differed from that of all other women. As Barbara A. Hanawalt puts it: 'widows were an object of concern in medieval society. On the one hand, they could be vulnerable, but, on the other, they were potentially independent, powerful individuals.'[13] It is independence which grants medieval English widows their potential power. Whereas wives had no control over property during their marriages, and their husbands acted legally for them under the common law,[14] widows, in contrast, were legally and financially independent.

Ecclesiastical suspicion of widows finds expression in concern at their status as sexually experienced but unmarried women. The Church encouraged women to take vows of chastity rather than remarry, chaste widowhood occupying a position in the three grades of chastity superior to marriage, although inferior to that of virginity. Jack Goody suggests that the Church's aversion to the remarriage of widows stems from a time when widows and orphans were cared for by the Christian community to prevent their remarriage to pagans,[15] and James A. Brundage suggests that the Church in the later Middle Ages might still have been under an obligation to assist widows as 'disadvantaged persons.'[16] Two examples of widows taking vows of chastity and being dispensed from them afterwards are seen firstly in a papal letter of May 1354 to the bishop of Lichfield, and secondly in a letter of June 1403 from the pope to the prior of Holy Trinity, York. The first letter permits the marriage of John de Gresley and Joan Warteneys, despite the fact that Joan took a vow of chastity on the death of her first husband, John Warteneys, and received a ring and a mantle in token of her vow.[17] The second letter allows Margaret, widow of William de Slengesby, to commute the vow of chastity that she hastily made after her husband's death into other works of piety, on the grounds that because of the frailty of the flesh she feared that she would not be able to keep her vow, and therefore desired to marry.[18]

---

[13] Barbara A. Hanawalt, 'Remarriage as an Option for Urban and Rural Widows in Late Medieval England,' in *Wife and Widow in Medieval England*, ed. Sue Sheridan Walker (Ann Arbor: University of Michigan Press, 1993), pp. 141–64 (p. 141).

[14] *Britton*, I, 227, 339–40; *Bracton*, III, 358–59; Pollock and Maitland, I, 485.

[15] Goody, p. 65.

[16] James A. Brundage, 'Widows as Disadvantaged Persons in Medieval Canon Law,' in *Upon My Husband's Death: Widows in the Literature and Histories of Medieval Europe* (Ann Arbor: University of Michigan Press, 1992), pp. 193–206.

[17] *Papal Letters. Vol. III. A.D.1342–1362*, ed. Bliss and Johnson, p. 561.

[18] *Calendar of Entries in the Papal Registers relating to Great Britain and Ireland. Papal Letters. Vol. V. AD 1396–1404*, ed. W. H. Bliss and J. A. Twemlow (London: HMSO, 1904), p. 536; on the commuting of vows of chastity, see Elliott, pp. 158–62.

While chaste widowhood was regarded by the Church as preferable to remarriage, which it termed 'bigamy,' remarriage was regarded as preferable to fornication, and the frailty of the flesh of widows in particular finds Biblical expression. To quote from the First Epistle of St Paul to Timothy:

5:9. Vidua eligatur non minus sexaginta annorum quae fuerit unius viri uxor.

5:10. In operibus bonis testimonium habens si filios educavit si hospitio recepit si sanctorum pedes lavit si tribulationem patientibus subministravit si omne opus bonum subsecuta est.

5:11. Adulescentiores autem viduas devita cum enim luxuriatae fuerint in Christo nubere volunt.

5:12. Habentes damnationem quia primam fidem irritam fecerunt.

5:13. Simul autem et otiosae discunt circumire domos non solum otiosae sed et verbosae et curiosae loquentes quae non oportet.

5:14. Volo ergo iuveniores nubere filios procreare matres familias esse nullam occasionem dare adversario maledicti gratia.

5:15. Iam enim quaedam conversae sunt retro Satanan.

5:9. Let a widow be chosen of no less than threescore years of age, who hath been the wife of one husband.

5:10. Having testimony for her good works, if she have brought up children, if she have received to harbour, if she have washed the saints' feet, if she have ministered to them that suffer tribulation, if she have diligently followed every good work.

5:11. But the younger widows avoid. For, when they have grown wanton in Christ, they will marry;

5:12. Having damnation, because they have made void their first faith.

5:13. And, withal being idle, they learn to go about from house to house; and are not only idle, but tattlers also and busy-bodies, speaking things which they ought not.

5:14. I will, therefore, that the younger should marry, bear children, be mistresses of families, give no occasion to the adversary to speak evil.

5:15. For some are already turned aside after Satan.

Paul's fear of widows wandering from house to house finds an echo in medieval representations of chaste widows as leading secluded lives: one sermon story represents Judith as 'a clene wedowe, and sche held hir priveliche in clos in hir hous with hir women and wolde noght goon out.'[19] In Chaucer's *Troilus and Criseyde*, Criseyde, when invited to dance by her uncle, suggests (perhaps tongue in cheek) that it would be more appropriate to her status as a widow for her to sit in a cave, to pray, and to read the lives of saints.

English ecclesiastical statutes of the thirteenth century clearly display the Church's disapproval of second and subsequent marriages. They did not prevent

---

[19] Owst, p. 119.

widows from remarrying, but they did impose penalties on priests who blessed second or subsequent marriages. To quote from 3 Worcester 26 (1240):

> Provideant insuper capellani quod secundo nubentibus benedictionem solemnpnem decetero non inpendant sicut penas canonicas voluerint evitare.[20]

> Chaplains shall see, moreover, that they do not bestow from now on a solemn blessing on women who remarry, just as they shall have wished to avoid canonical penalties.

That penalties were imposed on English priests who blessed second marriages seems clear from a letter of November 1353 from the pope to the bishop of Exeter, granting him permission to absolve certain priests who had incurred censure by blessing second marriages.[21] One version of 2 Exeter 7, dating from 1287, forbids the blessing of second marriages of both male and female 'bigamists,' i.e. persons who remarry, as follows:

> Caveant enim sacerdotes ne bigamum vel bigamiam transeuntes ad secunda vota benedicere presumant sub pena canonica, quia secunde nuptie benedici non debent [. . .].

> For priests should beware that they do not dare to bless, under canonical penalties, bigamists, male or female, crossing towards second vows, because it is not becoming for a second marriage to be blessed [. . .].[22]

The statute then goes on to cite a decretal of Alexander III, which is included in the canonical collection *Decretals of Gregory IX*. The second statutes of Durham (1241 × 1249) give a slightly paraphrased extract from the same decretal:

> Item, ne vir nec mulier ad bigamiam transiens a presbitero benedicatur, quia, cum alia vice sint benedici, benedictio eorum iterari non debet.

> Likewise, a man or a woman passing into bigamy should not be blessed by a priest, because, since they have been blessed on another occasion, it is not fitting for their blessing to be repeated.[23]

The disapproval of bigamy expressed in these later medieval statutes echoes similar opinions from the early medieval period.[24] The medieval Church, then, adopts a role as a protector of widows, but is suspicious of their status as unmarried but sexually experienced women. It therefore tries to steer them into religious life through vows of chastity, or, despite its unease about bigamy, into remarriage.

---

[20] Powicke and Cheney, I, 302.
[21] *Papal Letters. Vol. III. AD 1342–1362*, ed. Bliss and Johnson, p. 513.
[22] Powicke and Cheney, I, 997, note 'q'.
[23] Powicke and Cheney, I, 433.
[24] See McNeill and Gamer, pp. 195–96 on early medieval penances for bigamy.

Widows and property

Anglo-Saxon laws which mention widows are largely concerned with their protection. The seventh-century laws of Æthelbert of Kent offer protection for widows and their property:

> 75. Mund þare betstan widuwan eorlcundre L scillinga gebete.
> 75.1. Ðare oþre XX scll', ðare þriddan XII scll', þare feorðan VI scll'.
> 76. Gif man widuwan unagne genimeþ, II gelde seo munde sy.

> 75. The compensation to be paid for the violation of the *mund* of a widow of the best class, [that is, of a widow] of the nobility, shall be 50 shillings.
> 75.1. For violation of the *mund* of a widow of the second class, 20 shillings; of the third class, 12 shillings; of the fourth class, 6 shillings.
> 76. If a man takes a widow who does not [of right] belong to him, double the value of the *mund* shall be paid.[25]

Carole Hough notes that the consensus of scholarly opinion is that clauses 75 and 76 deal with the abduction of widows, who apparently occupied a subordinate position under the protection or guardianship of members of their kin. She argues that in fact the correct interpretation is the reverse of that, and that it was the widows who extended protection to their household. Hough translates these clauses as follows:

> 75. The right of protection of a widow of the highest class of the nobility is to be compensated for at 50 shillings.
> 75.1. That of one of the second class, at 20 shillings; of one of the third class, at 12 shillings; of one of the fourth class, at 6 shillings.
> 76. If anyone takes a widow who is not his own [legal wife], [the penalty] is twice the value of the right of protection.[26]

The early eleventh-century laws of Cnut also discuss the status of widows, specifying that they should not remarry for a year after their bereavement, but allowing them free choice thereafter.[27] They also allow widows up to a year to pay the heriot on their property.[28] Neither, the laws specify, should widows be consecrated as nuns with excessive haste. The laws dictate that if a widow does choose to marry within a year of bereavement she loses her morning gift and property from the

---

[25] Attenborough, pp. 14, 15.
[26] Hough, 'The Widow's *Mund*,' p. 16; for the alternative interpretation, see Fell, p. 61.
[27] The *Penitential of Theodore* contains a clause stating that a widow can remarry after a year, but a widower after a month: McNeill and Gamer; Fell, p. 61, notes that Cnut's laws repeat Æðelræd's code of 1008 in their regulations concerning widows, as does Whitelock, p. 429 n. 2.
[28] *MED* s.v. *heriet* (n.) '(a) A payment made, by the heir(s to the lord of the manor, upon the death of a tenant.'

first marriage. This applies even if the marriage has taken place through force, unless the widow is willing to leave the man and return home (implying perhaps that some widows might consent to their own abduction).[29]

Magna Carta guarantees the widow the property which her husband endowed her with when they married and any inherited property held by both spouses. On the question of remarriage, it balances the doctrine of consent against the *realpolitik* of feudal politics in stating that widows would not be forced to marry, but that, if they do wish to do so, they must obtain the consent of the lords to whom they owe homage.[30] This condition was enforced: an example is the agreement of Margaret, widow of Hugh de Courtenay, earl of Devon, not to marry without Richard II's licence.[31]

Later medieval English law provides extensive and detailed regulations concerning dower: the existence of extensive regulations relating to dower contrasts with the lack of regulation attached to curtesy, the equivalent life tenancy for the husband who survives his wife in his wife's property, but, as Milsom points out: 'Curtesy was not, like dower, itself a tenure, and was not held of the heir as an internal arrangement within the wife's inheritance. Indeed it was not really a separate entity, and was slow to acquire even a name. Nor was it a frequent object of litigation because the husband never had to sue for the land: he had held it since the day of his marriage.'[32]

The property which a widow held in dower was held in free tenure for life, and would revert to the heir after her death. Consequently, there were limitations on what might be done with the property: the widow was entitled to use and enjoy it, but without waste, destruction, or exile.[33] The Statute of Gloucester (1278) makes provision for recovery against widows who commit waste, or who sell or grant away their tenements held in dower.[34] Because the widow holds her dower through a life tenure, in legal actions concerning the property in dower, she vouches to warranty: the role of the warrantor (the heir) is to defend the widow and her property against the plaintiff.[35] Widows could not sue in actions concerning their dower without their warrantor,[36] but this was not a general limitation on the legal standing of widows comparable to the ban on wives suing without their husbands: it applied only to actions concerning dower. The failure of the warrantor to appear in court did not adversely affect the widow's action.[37] Neither did the warrantor's granting of land that constituted dower to a third party adversely affect either the widow or the third party, for one kept the land,

---

[29] Whitelock, p. 429.

[30] Rothwell, p. 318.

[31] *Calendar of Close Rolls: Richard II. Vol. I* (London: HMSO, 1914), p. 33; for the writ brought against widows married contrary to *Magna Carta*, see *Novae Narrationes*, ed. Shanks and Milsom, p. 271.

[32] Milsom, pp. 168–69; For local customs relating to curtesy, see Bateson, II, 112–15.

[33] *Bracton*, ed. Woodbine, trans. Thorne, III, 405.

[34] Rothwell, p. 417.

[35] *Britton*, ed. Nicholls, II, 272.

[36] *Bracton*, ed. Woodbine, trans. Thorne, III, 358–59.

[37] *Bracton*, ed. Woodbine, trans. Thorne, III, 364–65.

and the other was provided with *escambium* (land to replace that lost) by the war-rantor.[38] The nature of the widow's tenure, however, did mean that there were limi-tations on the types of plea that were admissible in her (manorial) court.[39]

It was not possible to increase or decrease the dower constituted at the church door.[40] That dower could not be decreased, however, was to the widow's advan-tage. Dower was exempted from paying the debts due on the estate of the deceased: all debts were paid from the inheritance.[41] Land from a specified dower alienated by the husband through the king's court by means of a fine was recov-erable by the widow (the heir was obliged to grant *escambium* to the feoffee).[42] Even where the land was lost through a legal judgment, if the widow could prove deceit or negligence on the part of her husband in losing the case, she could recover the property.[43] As Holdsworth points out, dower receives a greater level of protection than that accorded to the property due to the heir.[44] The level of pro-tection accorded to dower by the common law, however, was sometimes under-mined by local custom. In Lincoln, for example, a custumal from 1240 states that a husband might sell the land that he had promised his wife in dower in case of necessity. Similar customs survive from the custumals of Bury St Edmund's (1304), Bury (1327), Godmanchester (1324), Nottingham (1276–1301), and Nottingham (1358).[45] Some of the customs insisted that the wife had to benefit from the sale of the land promised to her in dower, others did not. All undermined the protection accorded to dower by the common law.

Magna Carta states that the widow's dower should be assigned to her within forty days of her husband's death, a statement echoed by the legal treatises.[46] Should the widow fail to receive her dower, or fail to receive her dower in full, a number of writs were available to her for its recovery, depending on the circumstances of the case. Of these, the most important were the writ of dower *unde nihil habet*, pleaded in the king's court, where the widow had not received any of her dower, and the writ of right of dower, where the widow had received part of her dower, which could be pleaded in the lord's court.[47] The pleading of writs of right in the lord's court does not mean that the king relinquished authority: in the writ, the king orders the lord to do right by the widow, and states that, if the lord will not, the sheriff will.[48]

---

38 *Bracton*, ed. Woodbine, trans. Thorne, III, 365–67.
39 *Bracton*, ed. Woodbine, trans. Thorne, II, 281; *Britton*, ed. Nichols, II, 252; *Fleta, Volume IV: Book V and Book VI*, ed. and trans. G. O. Sayles, Selden Society vol. 99 (London: Selden Society, 1984), p. 79.
40 *Britton*, ed. Nichols, II, 245, 269–70.
41 *Bracton*, ed. Woodbine, trans. Thorne, II, 180, 281.
42 *Bracton*, ed. Woodbine, trans. Thorne, III, 370.
43 *Bracton*, ed. Woodbine, trans. Thorne, III, 392–93.
44 Holdsworth, III, 162.
45 Bateson, II, 103–5.
46 Rothwell, p. 318; *Bracton*, ed. Woodbine, trans. Thorne, II, 275–76; *Britton*, ed. Nichols, II, 246; *Fleta*, p. 77.
47 *Britton*, ed. Nichols, II, 254–56, 292.
48 Milsom, pp. 124–25.

Where two or more women claimed dower, the matter was referred to the ecclesiastical court to decide which was the lawful wife, but limitations were placed upon that court's inquiries into the matter. *Bracton* states that a decision should be sent back to the king's court despite any appeal by the losing side.[49] This is partly through fear that appeals may cause the whole matter to be protracted indefinitely, something which we can also see in ecclesiastical legislation.[50] *Bracton* also clearly displays a concern, however, that the case should return to the secular jurisdiction speedily for fear of usurpation of its role by the ecclesiastical jurisdiction.[51] These regulations applied only where the case was referred from the secular courts to the ecclesiastical for a decision: when a dower case appeared in the secular court and a judgment on the validity of the marriage had already been made in the ecclesiastical court, appeals were taken into account.[52] Divorce invalidated the constitution of dower, as did adultery.[53] Subsequent reconciliations were acceptable to the secular jurisdiction only as long as they were not reconciliations enforced by the ecclesiastical courts.[54]

Despite the existence of many laws protecting them and their property, however, propertied widows might still be vulnerable to exploitation in the later Middle Ages. A papal letter of December 1363 to the bishop of Lincoln concerns the case of Margaret de Boslingthorpe, a widow, whose property was seized by Roger Haunstredi, a knight, who alleged a previous contract of marriage between them. The papal letter indicates that Roger has destroyed buildings and manor walls, wasted the woods, and alienated Margaret's land and possessions. The pope instructs the bishop to take control of Margaret's property while the case is pending, and to pay a portion of the income from the property to Roger.[55] This reads like a slightly updated version of the abduction of widows in Anglo-Saxon England: Roger seizes the property, alleges a clandestine marriage, and spends the proceeds while waiting for the Church courts to decide the issue.

The economics of remarriage

The law's guarantee of the right of widows not to remarry makes a difference at the top end of medieval English society. Rowena Archer's survey of 151 fifteenth-century noble holdings estimates that of the 495 holders of these titles, 375 were

---

[49] *Bracton*, ed. Woodbine, trans. Thorne, III, 385.

[50] E.g. The archbishop of Canterbury's outlawing of tuitorial appeals in marriage cases in 1342: Wilkins, II, 683.

[51] Cf. the similar concern expressed in different circumstances in *Bracton*, ed. Woodbine, trans. Thorne, III, 373.

[52] *Bracton*, ed. Woodbine, trans. Thorne, III, 385–86.

[53] *Bracton*, ed. Woodbine, trans. Thorne, II, 266, III, 372; *Britton*, ed. Nichols, II, 281–82; *Fleta* ed. Sayles, p. 74.

[54] *Britton*, ed. Nichols, II, 281–82.

[55] *Papal Letters. Vol. IV. AD 1362–1404*, ed. Bliss and Twemlow, pp. 44–45.

widows: therefore 76% of noble holdings were reduced by at least one third (the minimum endowment) for an average of seventeen years between 1400 and 1500.[56] Joel T. Rosenthal's examination of the 1436 parliamentary assessment of landed incomes also shows noble widows to be prominent: the 1436 assessment shows thirty-four peerages in male hands, thirteen shared between male heirs and dowager peeresses, and five under the control of dowagers. Rosenthal's survey of fifteenth-century peerages finds that 46% remarried, with over half of the younger widows remarrying, and with a tendency to remarry within a year or two of bereavement or not at all.[57]

At the other end of the social scale, the existence of remarriage as an option for widows seems to have varied depending on demographic and economic factors. J. Z. Titow shows that on the manor of Taunton in the thirteenth century, scarcity of land meant that marrying widows was an important means of access to property for men. His statistics for Taunton from 1270 to 1315 show that between 8.1% and 12.3% of holdings acquired in this period were obtained through marriages with widows, which account for between 21.6% and 32.6% of all marriages found. This contrasts with lower figures for manors where land reclamation meant easier access to land in the same period.[58] But if men married widows to gain control of their property in the later thirteenth and early fourteenth centuries, there is evidence for a collapse in the demand for property-holding widows in rural England after the plague. In his analysis of the manor of Halesowen, Zvi Razi argues that the post-plague period saw a greater availability of land, and a decline in the age at first marriage for women.[59] Of the widows noted in the court rolls of Halesowen between 1349 and 1400, 26% remarried, but this contrasts with a figure of 63% for the period 1270 to 1348.[60] Also, four of the nine *leyrwites*, manorial fines for fornication, recorded between 1349 and 1396 were paid by widows, in contrast with a figure of 8% for the pre-plague period, when there was a much larger number of *leyrwites* in total.[61] This suggests a much lower percentage of young unmarried women having premarital sex, suggesting perhaps that it was easier for young women to get married in the second half of the century, and that they married younger. Jack Ravensdale's analysis of the Cambridgeshire manor of Cottenham suggests that, before the plague, high fines

---

[56] Rowena E. Archer, ' "How ladies ... who live on manors ought to manage their households and estates": Women as Landholders and Administrators in the Later Middle Ages,' in *Woman is a Worthy Wight: Women in Medieval English Society, c. 1200–1500*, ed. P. J. P. Goldberg (Stroud: Sutton, 1992), pp. 149–81 (p. 162).

[57] Joel T. Rosenthal, 'Fifteenth Century Widows and Widowhood: Bereavement, Integration, and Life Choices,' in *Wife and Widow in Medieval England*, ed. Sue Sheridan Walker (Ann Arbor: University of Michigan Press, 1993), pp. 33–58 (pp. 36–37, 42).

[58] J. Z. Titow, 'Some Differences between Manors and their Effects on the Condition of the Peasant in the Thirteenth Century,' *The Agricultural History Review* 10 (1962), 1–13 (pp. 8–9).

[59] Razi, pp. 135–37.

[60] Razi, p. 138.

[61] Razi, p. 139.

were extracted from those marrying widows with lands, and that these are an indication of land values: these fines collapse after the plague.[62] It would appear that widows and their lands were no longer the valuable commodity on the marriage market in the second half of the fourteenth century that they were in the first.[63] Ravensdale suggests, however, that widows in the second half of the fourteenth century might have used their economic independence to sell their land.[64] Although no longer is the same demand on the marriage market as previously, their economic status may have provided them with other options.

The literary widow: Chaucer's Wife of Bath

Widows may have presented a very visible exception to authoritative ideologies of female disability in later medieval England. Their freedom to exercise legal and economic rights otherwise restricted almost entirely to men would have obtained increased visibility as they were excluded from the marriage market by demographic factors in rural post-plague England. The exceptional position of widows might have been further highlighted given that they were the focus of sexual suspicion from the Church. With this evidence in mind, I want to turn to a literary text to see if we can link what I would argue to be its hostile portrayal of widows with the evidence that we have gathered elsewhere about the actual social position of widows and authoritative attitudes towards them. I want to argue that Chaucer's *Canterbury Tales* gives some prominence to widows, to show that the representation of widows in the *Canterbury Tales* re-presents authoritative antifeminist and antividual ideologies, and to suggest that this may have something to do with the real change in circumstances for widows in later fourteenth-century England argued for earlier.

The first widows that we come across in the *Canterbury Tales* are the two mothers-in-law of the *Man of Law's Tale*. Since there is no mention of their husbands, and since their sons hold power, it seems safe to assume that the Sultaness and Donegild, the mothers of Custance's two intended husbands, are widows. They are shown in a less than positive light. The Sultaness is described as 'Virago' and 'Semyrame the seconde' (II. 359). The *Riverside Chaucer* notes that, in Diodorus Siculus, Semiramis persuaded her husband to yield power to her for five days and then threw him in prison, and that in Boccaccio she usurps the throne from her son, and argues that 'virago' may be interpreted here as a woman usurping a man's office, citing the similar censure of Donegild at II. 782 as 'mannysh.'[65]

---

[62] Ravensdale, pp. 209–10.

[63] With the exception of London: see Hanawalt, 'Remarriage as an Option,' pp. 150–51.

[64] Ravensdale, pp. 213, 214.

[65] *Riverside Chaucer*, ed. Benson, p. 860; Cf. the contrary argument in Mann, *Geoffrey Chaucer*, p. 131, who argues that 'The active independence of the two "mannish" women [...] appears as mere illusion. [...] The Sultaness acts as the "instrument" of Satan's will; her independence becomes the tool of his designs.'

This description then casts doubt upon the Sultaness's nature as a woman: she is described as a 'serpent under femynynytee' (II. 360). A real hostility to widows may underlie the description of the Sultaness and Donegild: widows' exercising of economic and legal rights available to men, but not to wives and daughters, together with an increase in the number of widows who did not remarry and hence might exercise these rights, may have led to widows being regarded as usurping male roles, and so the characterization of these two widows as 'viragos' here is worth noting.[66] But these two characters are not central to the *Canterbury Tales*. If a real masculine hostility towards widows does underlie their character-ization in Chaucer's poem, then it must be regarded as centred on the Wife of Bath.

The translation of Middle English *wyf* as Modern English 'wife' is only par-tially accurate, both linguistically and as a definition of the character of the Wife of Bath. While Alison is, as Helen Cooper puts it, 'a *wife*, by both profession and vocation,'[67] she is also frequently a widow. D. J. Wurtele argues that husband number five, Jankyn, is not dead when she appears on the Canterbury pilgrim-age:[68] the reference in the Wife's tale to wise widows (III. 1027), if intended to be a humorous reference to the tale's narrator, would suggest that she is a widow, but, whatever her marital status when she appears in the poem, it is clear that she has often been widowed. Read in the context of the economic and demographic evidence already presented, David Aers's description of the Wife as working within the context of market relations by accumulating property and selling her body may well be a thing of the past by the time Chaucer is writing, because there may literally no longer be a market for widows.[69] In reality, a widow with 'lond and fee' (III. 631) might not have been such an attractive proposition in post-plague England. Nonetheless, the exercising by widows of economic and legal rights otherwise available only to men may underlie the portrayal of the Wife of Bath as demanding mastery in marriage, which the Church defines clearly as the husband's role.[70] Like the two widows of the *Man of Law's Tale*, in this respect she clearly acts as a virago.

Chaucer's portrayal of the Wife of Bath is part of a lengthy literary tradition of satirical treatment of widows: Alcuin Blamires traces this tradition from Ovid's description of the bawd Dipsas, through the passage from St Paul quoted earlier in this chapter, Gautier le Leu's thirteenth-century poem *La Veuve*, Jean de Meun's portrait of *la Vieille* in the *Roman de la Rose*, and Jehan le Fèvre's

---

[66] See J. C. Ward, *English Noblewomen in the Later Middle Ages* (Essex: Longman, 1992), pp. 2, 3; J. M. Bennett, 'Public Power and Authority in the Medieval English Countryside,' in *Women and Power in the Middle Ages*, ed. M. Erler and M. Kowaleski (London: University of Georgia Press, 1988), p. 23.

[67] Helen Cooper, *Oxford Guides to Chaucer: The Canterbury Tales* (Oxford: Oxford University Press, 1989), p. 143.

[68] D. J. Wurtele, 'Chaucer's Wife of Bath and the Problem of the Fifth Husband,' *Chaucer Review* 23 (1988), 117–28 (p. 119).

[69] David Aers, *Chaucer* (Brighton: Harvester, 1986), p. 70.

[70] As directly stated in canon law: Friedberg, I, 1254; English translation, Blamires, p. 84.

fourteenth-century translation of Mathieu of Boulogne's *Lamentations of Matheolus,* to Chaucer's poem.[71] Indeed, the tradition continues beyond Chaucer (and is indebted to him) in William Dunbar's fifteenth-century poem *The Tretis of the Twa Mariit Wemen and the Wedo.* The Wife's prologue also displays a debt to the values of *fabliau* in its use of sexual material for humour. That Chaucer's poem fits into traditions of *fabliau* and antividual satire might suggest that we should not read the portrait as being in some way a response to the realities of later medieval England. But while Chaucer's portrait engages with literary tradition, it also seems very specifically framed to portray the Wife as breaching contemporary ecclesiastical law.

The Wife's five marriages at the church door are mentioned twice: firstly in the portrait of the Wife in the *General Prologue* (I. 460–62) and later at the beginning of the *Wife of Bath's Prologue* (III. 6). Initially, the repeated reference to the marriages taking place at the church door seems like a realistic detail, but when we recall that priests were forbidden to bless the marriages of bigamists by several sets of synodal statutes, quoted earlier, the mention of the church door would seem instead to be designed to call attention to the fact that such marriages should not take place there, specifically because of the denunciations of bigamy that the Wife mentions at her prologue's outset (III. 9–20). We are told again in the description of her wedding to her fifth husband that it was celebrated with 'greet solempnytee' (III. 629).

The first reference to her marriages at the church door (I. 460) precedes the suggestion that she had committed fornication prior to her marriage (I. 461), which itself suggests that the mention of age twelve at III. 4 is not intended to provide her age at first marriage, but is a reference to the age at which marriage was canonically permitted – the age of consent. The mention of the church door, then, reinforces the suggestions made early in the Wife's prologue that she has behaved improperly in marrying five times, and may be intended to emphasize the portrayal of the Wife as lustful: she has married five times in violation of the Church's disapproval of bigamy.

The references to the church door may also have another significance, related to the Wife's accumulation of wealth. A husband's constitution of dower for his wife had to take place at the church door, and no exceptions were allowed. If the endowment was being made out of someone else's lands, they were required to assent at the church door to the endowment.[72] A written endowment made elsewhere had to be repeated at the church door to be valid.[73] The condition applied even under an interdict.[74] The insistence upon the endowment taking place at this specific location was due to the presence of the words 'at the church door' in the writs used to bring dower cases to court.[75] M. Teresa Tavormina has suggested that

[71]   Blamires, pp. 135–36, argues for the connections; the relevant texts are on pp. 21–23, 37, 135–44, 159–63, 187–88.
[72]   *Britton,* ed. Nichols, II, 244.
[73]   *Britton,* ed. Nichols, II, 276.
[74]   *Britton,* ed. Nichols, II, 268 and note 'm'.
[75]   *Britton,* ed. Nichols, II, 265; *Novae Narrationes,* ed. Shanks and Milsom, pp. 51, 224–26.

property transfers other than dower probably took place during the marriage cere-mony also.[76] The Wife tells us that she is rich (III. 606), and that her wealth was given to her, presumably by her husband in marriage, just as she in turn gives it to Jankyn, her fifth husband, at their wedding (III. 629–32). These references to mar-riage and property transfer, then, give the references to the church door a further resonance.

The Wife's fifth marriage is also portrayed as being contracted in a suspicious manner. The contract to marry is made by Alison and Jankyn, through words of consent spoken in the future tense, with a condition attached, before the death of her fourth husband:

> I spak to hym and seyde hym how that he,
> If I were wydwe, sholde wedde me.   (III. 567–68)

This contract, because it was entered into before the death of Alison's fourth hus-band, might in fact create an impediment to their marriage. 1 Salisbury 79 defines the impediment of crime as follows:

> De matrimonio prohibito.
> Moneant et prohibeant sacerdotes ne quisquam cum ea contrahat matrimonium quam vivente marito suo polluit per adulterium; et hoc si adulter fidem dederit adultere de ea ducenda adhuc viro suo vivente, vel etiam si ipsa adultera vel adulter in mortem viri machinati sunt.[77]

> Concerning forbidden marrriage.
> Priests are to warn and forbid anyone to marry a woman whom he has defiled through adultery while her husband was still alive; and likewise if an adulterer has promised an adulteress that he would marry her while her husband was still alive, and also if the adulteress herself or the adulterer plotted the death of the husband.

The impediment exists if there is adultery and either a contract of marriage between the adulterers while the husband is still alive, or a plot to kill the husband. There is certainly a contract of marriage between Alison and Jankyn: the question is whether or not they have also committed adultery. The Wife's berating of her earlier husband suggests that they might have done:

> And yet of oure apprentice Janekyn,
> For his crispe heer, shynynge as gold so fyn,
> And for he squiereth me bothe up and doun,

---

[76] Tavormina, p. 16 n. 36.

[77] Powicke and Cheney, I, 85–86; cf. the similar formula in Peter Lombard, *Sententiae*, II, 472; for judgments of Alexander III implementing this formula in actual cases, see Friedberg, II, 687–88; Helmholz, *Marriage Litigation*, p. 97, finds no cases of English divorces granted because of this impediment; Charles Donahue, Jr., 'Female Plaintiffs,' p. 189, finds four cases where the impediment is offered as a defence.

> Yet hastow caught a fals suspecioun.
> I wol hym noght, thogh thou were deed to-morwe!   (III. 303–7)

The tongue-in-cheek statement of III. 307 seems to find fulfilment later in the tale (assuming, that is, that Janekyn the apprentice (III. 303) and Jankyn the clerk (III. 629) are one and the same), but the sexual innuendo of III. 305 seems to suggest that something is already going on. Being 'squired' up and down may not seem a very innocent activity, especially given suggestions about the nocturnal activities of the Squire of the *General Prologue*. In her study of the portraits of the Monk and the Friar in the *General Prologue*, Jill Mann has suggested that Chaucer tends to offer linguistic suggestions of sexual licence rather than explicit description, and this seems to be the case here also.[78] There is a strong suggestion that Alison and Jankyn have contracted illegally, but it is not explicitly stated. Read in the context of contemporary ecclesiastical marriage law, then, the characterization of the Wife seems deliberately designed to suggest deviation from that law. Such a reading seems justified given the explicit construction of the *Wife of Bath's Prologue* in relation to textual authorities that underlie it.

The Wife's 856-line prologue overshadows her 408-line tale in a manner not found elsewhere in the *Canterbury Tales*. Effectively, two tales are allocated to the Wife, but placed on different narrative levels. The longer of the two is told within the context of a framing narrative, which is explicitly constructed as a representation of an external reality, and is presented in an autobiographical or confessional manner. Insofar as this is possible within a fiction, it is given the status of fact. The opening lines of the prologue present her character in the context of experience rather than authority:

> Experience, though noon auctoritee
> Were in this world, is right ynogh for me
> To speke of wo that is in mariage;   (III. 1–3)

As Helen Cooper points out, the Wife's prologue contains more material from textual authorities than any other part of the *Canterbury Tales*, with the exception of *Melibee*; even the lines just quoted in praise of experience over authority are an allusion to a similar argument in the *Roman de la Rose*.[79] But what is the authoritative status of the Wife's text in relation to the texts she cites? The character of the Wife is represented as invoking and transgressing against all manner of textual authorities, including, as we have just seen, ecclesiastical marriage law. Does authority reside with her text or with the authorities underlying it?

---

[78] Jill Mann, *Chaucer and Medieval Estates Satire: The Literature of Social Classes and the General Prologue to the Canterbury Tales* (London: Cambridge University Press, 1973), pp. 25, 42.
[79] Cooper, p. 144; Guillaume de Lorris and Jean de Meun, *The Romance of the Rose*, trans. Frances Horgan (Oxford: Oxford University Press, 1994), pp. 197–98.

A. J. Minnis states that for a text to possess *auctoritas*, authority, in a literary context, it had to have intrinsic worth, to say the right things, to conform with Christian truth.[80] Not all texts were equal in authority. The Bible was the most authoritative of texts, but the New Testament was more authoritative than the Old. Christian texts were more authoritative than pagan texts.[81] When a fourteenth-century vernacular text invokes authorities such as St Paul, St Jerome, and canon law, it is clear enough where authority lies according to late medieval literary theory. Minnis also notes Chaucer's fictional stance of not being the author, but rather the compiler of the *Canterbury Tales*, denying his responsibility for the words spoken by the Miller (I. 3167–75).[82] Such a fiction tends to suggest that the characters themselves are responsible for the authoritative status of each text: a suggestion that seems to be taken up by Thomas Hoccleve in his reference to the Wife as *auctrice*.[83] This raises the problem of female authority. In 1 Timothy 2:12, St Paul states: *Docere autem mulieri non permitto neque dominari in virum sed esse in silentio*, 'But I suffer not a woman to teach, nor to use authority over the man; but to be in silence.' Paul's injunction seems to make female authority an impossibility.

There is a long-standing critical divide on the question of positive or negative readings of the Wife of Bath. Mary Carruthers argues in a 1994 afterword to her famous essay on the Wife that it is contemporary critics rather than Chaucer's text who attempt to silence the Wife's powerful performance:

> The newness of Chaucer's Wife as a literary text lies in the fact that such power has been given to a female voice, without any effort on Chaucer's part to shut her up. Here the comparison with the Pardoner is again instructive, for he is silenced *within the text itself*. The impulse to shut the Wife up comes from readers, whom she variously frightens, repels and attracts, as we variously respond to her power.[84]

Carruthers's reading of the Wife is positive and compelling, but I think that in fact we can identify several ways in which the text tries to undermine the Wife and what she has to say. The Wife's prologue, already problematized in what it has to say by the textual authorities it draws upon, is further undermined by subsequent *Canterbury Tales*. The Wife's text is greatly concerned with the practice of glossing, and the relationship of text and gloss (see III. 26, 119, 509): Carolyn Dinshaw argues that the Wife mimics glossators in the interpretations that she places upon the sources underlying her text.[85] But further to this, the Wife's Prologue and Tale forms a text that is itself glossed as subsequent tales respond to her arguments. Cooper

---

[80] A. J. Minnis, *Medieval Theory of Authorship: Scholastic Literary Attitudes in the Later Middle Ages*, 2nd ed. (Aldershot: Scolar, 1988), p. 10.

[81] Minnis, pp. 112–16.

[82] Minnis, pp. 192, 199.

[83] Thomas Hoccleve, *Hoccleve's Works: The Minor Poems*, ed. F. J. Furnivall and I. Gollancz, rev. J. Mitchell and A. I. Doyle, EETS, e.s. 61, 73 (London: Oxford University Press, 1970), p. 135.

[84] Carruthers, p. 44.

[85] Dinshaw, *Chaucer's Sexual Poetics*, p. 123.

notes that she alone of all the Canterbury pilgrims appears in the tales of others:[86] there are direct references at IV. 1170 and IV. 1685. Nor does an argument for the Wife's text as an independent unit seem justified given that there are no manuscripts containing the Wife's text alone. The one separate manuscript of all of Fragment III also includes the *Clerk's Tale*, one of the tales that explicitly acts as a gloss to the Wife's prologue and tale.[87] The example of Heloise, cited by the Wife at III. 677, to some extent parallels that of the Wife herself. Like the Wife, Heloise cited Jerome's *Adversus Jovinianum*, putting it to a use for which it was certainly not intended, in her defence of fornication rather than marriage.[88] In the *Roman de la Rose*, although Heloise is described as an exceptional woman, whose erudition enabled her to overcome the qualities attributed to women in antifeminist literature, her citing of this literature is explained by her recognition of these qualities in herself:

> Car les livres avait veüz
> E estudiez e seüz,
> E les meurs femenins savait,
> Car trestouz en sei les avait.   (lines 8773–76)

For she had seen and studied and understood the books and she understood feminine ways, for she had them all in herself. [. . .].[89]

Jean de Meun's antifeminist gloss, and that gloss alone, is picked up by Chaucer. When she appears in Chaucer's *Wife of Bath's Prologue*, Heloise is just another entry in Jankyn's book of wicked wives: she has herself become an example of antifeminist literature. This example of an antifeminist gloss on a text that itself attempted to subvert antifeminist authorities parallels what happens to the Wife's text. The Wife's text cannot triumph over its antifeminist material because it is itself designed to be the subject of antifeminist comment.

At the end of the *Clerk's Tale*, the Clerk suggests that his tale is not to be taken literally, for it would be *inportable*, insufferable, if wives acted as the obedient Griselda did (IV. 1142–44). This implies that Griselda is not an ideal figure whose behaviour is intended for imitation by contemporary women, and that an allegorical reading of her behaviour is more appropriate (IV. 1145–62). The impossibility of imitating Griselda also suggests, however, that contemporary women are incapable of obedience (IV. 1163–1212). In a reversal of the position taken a few lines earlier in the poem, Griselda is now held up as an example of perfection which can after all be read literally rather than allegorically, an example against

---

[86]   Cooper, p. 149.

[87]   Cooper, p. 140.

[88]   *The Letters of Abelard and Heloise*, trans. Betty Radice (Harmondsworth: Penguin, 1974), pp. 71, 73. The arguments referred to are cited by Abelard in his *Historia Calamitatum*, but confirmed by a subsequent letter of Heloise's referring to this work (p. 114).

[89]   *Le Roman de la Rose*, ed. Ernest Langlois, 3 vols (Paris: Champion, 1914–21), III, 95; *Romance*, trans. Horgan, p. 135.

which the Wife of Bath 'and al hire secte' are contrasted (IV. 1170–71). A passage which can easily be read as a condemnation of the Wife has already been placed in Griselda's mouth:

> Til I be deed my lyf ther wol I lede,
> A wydwe clene in body, herte, and al.
> For sith I yaf to yow my maydenhede,
> And am youre trewe wyf, it is no drede,
> God shilde swich a lordes wyf to take
> Another man to housbonde or to make!   (IV. 835–40)

When Walter dismisses her, supposedly so that he may remarry, Griselda declares here that she will live the rest of her life as 'a wydwe clene in body, herte, and al': she portrays herself as a chaste widow, despite the fact that her husband is still alive. At the end of the tale, it is suggested that real women are not like Griselda, they are like the Wife (IV. 1163–1212). This is echoed by the Host at IV. 1212 a–g, and the Merchant at IV. 1213–25: their wives are nothing like Griselda. It is interesting that Griselda, the virtuous widow, is affirmed not to exist. Later in the *Canterbury Tales*, Prudence in the *Tale of Melibee* seems to distance herself from the Wife in terms that echo both the Wife and St Jerome (VII. 1084–88). Prudence, like Griselda an ideal image of wifehood, is also unlike real wives (VII. 1891–96).

This commentary process that undermines the Wife and her attempt to appropriate antifeminist texts to other ends is one that extends beyond the *Canterbury Tales* itself. John Scattergood, writing of *Lenvoy de Chaucer a Bukton*, notes not only the quotation of passages from the Wife, as well as a direct reference, but also a parallel between *Chaucer a Bukton* 13–14 and *Canterbury Tales* IV. 1226–27: the Merchant's complaints about his wife which follow his assertion that she is nothing like Griselda.[90] Scattergood reads *Chaucer a Bukton* as being based almost entirely on proverbial wisdom, and provides proverbial, literary, biblical and exegetical parallels for some of the lines from *Chaucer a Bukton* that are paralleled in the *Canterbury Tales*, mostly in the Wife's text.[91] But if Chaucer explicitly characterizes this short poem as being based on proverbial wisdom (line 25), he also invokes the Wife as a source (line 29). The Wife is simultaneously invoked as a real person, and dismissed as a source of authority, which is shown instead to lie in the proverbial and antifeminist wisdom that underlies her text, and has been extracted from it for this short poem advising a real widower not to marry.

The Wife is portrayed as a lecherous widow, and we are told that this is what women are really like. This portrayal may be placed within a larger context of

---

[90] John Scattergood, '*Chaucer a Bukton* and Proverbs,' *Nottingham Medieval Studies* 31 (1987), 98–107 (pp. 103, 104, 105, 107). *Chaucer a Bukton* 13–14 and *Canterbury Tales* IV. 1226–27 both describe marriage as a denial of freedom.

[91] Scattergood, '*Chaucer a Bukton* and Proverbs,' pp. 99, 103–5.

antifeminism, but the representation of widows in Chaucer's text, and its re-presentation of authoritative antifeminist ideologies, may have something to do with a real change in circumstances for widows in later fourteenth-century England. Increased numbers, access to legal and property rights, and ecclesiastical suspicion, may have simultaneously made them a marginalized grouping, and, paradoxically, a visible challenge to masculine authority in the second half of the fourteenth century.

Conclusion

This book opened by arguing that some continuities in thinking about marriage are visible to a greater or lesser extent across the medieval period. Anglo-Saxon texts suggest that consent is important in marriage, at least as an ideal, long before the Church formulates its consensual model. Likewise, the importance of property in making marriages and the notion of marriage as alliance survive the introduction of the Church's emphasis on the consent of the partners. That love should be encouraged between spouses is a feature of thinking about marriage from Saint Paul to the later Middle Ages. Unease about the role of sex within marriage is found in Christian thinking throughout the medieval period. Attempts to make marriage both monogamous and indissoluble also persist. This is not to argue against the existence of historical change in medieval thinking about marriage. We can see movement, for example, from endogamous marriage to exogamous marriage, from limited polygamy towards monogamy, and a tendency away from bilineal notions of kinship and towards patrilineage. In the later medieval period, marriage becomes the subject of a body of law, secular and ecclesiastical, which is increasingly comprehensive and presumably influential. We might assume, therefore, that the Church in particular is more effective in implementing its views on marriage in the later part of the Middle Ages – but those views are still indebted to earlier medieval thinking. Continuities are visible across the medieval period, and changes that take place in medieval thinking about marriage are often changes of emphasis between elements that coexist in medieval marriage.

That is not to suggest, however, that we can construct a single model of marriage that will hold across the medieval period, or, indeed, at any moment during it. Far from it. Marriage fulfils a variety of roles: social, spiritual, emotional, sexual and economic, among others. It is not surprising, then, that there should be sustained debate and differences of opinion about its role and purpose, in the medieval period as now. While this book has attempted to demonstrate continuities across the Middle Ages in marital ideology and practice, then, it has also pointed to a significant number of areas where there are important contradictions within medieval thinking on marriage. Such contradictions are clearest in later medieval England, where marriage is subject to two systems of law with very different objectives. The Church's jurisdiction is primarily interested in marriage as it relates to the salvation of the individual, whereas the secular jurisdiction is interested in marriage primarily as the location of transfers of property related to inheritance strategies. We can identify several contradictions between the ideologies of marriage outlined by the secular and ecclesiastical jurisdictions. The ecclesiastical position on freedom of choice of marriage partner is problematized by secular legislation and practice relating to the marriages of widows and wards: although statute law conceded that neither widows nor wards would be forced to marry, their lords retained an economic interest in their marriages which meant that freedom of choice had to be paid for, if it was to be exercised at all. Another conflict between the jurisdictions concerns the property rights and testamentary rights of married women. Married women were unable to make wills without the permission of their husbands because of their proprietary disability under the common law. Common law restrictions of the rights of married women are indebted to antifeminist restrictions of the legal position of married women in the canon law, but ecclesiastical law insisted on the testamentary rights of married women. Here the Church's belief in the right of all Christians to give alms for the benefit of their souls overcame its belief in the role of married women as subject to their husbands, which resulted in a direct conflict between secular and ecclesiastical jurisdictions. The refusal of the common law courts to recognize reconciliations between partners by order of the ecclesiastical courts where dower had been forfeited through adultery is a further division between the two, as is the existence of two separate sets of regulations concerning legitimacy. This tension between the spiritual and worldly aspects of marriage does not arise as a result of the division in jurisdictions, however: that division is a symptom rather than a cause of the difference in outlook.

The overdetermination of marriage is not merely a binary phenomenon, however, for two reasons. Firstly, there are some traces in the texts available to us of other ideologies which render overdetermination yet more complex. There have been glimpses throughout of people behaving in a manner which resists legal prescription, and we might well presume that the existence of legal prescription often suggests the existence of the practices that it seeks to modify. As David Aers comments in a more general context:

> [. . .] Were the practices, doctrines and apparatuses of the ruling groups actually able to constitute subjects and achieve anything like the assumed hegemony, they would hardly need such continual and elaborate legitimation.[1]

In some cases, resistance to the ideologies of marriage prescribed by the law implies the existence of other ideologies of marriage current among the laity but

---

[1] Aers, *Community, Gender and Individual Identity*, p. 8.

not evident in the legal texts. R. H. Helmholz argues for a difference between formal law and popular attitude regarding the consensual model of marriage, and he argues that many lay people continued to regard a contract of marriage through words of present consent merely to constitute betrothal, despite the views of the Church.[2] There are also suggestions of people working around the prescribed rules – of clandestine unions, of 'self-divorce', of people using what means they could to get around inheritance rules.

Secondly, there are internal contradictions within the positions adopted by legal texts. There was significant contradiction within ecclesiastical law on the means by which the marital bond could be created, with the Church simultaneously recognizing and condemning clandestine unions. Despite the Church's insistence on freedom of choice, forced marriage persists in the later medieval practice of abjuration *sub pena nubendi*. Here the conviction that all extramarital intercourse was sinful, and the Church's need to exercise social control, won out over the ideology of marriage as a matter of free choice. The ban on underage unions, instituted partly because of the inability of children to consent (although the ability to consummate a marriage was also a factor), might be waived if the marriage was taking place to cement a peace treaty. Here the ideology of marriage as alliance between families wins out over the ideology of marriage as a union freely entered into between two people. There was also ambiguity in the Church's attitude to the sacramental status of marriage because of distinctions made between the prelapsarian and postlapsarian institution of marriage, where marriage was seen as a remedy for lust rather than a source of grace. Ecclesiastical unease about the sacramental status of marriage was related to the Church's conviction of the evil nature of postlapsarian desire, and hence an unease about sexual intercourse, even within marriage. Uncertainties about marital sex (and hence about the good of marriage) are visible from the very beginning of the Christian era, in St Paul, and in St Augustine. Canonists held a wide range of views on the nature of marital intercourse, but the conviction that marital intercourse could be at the very least venially sinful is found in writers as various as Augustine, Chaucer, and Margery Kempe. Ecclesiastical insistence on the indissolubility of marriage is subject to modification in the early Middle Ages, as seen in both Bede and the *Penitential of Theodore*. Here the Church appears to be prepared to modify doctrine in the context of conversion. Internal divisions also exist within the secular law in the later Middle Ages, mainly due to the divisions between the common law and local custom – the lack of any definite law of England. Such divisions, as exemplified in the existence of contradictory sets of regulations concerning dower and the property rights of women, embody a variety of ideologies, often conflicting, brought to bear on the practice of marriage.

So much for the positions adopted by the legal texts. What is the contribution of literature to medieval ideologies of marriage? As suggested in the introduction,

---

[2] Helmholz, *Marriage Litigation*, p. 31.

recent work on law and literature has emphasized similarities rather than differences in the way that legal and literary texts work. Here we can sometimes see law and literature addressing the same issues: as is the case where texts like *Beowulf*, the *Knight's Tale*, and ecclesiastical statutes address the possibility of marriages being contracted for the purpose of establishing peace. We can also see literature engaging critically with legal issues, as with Langland, whose discussion of marriage and property adopts material from the marriage liturgy and the format of a charter to satirize the practice of marriage for money.[3] Something similar can be seen in the Harley manuscript poem *In the Ecclesiastical Court* which satirizes the practice of abjuration *sub pena nubendi*.

But does literature exercise an influence on practice? Such influence is difficult to trace, although there are possibilities we can point to. We can see Chaucer referring to his own poem on the Wife of Bath in advising a real widower not to marry in *Chaucer a Bukton*. More concrete evidence comes from Margery Kempe, whose life as represented in her *Book* imitates models of female perfection found in hagiographical texts. Concern about the potential influence of literary representations of marital practice may also be seen in John Audelay's falsification of the reality of St Bridget's life in his poem about the saint, and in Wynkyn de Worde's abridgement of Kempe's *Book*, with all autobiographical material removed. For the most part, however, the influence of literary texts on practice is not easily traced. Their attempts at shaping opinions and practice are subtler in operation than legal texts, and are more difficult to trace as a result. It is clear that they do intervene in the same debates that the legal texts enter into, and that their objective in doing so is broadly similar to that of the legal texts: to influence the practice of contemporaries. But the ideologies present in literary texts are no less overdetermined than those of legal texts.

If marriage is overdetermined, what are the consequences of that overdetermination? As we might expect, one of the consequences is uncertainty. For example, doubt regarding the good of marriage in relation to the perceived evil of sexual intercourse arises in early Christian writing and persists through the Middle Ages. Likewise, love is regarded as appropriate within marriage, but only in moderation, for it too may lead to excess. Langland's satire of financial interests in marriage draws the spiritual value of marriage into question by highlighting the incompatibility between ideologies of marriage based on spiritual values and ideologies based on property transfer. The construction of widows as both vulnerable and potentially powerful leads to laws guaranteeing their protection but it leads also to nervousness, expressed in literary and ecclesiastical sniping.

There are also positive consequences, however. In some cases, the end result of overdetermination is the chance to exercise personal freedom, albeit at a cost. A concrete example might be the marriage of Margery Paston and Richard Calle.

---

[3]   Langland also makes extensive use of legal language, on which see John A. Alford, *Piers Plowman: A Glossary of Legal Diction* (Cambridge: Brewer, 1988).

Despite C. S. Lewis's argument that property interests and the ideology of marriage as alliance work against freedom of choice in marriage, such freedom did exist. The Paston family's policy of basing marriage unions on property transfer and of marrying only within their own class (a view of marriage supported by the secular law) is rejected by Margery Paston, who clandestinely marries Richard Calle, the family bailiff (clandestine marriage receiving the recognition of the ecclesiastical law, possibly because of its acceptance of a model of marriage based on free consent). Because the Church's consensual model recognizes clandestine marriage (albeit while simultaneously condemning it), the marriage is seen as valid by the bishop of Norwich's inquiry into the marriage. However, this does not prevent Margery Paston's family from retaliating against her by casting her out of the family. Another example of an individual exercising personal freedom is that of Margery Kempe, who, owing to her economic independence from her husband (which contravened common law), was able to persuade her husband to agree to a vow of chastity by paying his debts, and so to reposition herself in the context of a tradition of chaste married women, upheld by the Church because of its unease about the role of intercourse, even within marriage. This tradition is itself overdetermined, because writers such as Jacques de Vitry use it to exemplify a female perfection that it was not feasible for married women to imitate. Kempe does imitate it, although not without cost, as indicated by the hostility shown towards her that is recorded in her text.

The consequences of overdetermination are perhaps best viewed in terms of the definition of power formulated by Michel Foucault, who states that power is 'the multiplicity of force relations immanent in the sphere in which they operate and which constitute their own organization.'[4] These force relations, we might argue, are produced by determining factors. Overdetermination leads to the potential for local alterations in force relations which are not intended by those in control of the determining forces: an unexpected change in power relations. Hence Margery Paston is able to marry clandestinely to escape her family's policy of pursuing marriage alliances based on property and political advantages. Likewise, Margery Kempe is able to exploit hagiographical example and economic innovation to her own advantage. Neither of these people are freed from the power structures which affect their lives, but they are able to make unexpected moves within them.

Marriage in medieval England is represented in multiple ways by a variety of different sorts of text. In discussing marriage, all of these texts try to define marriage and its boundaries, and to determine marital practice. Because they come from a wide range of perspectives, contradictions result, and those contradictions sometimes have unexpected consequences. For these reasons, and despite the continuities that we can trace in thinking about marriage across the medieval period,

---

[4] Michel Foucault, *The History of Sexuality: An Introduction*, trans. by Robert Hurley (Harmondsworth: Penguin, 1981), p. 92.

medieval marriage is best read in terms of a variety of representations: however convenient it might be to try to offer a single definition of normative marriage practice in medieval England, such a definition runs the risk of being reductive and of ignoring the variety that is an important characteristic of the subject. Marriage, consent, inheritance, love, sex, family, bereavement, and the many other related topics that have been touched on in the course of this book, were the subject of debate rather than consensus in the Middle Ages. It is the representation of the variety and contradiction to be found in medieval texts on marriage, rather than any attempt to arrive at a norm, that most accurately reflects medieval thought and practice.

Bibliography

PRIMARY SOURCES

Adams, Norma, and Charles Donahue, Jr. (eds), *Select Cases from the Ecclesiastical Courts of the Province of Canterbury, c. 1200–1301* (London: Selden Society, 1981)

Alighieri, Dante, *The Divine Comedy of Dante Alighieri*, trans. Charles S. Singleton, Bollingen Series LXXX, 3 vols (Princeton, NJ: Princeton University Press, 1973)

Amt, Emilie (ed.), *Women's Lives in Medieval Europe: A Sourcebook* (London: Routledge, 1993)

Anderson, J. J. (ed.), *Sir Gawain and the Green Knight, Pearl, Cleanness, Patience* (London: Dent, 1996)

Andreas Capellanus, *On Love*, ed. and trans. P. G. Walsh (London: Duckworth, 1982)

Attenborough, F. L. (ed. and trans.), *The Laws of the Earliest English Kings*, (Cambridge: Cambridge University Press, 1922)

St Augustine, *Confessions*, trans. R. S. Pine-Coffin (Harmondsworth: Penguin, 1961)

—— *The City of God against the Pagans*, ed. and trans. T. E. Page et al., Loeb Classics, 7 vols (London: Heinemann, 1966)

—— *De bono coniugali, de sancta virginitate*, ed. and trans. P. G. Walsh (Oxford: Clarendon, 2001)

Bateson, Mary (ed.), *Borough Customs*, 2 vols (London: Quaritch, 1904–06)

St Bede, *Ecclesiastical History of the English People*, trans. L. Sherley Price, R. E. Latham, D. H. Farmer, revised ed. (Harmondsworth: Penguin, 1990)

Blamires, Alcuin, with C. W. Marx and Karen Pratt (eds), *Woman Defamed and Woman Defended: An Anthology of Medieval Texts* (Oxford: Oxford University Press, 1992)

Bliss, W. H. (ed.), *Calendar of Entries in the Papal Registers Relating to Great Britain and Ireland. Petitions to the Pope. Vol. I. AD 1342–1419* (London: HMSO, 1896)

Bliss, W. H., and C. Johnson (eds), *Calendar of Entries in the Papal Registers Relating to Great Britain and Ireland. Papal Letters. Vol. III. AD 1342–1362* (London: HMSO, 1897)

Bliss, W. H., and J. A. Twemlow (eds), *Calendar of Entries in the Papal Registers Relating to Great Britain and Ireland. Papal Letters. Vol. IV. AD 1362–1404* (London: HMSO, 1902)

—— *Calendar of Entries in the Papal Registers Relating to Great Britain and Ireland. Papal Letters. Vol. V. AD 1396–1404* (London: HMSO, 1904)

Bryan, W. F., and Germaine Dempster (eds), *Sources and Analogues of Chaucer's Canterbury Tales* (Chicago: University of Chicago Press, 1941)

Calendar of Close Rolls: Richard II. Vol. I (London: HMSO, 1914)

Cartlidge, Neil (ed. and trans.), *The Owl and the Nightingale: Text and Translation* (Exeter: University of Exeter Press, 2001)

Chaucer, Geoffrey, *The Franklin's Tale from the Canterbury Tales*, ed. Gerald Morgan (Dublin: Irish Academic Press, 1980, repr. 1992)

Chaucer, Geoffrey, *The Riverside Chaucer*, ed. Larry D. Benson and others (Boston: Houghton Mifflin, 1987)

Cumming, William Patterson (ed.), *The Revelations of Saint Birgitta*, EETS, o.s. no. 178 (London: Oxford University Press, 1929)

D'Avray, David L., *Medieval Marriage Sermons: Mass Communication in a Culture without Print* (Oxford: Oxford University Press, 2001)

Davies, R. T. (ed.), *Medieval English Lyrics* (London: Faber, 1963)

Davis, Norman (ed.), *Paston Letters and Papers of the Fifteenth Century* (Oxford: Oxford University Press, 1971–76)

Douglas, David C., and George W. Greenaway (eds), *English Historical Documents, Volume 2: 1042–1189* (London: Eyre & Spottiswoode, 1953)

Ellis, Roger (ed.), *The Liber Celestis of St Bridget of Sweden* (Oxford: Oxford University Press, 1987)

Friedberg, Emil (ed), *Corpus Iuris Canonici*, 2 vols (Leipzig: 1879)

Furnivall, Frederick J. (ed.), *The Babees Book* (London: Early English Texts Society, 1868)

—— (ed.), *The Fifty Earliest English Wills in the Court of Probate, London*, EETS, o.s. no. 78 (London: Oxford University Press, 1964)

Gairdner, James (ed.), *The Paston Letters*, 6 vols (1904; repr. Stroud: Sutton, 1983)

Giraldus Cambrensis, *The History and Topography of Ireland*, trans. John J. O'Meara (Harmondsworth: Penguin, 1982)

Gower, John, *The English Works of John Gower*, ed. G. C. Macaulay, EETS, e.s. 81, 82 (Oxford: Oxford University Press, 1900)

Guillaume de Lorris and Jean de Meun, *Le Roman de la Rose*, ed. Ernest Langlois, 3 vols (Paris: Champion, 1914–21)

—— *The Romance of the Rose*, trans. Frances Horgan (Oxford: Oxford University Press, 1994)

Hair, Paul (ed.), *Before the Bawdy Court: Selections from Church Court and Other Records relating to the Correction of Moral Offences in England, Scotland, and New England* (London: Elek, 1972)

Hamer, Richard (ed. and trans.), *A Choice of Anglo-Saxon Verse* (London: Faber, 1970)

Havely, N. R. (ed. and trans.), *Chaucer's Boccaccio: Sources of* Troilus *and the* Knight's *and* Franklin's Tales (Cambridge: Brewer, 1980)

Hoccleve, Thomas, *Hoccleve's Works: The Minor Poems*, ed. F. J. Furnivall and I. Gollancz, rev. J. Mitchell and A. I. Doyle, EETS, e.s. 61, 73 (London: Oxford University Press, 1970)

Horstmann, C., 'Prosalegenden: Die Legenden des ms. Douce 114,' *Anglia* 8 (1885), 102–96

Hugh of Saint Victor, *On the Sacraments of the Christian Faith*, trans. Roy J. Deferrari (Cambridge, MA: Medieval Academy of America, 1951)

St Jerome, *The Principal Works of St Jerome*, trans. W. H. Fremantle (Oxford: James Parker, 1893)

Kempe, Margery, *The Book of Margery Kempe*, ed. Sanford Brown Meech and Hope Emily Allen, EETS, o.s. no. 212 (London: Oxford University Press, 1940)

—— *The Book of Margery Kempe*, trans. B. A. Windeatt (Harmondsworth: Penguin, 1985)

Langland, William, *Piers Plowman: The A Version*, ed. George Kane, revised edn. (London: Athlone, 1988)

Langland, William, *Piers Plowman: The Prologue and Passus I–VII of the B Text as found in Bodleian MS. Laud Misc. 581*, ed. J. A. W. Bennett (Oxford: Oxford University Press, 1972–76)

—— *The Vision of Piers Plowman: A Critical Edition of the B Text*, ed. A. V. C. Schmidt, revised edn. (London: Dent, 1987)

—— *Piers Plowman: The C Text*, ed. Derek Pearsall (York, 1988, repr. Exeter: University of Exeter Press, 1994)

Larrington, Carolyne, *Women and Writing in Medieval Europe: A Sourcebook* (London: Routledge, 1995)

Lyndwood, William, *Provincialis Wilhelmi Lyndewode* (Paris, 1501)

Manuale et Processionale ad Usum Insignis Ecclesiae Eboracensis, Surtees Society vol. 63 (London, 1875)

McCarthy, Conor (ed.), *Love, Sex and Marriage in the Middle Ages: A Sourcebook* (London: Routledge, 2004)

McNeill, J. T., and H. M. Gamer (ed. and trans.), *Medieval Handbooks of Penance* (New York: Columbia University Press, 1938; repr. New York: Octagon, 1965)

Millett, Bella, and Jocelyn Wogan-Browne (ed. and trans.), *Medieval English Prose for Women: Selections from the Katherine Group and Ancrene Wisse* (Oxford: Clarendon, 1990)

Nichols, F. M. (ed. and trans.), *Britton* (London: Macmillan, 1865)

Peter Lombard, *Sententiae in IV Libris Distinctae*, ed. Pontificale Collegium S. Bonaventurae Ad Claras Aquas (Rome: Grottaferrata, 1971–81)

Poos, L. R., and Lloyd Bonfield (ed. and trans.), *Select Cases in Manorial Courts, 1250–1550: Property and Family Law* (London: Selden Society, 1998)

Powicke, F. M., and C. R. Cheney (eds), *Councils and Synods with Other Documents relating to the English Church, AD 1205–1313* (London: Oxford University Press, 1964)

Radice, Betty (trans.), *The Letters of Abelard and Heloise* (Harmondsworth: Penguin, 1974)

Robertson, A. J. (ed. and trans.), *The Laws of the Kings of England from Edmund to Henry I* (Cambridge: Cambridge University Press, 1925)

—— *Anglo-Saxon Charters* (Cambridge: Cambridge University Press, 1956)

Rothwell, Harry (ed.), *English Historical Documents, 1189–1327* (London: Eyre & Spottiswoode, 1975)

Sayles, G. O. (ed. and trans.), *Fleta: Volume IV: Book V and Book VI*, Selden Society vol. 99 (London: Selden Society, 1984)

Shanks, E., and S. F. C. Milsom (eds), *Novae Narrationes*, Selden Society no. 80 (London: Quaritch, 1963)

Swanton, Michael (ed. and trans.), *Anglo-Saxon Prose* (London: Dent, 1975)

—— (ed. and trans.), *Beowulf* (Manchester: Manchester University Press, 1978)

Talbot, C. H. (ed. and trans.), *The Life of Christina of Markyate: A Twelfth Century Recluse* (Oxford: Clarendon, 1959)

Tanner, N. P. (ed.), *Decrees of the Ecumenical Councils* (London: Sheed and Ward, 1990)

St Thomas Aquinas, *Summa Theologiae*, ed. T. Gilby and others, 61 vols (London: Blackfriars, 1964–81)

Turville-Petre, Thorlac (ed.), *Alliterative Poetry of the Later Middle Ages* (London: Routledge, 1989)

Whitelock, Dorothy (ed.), *English Historical Documents, 500–1042*, 2ⁿᵈ ed. (London: Eyre Methuen, 1974)

Wilkins, David (ed.), *Concilia Magnae Brittaniae et Hiberniae* (London: 1737)

Woodbine, G. E. (ed.), trans. S. E. Thorne, *Bracton: On the Laws and Customs of England* (Cambridge, MA: Harvard University Press, 1968–77)

Wyclif, John, *Select English Writings of John Wyclif*, ed. Thomas Arnold, 3 vols (Oxford: Macmillan, 1869–71)

Year Books: 5 Edward II, Selden Society vol. 63 (London: Selden Society, 1944)

SECONDARY SOURCES

Aers, David, *Chaucer, Langland, and the Creative Imagination* (London: Routledge, 1980)

—— *Chaucer* (Brighton: Harvester, 1986)

—— *Community, Gender and Individual Identity: English Writing, 1360–1430* (London: Routledge, 1988)

Alford, John A., *Piers Plowman: A Glossary of Legal Diction* (Cambridge: Brewer, 1988)

Althusser, Louis, *Essays on Ideology* (London: Verso, 1984)

—— *For Marx*, trans. Ben Brewster (Harmondsworth: Penguin, 1969)

Archer, Rowena E., ' "How ladies . . . who live on manors ought to manage their households and estates": Women as Landholders and Administrators in the later Middle Ages,' in *Woman is a Worthy Wight: Women in Medieval English Society, c. 1200–1500*, ed. P. J. P. Goldberg (Stroud: Sutton, 1992), pp. 149–81

Ariès, Philippe, 'Love in Married Life,' in *Western Sexuality: Practice and Precept in Past and Present Times*, ed. Philippe Ariès and André Bejin, trans. Anthony Forster (Oxford: Blackwell, 1985)

Baldwin, Anna P., *The Theme of Government in Piers Plowman* (Cambridge: Brewer, 1981)

Barratt, Alexandra, 'The Characters "Civil" and "Theology" in *Piers Plowman*,' *Traditio* 38 (1982), 352–64

Bennett, H. S., *The Pastons and their England: Studies in an Age of Transition* (Cambridge: Cambridge University Press, 1922)

Bennett, Judith M., *Women in the Medieval English Countryside: Gender and Household in Brigstock before the Plague* (Oxford: Oxford University Press, 1987)

—— 'Public Power and Authority in the Medieval English Countryside,' in *Women and Power in the Middle Ages*, ed. M. Erler and M. Kowaleski (London: University of Georgia Press, 1988)

Boase, Roger, *The Origin and Meaning of Courtly Love: A Critical Study of European Scholarship* (Manchester: Manchester University Press, 1977)

Boswell, John, *Christianity, Social Tolerance, and Homosexuality: Gay People in Western Europe from the Beginning of the Christian Era to the Fourteenth Century* (London: University of Chicago Press, 1980)

Brand, P. A., P. R. Hyams, R. Faith and E. Searle, 'Debate: Seigneurial Control of Women's Marriage,' *Past and Present* 99 (1983), 123–60

Brewer, D. S., 'Love and Marriage in Chaucer's Poetry,' *The Modern Language Review* 49 (1954), 461–64

—— review of Kelly (1975), *Review of English Studies*, n. s. 28 (1977), 194–97 (p. 196)

Brooke, C. N. L., *The Medieval Idea of Marriage* (Oxford: Oxford University Press, 1989)

Brown, Peter, *The Body and Society: Men, Women and Sexual Renunciation in Early Christianity* (New York: Columbia University Press, 1988)

Brucker, Gene, *Giovanni and Lusanna: Love and Marriage in Renaissance Florence* (Berkeley: University of California Press, 1986)

Brundage, James A., 'Concubinage and Marriage in Medieval Canon Law,' in *Sexual Practices and the Medieval Church*, ed. Vern L. Bullough and James A. Brundage (Buffalo, NY: Prometheus, 1982), pp. 118–28

—— 'Adultery and Fornication: A Study in Legal Theology,' in *Sexual Practices and the Medieval Church*, ed. Vern L. Bullough and James L. Brundage (Buffalo, NY: Prometheus, 1982), pp. 129–34

—— *Law, Sex and Christian Society in Medieval Europe* (Chicago and London: University of Chicago Press, 1987)

—— 'Widows as Disadvantaged Persons in Medieval Canon Law,' in *Upon My Husband's Death: Widows in the Literature and Histories of Medieval Europe* (Ann Arbor: University of Michigan Press, 1992), pp. 193–206

Bullough, Vern L., 'Introduction: The Christian Inheritance,' in *Sexual Practices and the Medieval Church*, ed. Vern L. Bullough and James A. Brundage (Buffalo, NY: Prometheus, 1982), pp. 1–12

Bullough, Vern L., and James A. Brundage (eds), *Sexual Practices and the Medieval Church* (Buffalo, NY: Prometheus, 1982)

—— *Handbook of Medieval Sexuality* (London: Garland, 1996)

Burrow, Colin, 'C. S. Lewis and *The Allegory of Love*,' *Essays in Criticism* 53 (2003), 284–94

Burrow, J. A., *Medieval Writers and Their Work: Middle English Literature and its Background, 1100–1500* (Oxford: Oxford University Press, 1982)

—— *The Ages of Man: A Study in Medieval Writing and Thought* (Oxford: Oxford University Press, 1996)

Carruthers, Mary, 'The Wife of Bath and the Painting of Lions,' in *Feminist Readings in Middle English Literature: The Wife of Bath and All her Sect*, ed. Ruth Evans and Lesley Johnson (London: Routledge, 1994), pp. 22–53

Cartlidge, Neil, *Medieval Marriage: Literary Approaches, 1100–1300* (Cambridge: Brewer, 1997)

Chance, Jane, *Woman as Hero in Old English Literature* (Syracuse, NY: Syracuse University Press, 1986)

Cheney, C. R., 'Legislation of the Medieval English Church,' *English Historical Review* 50 (1935), 193–224, 385–417

Clark, Elizabeth A., ' "Adam's Only Companion": Augustine and the Early Christian Debate on Marriage,' in *The Olde Daunce: Love, Friendship, Sex and Marriage in the Medieval World*, ed. Robert R. Edwards and Stephen Spector (Albany: SUNY Press, 1991), pp. 15–31

—— (ed.), *Saint Augustine on Marriage and Sexuality* (Washington: Catholic University of America Press, 1996)

Clunies Ross, Margaret, 'Concubinage in Anglo-Saxon England,' *Past and Present* 108 (1985), 3–34

Coleman, Janet, '*The Owl and the Nightingale* and Papal Theories of Marriage,' *Journal of Ecclesiastical History* 38 (1987), 517–68

Cooper, Helen, *Oxford Guides to Chaucer: The Canterbury Tales* (Oxford: Oxford University Press, 1989)

Corbett, Percy Ellwood, *The Roman Law of Marriage* (London: Oxford University Press, 1930)

Cosgrove, Art, 'Marriage in Medieval Ireland,' in *Marriage in Ireland*, ed. Art Cosgrove (Dublin: College Press, 1985), pp. 35–50

Crawford, Sally, *Childhood in Anglo-Saxon England* (Stroud: Sutton, 1999)

Dauviller, Jean, *Le Mariage dans le Droit Classique de L'Eglise depuis le Decret de Gratien (1140) jusqu'a la mort de Clement V (1314)* (Paris: Sirey, 1933)

D'Avray, David L., 'The Gospel of the Marriage Feast of Cana and Marriage Preaching in France,' in *The Bible in the Medieval World: Essays in Memory of Beryl Smalley*, ed. Katherine Walsh and Diana Wood (Oxford: Blackwell, 1985), pp. 207–24

Dinshaw, Carolyn, *Chaucer's Sexual Poetics* (London: University of Wisconsin Press, 1989)

—— 'The Law of Man and its "Abhomynacions",' *Exemplaria* 1 (1989), 117–48

—— *Getting Medieval: Sexual Communities Pre- and Post-Modern* (Durham, NC: Duke University Press, 1999)

Donahue, Charles, Jr., 'Female Plaintiffs in Marriage Cases in the Court of York in the Later Middle Ages: What Can We Learn from the Numbers?,' in *Wife and Widow in Medieval England*, ed. Sue Sheridan Walker (Ann Arbor: University of Michigan Press, 1993), pp. 183–213

Donaldson, E. Talbot, *Piers Plowman: The C-Text and Its Poet* (London, 1949, repr. Cass: 1966)

DuBoulay, F. R. H., *The England of Piers Plowman: William Langland and His Vision of the Fourteenth Century* (Cambridge: Brewer, 1991)

Duby, Georges, *The Knight, the Lady, and The Priest: The Making of Modern Marriage in Medieval France*, trans. Barbara Bray (New York: Pantheon, 1983)

Elliott, Dyan, *Spiritual Marriage: Sexual Abstinence in Medieval Wedlock* (Princeton: Princeton University Press, 1993)

Ellis, Roger, ' "Flores ad fabricandam . . . coronam": An Investigation into the Uses of the Revelations of St Bridget of Sweden in Fifteenth Century England,' *Medium Aevum* 51 (1982), 163–86

Erdmann, Carl, *The Origin of the Idea of Crusade*, trans. by Marshall W. Baldwin and Walter Goffart (Princeton, NJ: Princeton University Press, 1977)

Evans, Ruth, and Lesley Johnson (eds), *Feminist Readings in Middle English Literature: The Wife of Bath and All her Sect* (London: Routledge, 1994)

Fell, Christine, *Women in Anglo-Saxon England* (London: British Museum, 1984)

Flake, Timothy H., 'Love, *Trouthe*, and the Happy Ending of the *Franklin's Tale*,' *English Studies* 77 (1996), 209–16

Foucault, Michel, *The History of Sexuality: An Introduction*, trans. Robert Hurley (Harmondsworth: Penguin, 1981)

Fowler, Elizabeth, 'Civil Death and the Maiden: Agency and the Conditions of Contract in *Piers Plowman*,' *Speculum* 70 (1995), 760–92

Frank, Roberta, 'Marriage in Twelfth- and Thirteenth-Century Iceland,' *Viator* 4 (1973), 473–84

Frantzen, Allen J., *Before the Closet: Same Sex Love from Beowulf to Angels in America* (Chicago and London: University of Chicago Press, 1998)

Goldberg, P. J. P., 'Marriage, Migration and Servanthood: The York Cause Paper Evidence,' in *Woman is a Worthy Wight: Women in English Society, c. 1200–1500*, ed. P. J. P. Goldberg (Stroud: Sutton, 1992), pp. 1–18

—— (ed.), *Woman is a Worthy Wight: Women in English Society, c. 1200–1500* (Stroud: Sutton, 1992)

Goodman, Anthony, *Margery Kempe and her World* (London: Longman, 2002)

Goody, Jack, *The Development of Marriage and the Family in Europe* (Cambridge: Cambridge University Press, 1983)

Green, Richard Firth, 'Chaucer's Victimized Women,' *Studies in the Age of Chaucer* 10 (1988), 3–21

—— 'Medieval Literature and Law,' in *The Cambridge History of Medieval English Literature*, ed. David Wallace (Cambridge: Cambridge University Press, 1999), pp. 407–31

—— *A Crisis of Truth: Literature and Law in Ricardian England* (Philadelphia: University of Pennsylvania Press, 1999)

Griffiths, Lavina, *Personification in Piers Plowman* (Cambridge: Brewer, 1985)

Hajnal, J., 'European Marriage Patterns in Perspective,' in *Population in History: Essays in Historical Demography*, ed. D. V. Glass and D. E. C. Eversley (London: Edward Arnold, 1975), pp. 101–53

Hanawalt, Barbara A., 'Peasant Women's Contribution to the Home Economy in Late Medieval England,' in *Women and Work in Preindustrial Europe*, ed. Barbara A. Hanawalt (Bloomington: Indiana University Press, 1986), pp. 3–19

—— *The Ties that Bound: Peasant Families in Medieval England* (Oxford: Oxford University Press, 1986)

—— 'Remarriage as an Option for Urban and Rural Widows in Late Medieval England,' in *Wife and Widow in Medieval England*, ed. Sue Sheridan Walker (Ann Arbor: University of Michigan Press, 1993), pp. 141–64

—— 'Female Networks for Fostering Lady Lisle's Daughters,' in *Medieval Mothering*, ed. John Carmi Parsons and Bonnie Wheeler (New York and London: Garland, 1996), pp. 239–58

—— 'Medievalists and the Study of Childhood,' *Speculum* 77 (2002), 440–60

Elaine Tuttle Hansen, *Chaucer and the Fictions of Gender* (Oxford: University of California Press, 1992)

Haskell, Ann S., 'The Paston Women on Marriage in Fifteenth Century England,' *Viator* 4 (1973), 459–84

Head, Thomas, 'The Marriages of Christina of Markyate,' *Viator* 21 (1990), 75–101

Helmholz, R. H., 'Bastardy Litigation in Medieval England,' in R. H. Helmholz, *Canon Law and the Law of England* (London: Hambledon, 1987), pp. 187–210 (pp. 203, 208) (first published in *American Journal of Legal History* 13 (1969), 360–83).

—— 'Abjuration *Sub Pena Nubendi* in the Church Courts of Medieval England,' in R. H. Helmholz, *Canon Law and the Law of England* (London: Hambledon, 1987), pp. 145–55 (p. 154) (originally published in *The Jurist* (1972): 80–90)

—— *Marriage Litigation in Medieval England* (London: Cambridge University Press, 1974)

—— 'Infanticide in the Province of Canterbury during the Fifteenth Century,' in R. H. Helmholz, *Canon Law and the Law of England* (London: Hambledon, 1987), pp. 157–68 (first published in *The History of Childhood Quarterly* 2 (1975), 379–90)

—— 'The Early Enforcement of Uses,' *Columbia Law Review* 79 (1979), 1503–13 (pp. 1504–7) (repr. in R. H. Helmholz, *Canon Law and the Law of England* (London: Hambledon, 1987), pp. 341–53).

—— *Canon Law and the Law of England* (London: Hambledon, 1987)

—— 'Married Women's Wills in Later Medieval England,' in *Wife and Widow in Later Medieval England*, ed. Sue Sheridan Walker (Ann Arbor: University of Michigan Press, 1993), pp. 165–82

Herlihy, David, *Medieval Households* (Cambridge, MA, and London: Harvard University Press, 1985)

—— 'Making Sense of Incest: Women and the Marriage Rules of the Early Middle Ages,' in David Herlihy, *Women, Family and Society in Medieval Europe: Historical Essays 1978–1991*, ed. A. Molho (Oxford: Berghahn, 1995), pp. 96–109 (first published in *Law, Custom, and the Social Fabric in Medieval Europe: Essays in Honor of Bryce Lyon*, ed. Bernard S. Bachrach and David Nicholas (Kalamazoo, MI, 1990), pp. 1–16.

—— 'Family,' in David Herlihy, *Women, Family and Society in Medieval Europe: Historical Essays 1978–1991*, ed. A. Molho (Oxford: Berghahn, 1995), pp. 113–34 (first published in *The American Historical Review* 96 (1991), 1–15).

—— 'The Making of the Medieval Family: Symmetry, Structure, and Sentiment,' in David Herlihy, *Women, Family and Society in Medieval Europe: Historical Essays 1978–1991*, ed. A. Molho (Oxford: Berghahn, 1995), pp. 135–53 (first published in *Journal of Family History* 8 (1983), 116–30).

—— 'The Family and Religious Ideologies in Medieval Europe,' in David Herlihy, *Women, Family and Society in Medieval Europe: Historical Essays 1978–1991*, ed. A. Molho (Oxford: Berghahn, 1995), pp. 154–73 (first published in *Journal of Family History* 12 (1987), 3–17)

Holdsworth, W. S., *A History of English Law*, 3 vols (London: Methuen, 1909)

Homans, George C., *English Villagers of the Thirteenth Century* (London: Norton, 1941, repr. 1973)

Holsinger, Bruce, 'The English Jurisdictions of *The Owl and the Nightingale*,' in *The Letter of the Law: Legal Practice and Literary Production in Medieval England*, ed. Emily Steiner and Candace Barrington (Ithaca and Cornell: Cornell University Press, 2002), pp. 154–84

Hornsby, Joseph Allen, *Chaucer and the Law* (Norman, Oklahoma: Pilgrim, 1988)

Hough, Carole, 'Alfred's *Domboc* and the Language of Rape: A Reconsideration of Alfred ch. 11,' *Medium Aevum* 66 (1997), 1–27

—— 'A New Reading of Alfred, ch. 26,' *Nottingham Medieval Studies* 41 (1997), 1–12

—— 'The Widow's *Mund* in Æthelbert 75 and 76,' *Journal of English and Germanic Philology* 98 (1999), 1–16

—— 'Two Kentish Laws Concerning Women: A New Reading of Æthelbert 73 and 74,' *Anglia* 119 (2001), 554–78

Howes, Laura L., 'On the birth of Margery Kempe's Last Child,' *Modern Philology* 90 (1992), 220–25

Jacquart, Danielle, and Claude Thomasset, *Sexuality and Medicine in the Middle Ages*, trans. Matthew Adamson (Princeton: Princeton University Press, 1988)

Jaski, Bart, 'Marriage Laws in Ireland and on the Continent in the Early Middle Ages,' in *'The Fragility of Her Sex'? Medieval Irishwomen in their European Context*, ed. Christine Meek and Katharine Simms (Dublin: Four Courts, 1996), pp. 16–42

Johnson, Lynn Staley, 'The Trope of the Scribe and the Question of Literary Authority in the Works of Julian of Norwich and Margery Kempe,' *Speculum* 66 (1991), 810–38

Karras, Ruth Mazo, *Common Women: Prostitution and Sexuality in Medieval England* (Oxford: Oxford University Press, 1996)

Kelly, Fergus, *A Guide to Early Irish Law* (Dublin: Dublin Institute for Advanced Studies, 1988)

Kelly, Henry Ansgar, *Love and Marriage in the Age of Chaucer* (Ithaca and London: Cornell University Press, 1975)

Kittredge, G. L., 'Chaucer's Discussion of Marriage,' in *Chaucer Criticism*, ed. R. J. Schoeck and Jerome Taylor, 2 vols (Indiana: University of Notre Dame Press, 1960), I, 130–58 (first published in *Modern Philology* 9 (1911–12), 435–67)

Klinck, Anne L., 'Anglo-Saxon women and the Law,' *Journal of Medieval History* 8 (1982), 107–21

Kooper, Erik, 'Loving the Unequal Equal: Medieval Theologians and Marital Affection,' in *The Olde Daunce: Love, Friendship, Sex, and Marriage in the Medieval World*, ed. Robert R. Edwards and Stephen Spector (New York: State University of New York Press, 1991), pp. 44–56

Kowaleski, Maryanne, 'Women's Work in a Market Town: Exeter in the Late Fourteenth Century,' in *Women and Work in Preindustrial Europe*, ed. Barbara A. Hanawalt (Bloomington: Indiana University Press, 1986), pp. 145–66

Lampe, David, 'Sex Roles and the Role of Sex in Medieval English Literature,' in *Handbook of Medieval Sexuality*, ed. Vern L. Bullough and James A. Brundage (London: Garland, 1996), pp. 401–22

Lancaster, Lorraine, 'Kinship in Anglo-Saxon Society,' *British Journal of Sociology* 9 (1958), 230–50, 359–77

Lévi-Strauss, Claude, *The Elementary Structures of Kinship*, ed. and trans. by James Harle Bell, John Richard von Sturmer and Rodney Needham, revised ed. (Boston: Beacon Press, 1969)

Lewis, C. S., *The Allegory of Love: A Study in Mediaeval Tradition* (Oxford: Oxford University Press, 1936)

Lochrie, Karma, *Margery Kempe and Translations of the Flesh* (Philadelphia: University of Pennsylvania Press, 1991)

Lucas, Angela M., *Women in the Middle Ages: Religion, Marriage and Letters* (Brighton: Harvester, 1983)

Lucas, Angela M., and Peter J. Lucas, 'The Presentation of Marriage and Love in Chaucer's *Franklin's Tale*,' *English Studies* 72 (1991), 501–12

Mann, Jill, *Chaucer and Medieval Estates Satire: The Literature of Social Classes and the General Prologue to the Canterbury Tales* (London: Cambridge University Press, 1973)

—— *Geoffrey Chaucer* (London: Harvester, 1991)

McCarthy, Conor, 'Love and Marriage in the *Confessio Amantis*,' *Neophilologus* 84 (2000), 485–99

McFarlane, K. B., *The Nobility of Later Medieval England: The Ford Lectures for 1953 and Related Studies* (Oxford: Oxford University Press, 1973)

McKinley, Richard, *Norfolk and Suffolk Surnames in the Middle Ages*, English Surnames Series II (London: Phillimore, 1975)

—— *The Surnames of Oxfordshire*, English Surnames Series III (London: Leopard's Head, 1977)

—— *The Surnames of Sussex*, English Surnames Series V (Oxford: Leopard's Head, 1988)

Medcalf, Stephen, 'Inner and Outer,' in *The Later Middle Ages*, ed. Stephen Medcalf (London: Methuen, 1981), pp. 108–71

Menuge, Noël James, *Medieval English Wardship in Romance and Law* (Cambridge: Brewer, 2001)

Mezger, F., 'Did the Institution of Marriage by Purchase Exist in Old Germanic Law?,' *Speculum* 18 (1943), 369–71

Milsom, S. F. C., *Historical Foundations of the Common Law*, 2nd ed. (London: Butterworths, 1981)

Minnis, A. J., *Medieval Theory of Authorship: Scholastic Literary Attitudes in the Later Middle Ages*, 2nd ed. (Aldershot: Scolar, 1988)

Minnis, A. J., with V. J. Scattergood and J. J. Smith, *Oxford Guides to Chaucer: The Shorter Poems* (Oxford: Oxford University Press, 1995)

Mirrer, Louise (ed.), *Upon my Husband's Death: Widows in the Literature and Histories of Medieval Europe* (Ann Arbor: University of Michigan Press, 1992)

Morgan, Gerald, 'Natural and Rational Love in Medieval Literature,' *Yearbook of English Studies* 7 (1978), 43–52

—— 'Langland's Conception of Favel, Guile, Liar and False in the First Vision of *Piers Plowman*,' *Neophilologus* 71 (1987), 626–33

Murphy, Colette, 'Lady Holy Church and Meed the Maid: Re-envisioning Female Personifications in *Piers Plowman*,' in *Feminist Readings in Middle English Literature: The Wife of Bath and All her Sect*, ed. Ruth Evans and Lesley Johnson (London: Routledge, 1994), pp. 140–64

Noonan, John T., Jr., 'Marital Affection in the Canonists,' *Studia Gratiana* 12 (1969), 479–509 (pp. 486–89)

—— 'Power to Choose,' *Viator* 4 (1973), 419–34

—— *Contraception: A History of its Treatment by the Catholic Theologians and Canonists*, enlarged ed. (Cambridge, MA: Belknap, 1986)

Ó Corráin, Donnchadh, 'Marriage in Early Ireland,' in *Marriage in Ireland*, ed. Art Cosgrove (Dublin: College Press, 1985), pp. 5–24

Oppel, John, 'Saint Jerome and the History of Sex,' *Viator* 24 (1993), 1–22

Owst, G. R., *Literature and Pulpit in Medieval England*, 2nd ed. (Oxford: Blackwell, 1961, repr. 1966)

Palmer, Robert C., 'Contexts of Marriage in Later Medieval England: Evidence from the King's Court circa 1300,' *Speculum* 59 (1984), 42–67

Parsons, John Carmi, and Bonnie Wheeler (eds), *Medieval Mothering* (London: Garland, 1996)

Payer, Pierre J., *Sex and the Penitentials: The Development of a Sexual Code, 550–1150* (Toronto: University of Toronto Press, 1984)

—— *The Bridling of Desire: Views of Sex in the Later Middle Ages* (Toronto: University of Toronto Press, 1993)

Plucknett, Theodore F. T., *A Concise History of the Common Law* (London: Butterworths, 1956)

Pollock, Frederick, and Frederic William Maitland, *The History of English Law Before the Time of Edward I*, 2nd ed., 2 vols (Cambridge: Cambridge University Press, 1898)

Ravensdale, Jack, 'Population Changes and the Transfer of Customary Land on a Cambridgeshire Manor in the Fourteenth Century,' in *Land, Kinship and Life Cycle*, ed. Richard M. Smith (Cambridge: Cambridge University Press, 1984), pp. 197–226

Razi, Zvi, *Life, Marriage and Death in a Medieval Parish: Economy, Society and Demography in Halesowen, 1270–1400* (Cambridge: Cambridge University Press, 1980)

Richmond, Colin, 'The Pastons Revisited: Marriage and the Family in Fifteenth-Century England,' *Bulletin of the Institute of Historical Research* 58 (1985), 25–36

Rieder, Paula M., 'Insecure Borders: Symbols of Clerical Privilege and Gender Ambiguity in the Liturgy of Churching,' in *The Material Culture of Sex, Procreation, and Marriage in Premodern Europe*, ed. Anne L. McClanan and Karen Roscoff Encarnación (New York and Basingstoke: Palgrave, 2002), pp. 93–113

Robertson, D. W., Jr., *A Preface to Chaucer* (Princeton, NJ: Princeton University Press, 1962)

Rosenthal, Joel T., 'Fifteenth Century Widows and Widowhood: Bereavement, Integration, and Life Choices,' in *Wife and Widow in Medieval England*, ed. Sue Sheridan Walker (Ann Arbor: University of Michigan Press, 1993), pp. 33–58

Rubin, Gayle, 'The Traffic in Women: Notes on the "Political Economy" of Sex,' in *Towards an Anthropology of Women*, ed. by Rayna R. Reiter (New York: Monthly Review Press, 1975), pp. 157–210

Salisbury, Joyce E., *Medieval Sexuality: A Research Guide* (New York: Garland, 1990)

Saunders, Corinne, *Rape and Ravishment in the Literature of Medieval England* (Cambridge: Brewer, 2001)

Scattergood, John, 'Chaucer a Bukton and Proverbs,' *Nottingham Medieval Studies* 31 (1987), 98–107

—— 'The "Lewed" and the "Lerede": A Reading of *Satire on the Consistory Courts*,' in John Scattergood, *The Lost Tradition: Essays on Middle English Alliterative Poetry* (Dublin: Four Courts, 2000)

Searle, Eleanor, 'Seigneurial Control of Women's Marriage: The Antecedents and Functions of Merchet in England,' *Past and Present* 82 (1979), 3–43

Shahar, Shulamith, *Childhood in the Middle Ages*, trans. Chaya Galai (London: Routledge, 1990)

Sheehan, Michael M., 'The Influence of Canon Law on the Property Rights of Married Women in England,' *Mediaeval Studies* 25 (1963), 109–24 (reprinted in Michael M. Sheehan, *Marriage, Family and Law in Medieval Europe: Collected Studies*, ed. James K. Farge (Toronto: University of Toronto Press, 1996), pp. 16–37)

—— 'The Formation and Stability of Marriage in Fourteenth Century England: Evidence of an Ely Register,' in Sheehan, *Marriage, Family, and Law*, pp. 38–76 (p. 61) (first published in *Mediaeval Studies* 33 (1971), 228–63)

—— 'Marriage and Family in English Conciliar and Synodal Legislation,' in Sheehan, *Marriage, Family, and Law*, pp. 77–86 (p. 84) (first published in *Essays in Honour of Anton Charles Pegis*, ed. J. Reginald O'Donnell (Toronto: Pontifical Institute of Mediaeval Studies, 1974), pp. 205–14)

—— 'Choice of Marriage Partner in the Middle Ages: Development and Mode of Application of a Theory of Marriage,' in Michael M. Sheehan, *Marriage, Family, and Law in Medieval Europe: Collected Studies*, ed. James K. Farge (Toronto: University of Toronto Press), pp. 87–117 (p. 92) (first published in *Studies in Medieval and Renaissance History* 1: 1–33)

—— 'Marriage Theory and Practice in the Conciliar Legislation and Diocesan Statutes of Medieval England,' in Sheehan, *Marriage, Family, and Law*, pp. 118–76 (p. 123) (first published in *Mediaeval Studies* 40 (1978), 408–60).

—— 'Maritalis Affectio Revisited,' in The Olde Daunce: Love, Friendship, Sex and Marriage in the Medieval World, ed. Robert R. Edwards and Stephen Spector (Albany: State University of New York Press, 1991), pp. 34–44 (reprinted in Michael M. Sheehan, Marriage, Family and Law in Medieval Europe: Collected Studies, ed. James K. Farge (Toronto: University of Toronto Press, 1996), pp. 262–77).

—— Marriage, Family and Law in Medieval Europe: Collected Studies, ed. James K. Farge (Toronto: University of Toronto Press, 1996)

Simpson, James, Piers Plowman: An Introduction to the B Text (London: Longman, 1990)

Smith, Richard M., 'Geographical Diversity in the Resort to Marriage in Late Medieval Europe: Work, Reputation and Unmarried Females in the Household Formation Systems of Northern and Southern Europe,' in Woman is a Worthy Wight: Women in English Society, c. 1200–1500, ed. P. J. P. Goldberg (Stroud: Sutton, 1992), pp. 19–59

Stacey, Robin Chapman, 'Divorce, Medieval Welsh Style,' Speculum 77 (2002), 1107–27

Stargardt, Ute, 'The Beguines of Belgium, the Dominican Nuns of Germany and Margery Kempe,' in The Popular Literature of Medieval England, ed. Thomas J. Heffernan (Knoxville: University of Tennessee Press, 1985), pp. 277–313

Steiner, Emily, and Candace Barrington (eds), The Letter of the Law: Legal Practice and Literary Production in Medieval England (Ithaca and London: Cornell University Press, 2002)

Tasoulias, J. A., 'Wulf and Eadwacer Reconsidered,' Medium Aevum 65 (1996), 1–18

Tavormina, M. Teresa, Kindly Similitude: Marriage and Family in Piers Plowman (Cambridge: Brewer, 1995)

Titow, J. Z., 'Some Differences between Manors and their Effects on the Condition of the Peasant in the Thirteenth Century,' The Agricultural History Review 10 (1962), 1–13

Treggiari, Susan, Roman Marriage: Iusti Coniuges from the Time of Cicero to the Time of Ulpian (Oxford: Oxford University Press, 1991)

Turville-Petre, Thorlac, 'English Quaint and Strange in "Ne mai no lewed lued",' in Individuality and Achievement in Middle English Poetry, ed. O. S. Pickering (Cambridge: Brewer, 1997), pp. 73–83

Wack, Mary Frances, Lovesickness in the Middle Ages: The Viaticum and its Commentaries (Philadelphia: University of Pennsylvania Press, 1990)

Walker, Sue Sheridan, 'Free Consent and the Marriage of Feudal Wards in Medieval England,' Journal of Medieval History 8 (1982), 123–34

—— (ed.), Wife and Widow in Medieval England (Ann Arbor: University of Michigan Press, 1993)

Ward, J. C., English Noblewomen in the Later Middle Ages (Essex: Longman, 1992)

Williams, Raymond, Keywords: A Vocabulary of Culture and Society (Glasgow: Fontana, 1976)

Wormald, Patrick, The Making of English Law: King Alfred to the Twelfth Century. Volume I: Legislation and its Limits (Oxford: Blackwell, 1999)

Wurtele, D. J., 'Chaucer's Wife of Bath and the Problem of the Fifth Husband,' Chaucer Review 23 (1988), 117–28

Index

Footnotes containing comment are included in this index; footnotes for reference are not.